ROUTLEDGE LIBRARY EDITIONS: MODERN EAST AND SOUTH EAST ASIA

Volume 6

T0341043

THE PROSPECTS FOR A REGIONAL HUMAN RIGHTS MECHANISM IN EAST ASIA

THE PROSPECTS FOR A REGIONAL HUMAN RIGHTS MECHANISM IN EAST ASIA

HIDETOSHI HASHIMOTO

Routledge
Taylor & Francis Group

LONDON AND NEW YORK

First published in 2004 by Routledge

This edition first published in 2015
by Routledge
2 Park Square, Milton Park, Abingdon, Oxon, OX14 4RN

and by Routledge
711 Third Avenue, New York, NY 10017

Routledge is an imprint of the Taylor & Francis Group, an informa business

© 2004 Routledge

British Library Cataloguing in Publication Data
A catalogue record for this book is available from the British Library

ISBN: 978-1-138-89258-3 (Set)
eISBN: 978-1-315-69792-5 (Set)
ISBN: 978-1-138-90145-2 (Volume 6)
eISBN: 978-1-315-69779-6 (Volume 6)
Pb ISBN: 978-1-138-90146-9 (Volume 6)

Publisher's Note
The publisher has gone to great lengths to ensure the quality of this reprint but points out that some imperfections in the original copies may be apparent.

Disclaimer
The publisher has made every effort to trace copyright holders and would welcome correspondence from those they have been unable to trace.

EAST ASIA

HISTORY, POLITICS, SOCIOLOGY, CULTURE

Edited by
EDWARD BEAUCHAMP
UNIVERSITY OF HAWAII

A ROUTLEDGE SERIES

East Asia: History, Politics, Sociology, Culture
Edward Beauchamp, *General Editor*

Words Kill
Destruction of "Class Enemies" in China, 1949-1953
Cheng-Chih Wang

The Trifurcating Miracle
Corporations, Workers, Bureaucrats, and the Erosion of Japan's National Economy
Satoshi Ikeda

State Formation, Property Relations, & the Development of the Tokugawa Economy (1600–1868)
Grace H. Kwon

Opening the Door
Immigration, Ethnicity, and Globalization in Japan
Betsy Brody

The Politics of Locality
Making a Nation of Communities in Taiwan
Hsin-Yi Lu

Japan's Foreign Policy Maturation
A Quest for Normalcy
Kevin J. Cooney

Engineering the State
The Huai River and Reconstruction in Nationalist China, 1927–1937
David A. Pietz

Japanese Direct Investment in China
Locational Determinants and Characteristics
John F. Cassidy

Shōkō-Ken
A Late Medieval Daime Sukiya Style Japanese Tea-House
Robin Noel Walker

From Transition to Power Alternation
Democracy in South Korea, 1987–1997
Carl J. Saxer

History of Japanese Policies in Education Aid to Developing Countries, 1950s–1990s
The Role of the Subgovernmental Processes
Takao Kamibeppu

A Political Economy Analysis of China's Civil Aviation Industry
Mark Dougan

The Bible and the Gun
Christianity in South China, 1860–1900
Joseph Tse-Hei Lee

An American Editor in Early Revolutionary China
John William Powell and the China Weekly/Monthly Review
Neil L. O'Brien

Between Sacrifice and Desire
National Identity and the Governing of Femininity in Vietnam
Ashley Pettus

New Culture in a New World
The May Fourth Movement and the Chinese Diaspora in Singapore, 1919-1932
David L. Kenley

Alliance in Anxiety
Détente and the Sino-American-Japanese Triangle
Go Ito

State and Society in China's Democratic Transition
Confucianism, Leninism, and Economic Development
Xiaoqin Guo

In Search of an Identity
The Politics of History as a School Subject in Hong Kong, 1960s-2002
Edward Vickers

THE PROSPECTS FOR A REGIONAL HUMAN RIGHTS MECHANISM IN EAST ASIA

Hidetoshi Hashimoto

ROUTLEDGE
NEW YORK & LONDON

First published in 2004

Published 2015 by Routledge
2 Park Square, Milton Park, Abingdon, Oxon OX14 4RN
711 Third Avenue, New York, NY, 10017, USA

Routledge is an imprint of the Taylor & Francis Group, an informa business

Library of Congress Cataloging-in-Publication Data

Hashimoto, Hidetoshi.
   The prospects for a regional human rights mechanism in East Asia / by Hidetoshi
Hashimoto.
      p. cm. — (East Asia : history, politics, sociology, culture)
   ISBN 0-415-94809-6 (hardcover : alk. paper)
   1. Human rights—East Asia. I. Title. II. Series: East Asia (New York, N.Y.)
JC599.E18H37 2003
323'.095—dc21   2003013099

ISBN-13: 978-0-415-94809-8 (hbk)

Contents

ACKNOWLEDGMENTS   vii

CHAPTER I: INTRODUCTION   1

CHAPTER II: THEORETICAL FRAMEWORK   11

CHAPTER III: THE IMPACT OF GLOBALIZATION ON HUMAN RIGHTS   47

CHAPTER IV: PROSPECTS FOR A REGIONAL HUMAN RIGHTS
REGIME IN EAST ASIA   91

CHAPTER V: CONCLUSIONS   139

APPENDIX A: A COVER LETTER   149
APPENDIX B: A QUESTIONNAIRE SENT TO NONGOVERNMENTAL
ORGANIZATIONS   151
APPENDIX C: A QUESTIONNAIRE SENT TO INDIVIDUALS   153
NOTES   155
BIBLIOGRAPHY   207
INDEX   241

Acknowledgments

I WOULD LIKE TO EXPRESS MY GRATITUDE TO THE MEMBERS OF MY Dissertation Committee, Drs. Marcus Franda, Richard Pierre Claude, Edy Kaufman, David Crocker, Richard Quester, and Daniel Fallon. Among others, my sincere gratitude goes to Dr. Marcus Franda who agreed to chair the Committee without hesitation, although he was extremely busy as Director of International Affairs at the University of Maryland at the time.

I express my profound gratitude to Dr. Richard Pierre Claude for his overwhelming support through his countless and invaluable advice and suggestions. I must also express my gratitude to Dr. Edy Kaufman, who I came to know at UCLA in the summer of 1991, and who suggested that I move to the University of Maryland. If I had not met him, I do not know how my life would have evolved. I also must extend my gratitude to Dr. David Crocker for his thorough reading and critique of my dissertation.

My gratitude also goes to Mr. Charles Egleston for his friendship in these trying times. His unflinching friendship and encouragement during my graduate study helped me to persevere. I also express my gratitude to Dr. Andrew Au for his sympathetic ear whenever I needed someone to listen, and his Chinese wisdom, which helped me to persist. Furthermore, I express my gratitude to Mrs. Helen Plack and Ms. Janet Wickham for their kindness in renting their houses for a pittance while I was working on my dissertation. Their generosity and understanding have gone a long way for a financially deprived student like myself. I also extend my gratitude to Mr. Donald Hirsch, who has helped me to improve my English writing skill over the years. I must also express my deepest appreciation to Mrs. Angela Greer for her careful proofreading of my manuscript. Finally, I would like to thank my mother in Japan for her patience for my long "perpetual" student years.

Chapter I

Introduction

REGIONAL INTER-GOVERNMENTAL HUMAN RIGHTS INSTITUTIONS HAVE been in operation for some time in Europe, the Americas, and Africa. These regional human rights regimes are based on regional human rights treaties such as the European Convention on Human Rights, the Inter-American Convention on Human Rights, and the African Charter on Human and Peoples' Rights. They are enforced by such political organizations as the Council of Europe, the Organization of American States (OAS), and the Organization of African Unity (OAU).

Regional human rights mechanisms have proven to be more effective and useful in promoting and protecting human rights than the global human rights mechanisms available at the UN (e.g. the Human Rights Committee, the Committee against Torture) because they cannot only be complementary to the UN system but can also reflect regional particularities (e.g. the needs, priorities, and conditions of the regions). Regional human rights regimes are usually justified as essential elements in any successful international human rights system in a diverse, conflicted world.

This book is an investigation into the prospects of establishing a regional human rights mechanism in East Asia, with a focus on the contributions of NGOs to the development of such a regional institution. This study is significant because Asia is the only region where a regional human rights protection mechanism has not existed. NGOs' activities can and should lead to regional inter-governmental collaboration because 1) regional inter-governmental organizations (RIGOs) provide a common and convenient NGO forum for decision-making; 2) A RIGO makes it easier for NGOs to do together what they otherwise would or might not be able to do separately; 3) A RIGO might be able to substitute for distant Geneva and New York United Nations establishments; 4) A RIGO can often enhance the legitimacy of NGOs as international actors; 5) A RIGO may enhance the legitimacy of human rights norms; 6) A RIGO may ensure cultural mediation of what many otherwise often see as Europe-American human rights standards; 7) A RIGO provides conflict-management and remediation mechanism at a level closer to the local level than such an intergovernmental organization in distant places like New York and Geneva.

In order to better understand the development of RIGOs and their potential role in East Asian human rights regime-building, it is useful to examine some of the theoretical literature of political science designed to provide conceptual clarity in this and related areas. The focus of the present chapter will be on five theoretical approaches to organizational issues directly related to the development of regional human rights mechanisms, encompassing the political science literature on: 1) functionalism; 2) regional integration; 3) interdependence; 4) global civil society; and 5) Nongovernmental Organizations (NGOs). In each case, we hope to learn whether and in what ways the theoretical literature might be helpful in understanding the failure thus far to build a regional human rights organization in East Asia. In addition, we hope to identify aspects of the theoretical literature that could enable us to project future alternative developments that might lead either to the growth of a regional institution or to explain the continued failure to build such an organization.

FUNCTIONALISM

Functionalism is the term given to a body of literature that assumes the ability of people with common needs to unite across national boundaries. Its origins are generally attributed to the writings of David Mitrany in the 1940s. The functionalist assumption - that there are wide and significant areas of common need that can be met by common services - is often seen as the inspiration for the creation of the specialized agencies of the United Nations. Functionalist logic was also the basis for the formation and proliferation of many of the NGOs that came into being in the latter half of the 20th century.

Functionalists argue that because problems confronting the world today (e.g. gross human rights violations, environmental degradation) can no longer be solved solely within national boundaries, international cooperation has become imperative.

This is the explanation as to why so many interests bind together groups of persons in different nations. Functional organizations can be either intergovernmental (IGOs) or nongovernmental (NGOs). The development of IGOs and NGOs is a manifestation and institutionalization of functional integration. In this context, globalization, for example, in the international economy and human rights may be considered components of a functional integration. The crux of functionalism is the doctrine of "spill-over" which contends that the development of collaboration in one field leads to collaboration in other fields. Accordingly, economic inter-action spills over into political integration.

Functional cooperation contributes to "consensus-building" and "institution-building." Mitrany argues that there can be a gradual transfer of political loyalties to international organizations, by the pooling of sovereign authority. Thus, the functional approach foresees a weakening of the sovereign state. It should be pointed out that Mitrany himself did not view functionalism as a theory of regional integration. In fact, Mitrany made it clear that he saw regional organizations as something that might deflect attention away from the goal of international integration, which Mitrany saw as being far more important. From Mitrany's perspective, regional organizations might contribute to the development of superstates or regional federations, which would perpetuate the intense conflicts and problems associated with the era of nation-states.

Mitrany's writings were directed at finding an alternative to the nation-state system, based on functionalist principles. In fact, many of the ideas inherent in functionalism have given rise to the growth of regional organizations (governmental and nongovernmental) as well as to many truly international organizations like the specialized agencies of the United Nations. What is of particular interest to the present thesis is the question whether the functionalist theory can be helpful in explaining the inability thus far of the nations of East Asia to build a common regional organization for the protection of human rights. There are several possible alternative answers to this question:

1. One might argue that a regional human rights organization has not been developed in East Asia because people and leaders there have not seen the need for such an organization. Since the basis of the functionalist position is that perceived common needs are the catalyst for organizational creation across national boundaries, the absence of felt needs could be seen as a contributing factor to the absence of an organization. The absence of felt needs in the area of human rights might be attributed to a number of factors, including most prominently the prevalence of the Confucian tradition in East Asia's cultural past.

2. A more plausible explanation, using functionalist logic, might be that state leaders in East Asia have failed to see the need for a regional human rights organization because of their unwillingness to tolerate human rights movements and their determination to build regimes in which basic human rights are subordinated to other goals of the state. This being the case, the failure to build a regional human rights organization in East Asia might be the result of a conscious effort by East Asian leaders to quash any attempt to build such an organization.

3. Consistent with point two above, one might argue, following functionalist logic, that there is a felt need for a regional human rights organization among some individual citizens of the countries of East Asia, which has been a catalyst for the creation and maintenance of a number of regional NGOs in the human rights field. In this view, the seeds for the creation of a functionalist human rights organization of any kind, including a regional human rights organization, would most effectively be searched for in nascent human rights NGOs. These NGOs have made it possible for citizens to unite organizationally to meet functionalist needs across state boundaries, despite discouragement from doing so by the leaders of the nation-states in this region.

As indicated earlier, the present essay seeks to highlight the role of NGOs and IGOs in the development of concepts and ideas that can be conceived as forerunners of a regional human rights organization for East Asia. In this context, following the logic outlined above, it will be dependent in part on some elements of functionalist theory.

REGIONAL INTEGRATION

Some functionalists (like Mitrany) reject regionalism as the basis for legitimate organization and stress the need for a more cosmopolitan and global outlook, searching ultimately for a truly international organization in the tradition of the world peace movement. On the contrary, many neo-functionalists argue that the more homogeneous the group (e.g. in cultural background or language), the more likely it is to achieve integration than are organizations that have representatives from across the globe.

Unifying factors that have been identified as being conducive to regional integration are geographical proximity, common historical traditions, cultural heritage, and economic and political mutuality, among others. In order to ascertain and compare various levels of integration, Nye has suggested measurement of integration in terms of economic integration, social integration and political integration (Nye, 1977). The most successful attempt at regional integration thus far has been the development of the European Union, which is now entering the 21st century as a powerful economic factor in its own right, based essentially on its ability to construct a complex set of regional institutions out of common regional needs.

In the field of human rights, implementation of human rights mechanisms have been far more successful at the regional level than at the larger international level. Human rights treaties such as the European Convention on Human Rights (1953), the American Convention on Human Rights (1978) and the Banjul Charter on Human and Peoples' Rights (1981) have made it possible not only to outline and delineate what rights are but also to find ways of enforcing them. This is not to say that all human rights regional organizations have been successful. The 1975 Helsinki Accords, for example, did not live up to the promise they originally held for promoting human rights in the then Soviet Bloc. The Arab Commission on Human Rights (1969) has also led to scant progress.

What is striking about East Asia, of course, is that no regional human rights organization, convention or Accord has yet been developed. Based on theories of regional integration, one might have expected that the leaders of East Asian nations would have come together, either to develop a common framework for promoting human rights or, in the absence of consensus about such a framework, would have hammered out a convention or Accord providing minimal guidance on the subject. One of the goals of the present study is to try and understand, within the context of the regional integration theory, why a regional human rights organization has not emerged in East Asia.

INTERDEPENDENCE

A third theoretical approach to organizational issues relating to human rights regime building is interdependence theory. Interdependence theory furnishes the underpinnings of globalization theory since globalization of the world's capitalist economy has made the world economy more interdependent than before. An enhanced degree of interdependence results in nations being more vulnerable than before in significant ways to developments taking place beyond their borders. Today, no nation-state can insulate itself from global interdependence. In this situation, the isolated state is not adequate for solving many problems because of the interdependent nature of the contemporary world.

If isolated states cannot by themselves solve large and complex problems, then it makes sense that regional organizations become increasingly significant. Ohmae, for example, argues that nation-states were created to meet the needs of a much earlier historical period (Ohmae, 1995). He stresses that states are dysfunctional as actors in a global borderless economy. Ohmae calls the units that make sense for analytical purposes "region-states." Region-states are natural economic zones drawn by the invisible hand of the global market (Ohmae, 1995).

Because of modern communication and transportation technologies, territorial boundaries are no longer impregnable to the flow of information and its capacity to influence public opinion and diplomacy. In this context, interdependence theory provides ample explanation why East Asian nations have been increasingly interacting with each other economically in a regional cooperation. We want to determine the extent to which there has been a similar increase in the human rights field at the regional level in East Asia.

GLOBALIZATION

Technological advancement has created a shrinking world. Globalization points to the emergence of global human conditions and involves global production networks, globalization of social institutions (e.g. human rights NGOs), global cultural homogenization (global spread of Western modernity, namely, the Americanization of the world), international division of labor, language hegemonies, and the global communication system (radio, satellites, fax, the Internet, etc).

This multi-faceted globalization undermines the territoriality of the nation-state because it increases global interconnectedness and consciousness, carrying the message that "we share a common destiny." National cultures, national economies and national borders are dissolving. Naisbitt argues that this globalization process is positive because the greater the global whole, the more opportunities there are for each individual (Naisbitt, 1994).

With globalization and regionalization of a social network and movement have increasingly made China, Japan, Koreas, Taiwan and Mongolia mutually interdependent in many respects, these states have not yet come together to establish an organizational basis in the human rights area. Why is this the case? What are the factors involved in globalization preventing East Asian nations from moving in the direction of a regional human rights organization despite the increasing interdependence that results from forces of globalization?

GLOBAL CIVIL SOCIETY

A fifth theoretical approach that might be taken to explain the organizational development of human rights regime-building in East Asia grows out of recent literature on "civil society." Civil societies - i.e. loosely organized voluntary associations independent of the state - need not be conceived as exclusively national in scope. Civil societies have increasingly become regional and global, not only because groups are establishing strategic linkages across national borders but also because of the nature of the issues around which NGOs converge.

Today people communicate, collaborate, and build relationships across national boundaries in their particular issue areas (AIDS, anti-nuclear politics, land mines, environmental degradation, human rights, etc) through extensive transnational alliances and networks.

"Global civil society" might be made up of individuals and groups in voluntary associations without regard to their identities as citizens of any particular country (Christenson, 1997). In its most extreme version, a "global civil society" is considered a functional response to the undertaking of a variety of welfare tasks. In this sense, global civil society would be a system of "global governance" (Gordenker and Weiss, 1996) and would demand accountability and transparency. It might ever eventually replace a state system as a main source of global governance. What would be requisite for a truly global civil society to emerge would be global citizenship (planetary citizenship [World Assembly, 1994]) based on global solidarity, consciousness and responsibility.

To the extent that global civil society exists, government loses its sovereign position as the sole repository of all wisdom, concern and capacity to act for the common good (World Assembly, 1994). Some evidence of such a shift appears to be the transfer of power away from nation-states to corporations, international bodies, and NGOs (Mathews, 1997). Rosenau refers to NGOs as "sovereign-free actors" (Rosenau, 1990). He argues that NGOs have freedom to operate as they see fit in their dealing with issues. Many NGOs are not tied to the territoriality of the state and have established rich transnational networks. With regard to human rights issues, NGOs have been agents for the strengthening of civil society, with human rights NGOs facilitating democratization while building human rights cultures.

AN INTRODUCTORY OUTLINE

A major goal of the present study is to gauge the development of civil societies in East Asia and the impact of such development on the formation of a regional human rights organization. As mentioned previously, the role of NGOs will be a special concern of this book. Based on the political science approaches outlined above, the present study seeks to trace the influence of functionalism, regional integration, interdependence, global civil society, and the work of NGOs on the establishment of a regional human rights mechanism in East Asia. One of the major manifestations of the development of such a mechanism was the coming together in 1996 of the more than 200 NGOs who participated in the drafting of the Asian Human Rights Charter. In many ways, this event was a functional expression of the issues and concepts outlined above. A major purpose of the present work is to determine whether the Asian Human Rights Charter can be viewed as a plausible step in creating a regional human rights protection structure for East Asia. In basic outline, the inquiry will proceed as follows.

In Chapter III, the investigation turns to the impact of globalization on human rights. In this chapter, I examine such issues as growing acceptance of the universality of human rights, the increasing number of international human rights treaties and the expanding United Nations human rights mechanisms. In addition, human rights diplomacy of the U.S., other major countries and international lending institutions are investigated. Major questions asked are whether, to what extent, and in what ways East Asia has been impacted by globalization in the human rights field.

Since the end of World War II, the UN has established internationally recognized human rights standards and principles by adopting a large number of human rights treaties. In 1948 the Universal Declaration of Human Rights was adopted as "a common standard of achievement for all peoples and all nations." Its thirty articles cover a wide range of rights, including civil, political and economic, social and cultural rights. The principles of the Declaration have been incorporated into the constitutions of many states and the Declaration is considered the embodiment of the universality of human rights.

The international human rights law has been developing in an unprecedented way and has become a substantial part of international law. In this chapter I comment on the development of major human rights treaties and illustrate the significance of each treaty with special attention to their implications for regional integration.

In addition to codification efforts of human rights laws, the UN has organized various human rights treaty monitoring systems to implement human rights in the world. These mechanisms deal with various issues related to human rights such as racial discrimination, torture, women' rights, and children's rights. In order to protect human rights the UN has devised various procedures including reporting procedures, inter-state and individual communication.

The UN also has devised Resolution 1235 and 1503 procedures to examine "a consistent pattern of systematic gross violations of human rights." In addition, the UN has devised thematic mechanisms such as special rapporteurs and working groups to deal with human rights violations in more flexible ways than formal organizational structures. In addition, the UN special agencies such as the ILO and UNESCO have created comprehensive human rights monitoring procedures. In this chapter I explicate the development of implementation systems and methods used by the UN in the field of human rights. The expansion of the UN mechanism has contributed to the growing global human rights culture.

In chapter IV, I describe the human rights diplomacy of the US, the Netherlands, Norway, Canada, and Germany. These countries have incorporated human rights not only into their foreign policy but also into their foreign assistance programs.

Their "quiet diplomacy" has given human rights a prominent place in international relations and has had considerable impact on developing countries including countries in East Asia. I do not include Japan because lack of implementation of the provisions pertinent to human rights in the Official Development Aid (ODA) policy, although Japan has been the largest aid donor in the world in recent years. In this chapter I pay special attention to the historical development of human rights legislation and the diplomacy of the US as the sole remaining superpower, which has considerable influence in the world including the East Asian countries.

The World Bank has also adopted the policy of aid conditionality, which is the largest single lending institution for the Third World countries. The conditionality of aid is viewed as a legitimate intervention in the domestic affairs of borrowing countries. I will investigate the Bank's policy to demonstrate that it has contributed to the globalization of human rights. Finally, I will briefly look into the significance of humanitarian intervention because such action has challenged the traditional notion of state sovereignty and has raised human rights to a higher level as a legitimate concern of the international community.

Also in Chapter IV, I investigate prospects for a regional human rights regime in East Asia. First, I make an assessment of regional human rights regimes in Europe, the Americas and Africa, with a focus on NGOs' contributions to the regimes. The investigation is made with a view to looking into the experiences of these previously established models to determine whether they might be relevant for the would-be architect of a human rights protection arrangement in East Asia. I highlight institutional characteristics, strengths and limitations of respective human rights regimes and I analyze a number of proposals for a regional human rights regime in East Asia.

Second, Chapter IV investigates current human rights situations in East Asian countries such as the Democratic People's Republic of Korea (DPRK), the Republic of Korea (ROK), Japan, the Republic of China (ROC), the People's Republic of China (PRC), and the Mongolian Republic. The purpose of this chapter is to understand what human rights problems these East Asian countries have been facing so that we can discern why they have particular predispositions to a regional human rights enforcement arrangement in the region. In the following section of Chapter IV, I investigate past attempts to set up regional human rights mechanisms in Asia. The UN and NGOs have been organizing conferences, seminars, and workshops with a view to setting up a regional human rights mechanism in the Asia-Pacific region. Because of diverse religious, cultural, and philosophical traditions that exist in Asia, governments in the region have agreed to take "step-by-step" and "building-block approaches" based on sub-regional institutional arrangements (e.g. the Association of Southeast Asian Nations [ASEAN], the South Asian Association for Regional Cooperation [SAARC], South Pacific).

Finally, I assess human rights NGOs in East Asia. The final section of chapter IV identifies and examines human rights NGOs in the ROK, Japan, ROC, Hong Kong and Mongolia. The research methodology I employ relies on mail surveys and interviews to collect experts' opinions. The purpose of the investigation is to determine those activities of human rights NGOs that may provide an impetus to the establishment of a regional human rights mechanism in East Asia and also to clarify the reasons given and arguments in favor of RIGO development by those who are most active in its promotion.

Overall, I use eclectic methods to elucidate a field of action, for example, (a) an historical approach including moral argument to describe developments thus far; (b) participant-sourced information, including interviews and questionnaires (c) institutional approach that includes understanding of the UN framework and the conditions necessary for RIGO development; (d) a pre-scientific exploratory effort to identify theoretical variables that might be explicated in future research on RIGO development.It should be noted that the topic of this book has not been the focus of any previous thesis, and the literature on Asian RIGO development is scarce. Sources were selected so as to include the writings of a widely diversified group of authorities - all of whose findings will be made a part of the resultant conclusions.

Chapter II

Theoretical Framework

THIS CHAPTER INVESTIGATES AND EXAMINES FIVE ISSUES—NAMELY functionalism, regional integration, interdependence, global civil society and NGOs—in order to construct theoretical foundations. These issues, and the concepts outlined in Chapter I, will help explore the feasibility and desirability of establishing a regional human rights arrangement in East Asia. The overall attempt is to better understand the prospects for the establishment of a regional human rights mechanism in East Asia, or elsewhere in Asia. For this study, East Asia includes the Democratic People's Republic of Korea (DPRk), the Republic of Korea (ROK), Japan, the Republic of China (ROC), the People's Republic of China (PRC) and the Mongolian Republic. This area incorporates approximately a quarter of the world's population.

FUNCTIONALISM

The growing complexity of governmental systems has increased greatly the essentially technical, nonpolitical tasks facing governments (Mitrany, 1966). Mitrany argues that government is the sum of its functions. The chief concern in Mitrany's "A Working Peace System" (1966) is how to achieve lasting peace in a conflicted world. Mitrany finds a solution in the unification of the world by technology, which has increased the interactions of individuals and states. Mitrany's functionalism is an attempt to construct a viable supranational administrative structure to build a peaceful world community. Central to the functional approach is the idea of gradual functional transformation of the nation-state system into a global community to achieve a "working peace system." Mitrany links functionalism to the prevention of war and to the development of authoritative world political institutions. Functionalism is an assertion that the development of international economic, social and political cooperation is a major prerequisite for the ultimate solution of political conflicts and elimination of war. Mitrany believes that the functional approach is one of the best means to achieve world peace.

According to Mitrany's scheme, a supranational political organ would have to evolve from a growing network of welfare agencies that would gradually perform tasks formerly carried out by nations. Nations have found it economical and efficient to take joint action in connection with, for example, tariffs and customs, or international postal and telegraph matters. Functionalism expects transfer of loyalties to the international community in response to the growing usefulness of functional agencies (Claude, 1971, p.385). Functionalism is a workable system of globalism, which would overlay political divisions with a spreading web of international activities and agencies (Mitrany, 1966, p. 31, 38).

A key part of Mitrany's scheme is his argument that sovereignty can be transferred through a function (Mitrany, 1966, p. 31). Functionalism is based on the hypothesis that national loyalties can be diffused and redirected into a framework of international cooperation, that is through a web of international organizations and a sharing of sovereignty or a "pooling" of sovereign authority. Mitrany argues that states have been forced to work together at a supra-national level for reasons of self-preservation. The growth in importance of technical issues (e.g. communications, finance) has made necessary the creation of frameworks for international cooperation and a resulting "surrender of sovereignty" (Mitrany, 1966).

Mitrany's approach seeks to demonstrate that the urgent problems confronting the world (e.g. environmental issues) can no longer be solved solely within national boundaries, and that the scope and character of the world's problems have made the nation-state increasingly obsolete. A variety of international organizations have come into being that are designed to fulfill specific technical and functional needs. These cut across national boundaries and thus create a web of interdependence that has gradually, according to Mitrany, made state sovereignty increasingly weaker. There is no doubt that the functional approach foresees a weakening of the importance and power of the "middle man" between the individual and a world community, i.e. the sovereign state (Curtis, 1950).

The functionalists stress that the state is less and less a positive structure for man, but instead an increasingly restrictive, or negative limit on his possibilities. The global issues that have emerged as a result of advances in economy and science mean territoriality no longer is a solution. Functional activity leads to a transfer of political activity away from the old nation-states toward a new structure. Mitrany sought a system to supersede the nation-state and speculated that eventually there would be universality in legally binding rules of law.

Functionalism stresses a wide range of activities, including social, economic and humanitarian concerns. Morgenthau equates functionalism with the gradual emergence of supranational institutions designed to perform specific functions, which create a community of interests (Morgenthau, 1978).

Mitrany hypothesizes that the development of successive layers of functional collaboration creates deep and wide strata of peace, in Frederick L. Schuman's phrase "peace by pieces."[11] The benefit of the functional approach has been projected to be that people's material lives will improve because the artificial boundaries of states will no longer interfere with economic and scientific activities (Eastby, 1985, p.10).

Functionalists believe that non-political matters can be separated from the political aspects of international relations. Regional cultural associations and the promotion of health care (illustrated by the activities of the World Health Organization) are often cited as the initial co-operating efforts envisaged in functionalism.

But it should be stressed that functionalists recognize that rights and duties do not stop at the artificial boundary lines set by nation-states. They believe that functional matters on one side of border are closely tied to similar matters across the face of the globe. Particularly because of the need for cooperation in matters of economics, science and technology, interdependence has made all men neighbors, if not brothers (Curtis, 1950, p. 79).

This explains why even with so many diversified interests, persons in different nations coming together in an increasing number of transnational organizations. An international association is a spontaneous outgrowth for meeting the needs of diverse worldwide groups. Functionalists believe that cosmopolitanism, based on the idea of cooperation, is concrete and practical. In this context, adequate institutions must be created in order that international action may become real.

Mitrany's argument was based on the fact that technical organizations can only be effective if they are intergovernmental, rather than nongovernmental (Haas, 1964). However, the functional approach does not exclusively focus on intergovernmental organizations but allows for a network of specialized agencies, many of which could be non-governmental. It was assumed by Mitrany that co-operation across states was most easily achieved between private groupings of individuals or technical or professional experts rather than between governments. Nongovernmental organizations (NGOs), in their contact with intergovernmental organizations (IGOs), informal or formal, create popular participation. This technical democracy is a process, which Mitrany argues, should be encouraged and promoted.

Functionalists believe that national policies could be translated into effective international action by bringing officials into direct contact across national boundaries. In the functionalist perspective, such officials soon develop an esprit de corps with others who talk the same technical language. The resulting globalization of the economy and other networks results in functional integration (e.g. the World Trade Organization or WTO).

The functionalist approach increases the opportunities for international cooperation. Internationalization of administration has, in fact, been confirmed, for example, in the fields of communication, transportation, public health, finance, science, welfare, crime and sanitation (e.g. the Universal Telegraphic Union, the International Association for the Protection of Child Welfare, the Universal Postal Union, the International Telecommunications and the World Meteorological Organization). Mitrany argues that the functions of everyday social life - transportation, health care, communications, agriculture, industrial development, scientific development and so on - are no longer exclusively carried on within the confines of each sovereign state but are undertaken across frontiers on a regional, or universal level. In fact, the functional agencies of the United Nations (e.g. the International Labor Organization [ILO], World Health Organization [WHO], Food Agricultural Organization [FAO]) already have undertaken such co-operative tasks.

THE SPILL-OVER HYPOTHESIS

The crux of empirical functionalism is the doctrine of "ramification," which contends that the development of collaboration in one technical field leads to collaboration in other technical fields. For example, the common market gives rise to pressure for further collaboration on pricing, investment, transport, insurance, tax, social security, banking, monetary policies and so on.

Functionalism suggests that it is easier for states to cooperate in "low politics" areas, such as health care or cultural exchanges, than in "high politics" areas such as arms control and security matters. Mitrany contends that the initial co-operation in non-controversial areas by technicians and professionals will expand and eventually spill over into government co-operation on more controversial matters, including security issues. Mitrany argues that economic unification would build up the impetus for political agreement (Mitrany, 1966, p. 97).

Lindberg argues that "spill-over" denotes the process whereby a given action, related to a specific goal, creates a situation in which the original goal can be assured only by taking further actions, which in turn create a further condition and a need for more action (Lindberg, 1963, p. 10).

Elaborating further on the concept, Schmitter defines "spill over" as:

"the process whereby members of an integration scheme - agreed on some collective goals for a variety of motives but unequally satisfied with their attainment of these goals - attempt to resolve their dissatisfaction either by resorting to collaboration in another, related sector (expanding the scope of the mutual commitment) or by intensifying their commitment to the original sector (increasing the level of mutual commitment) or both" (Schmitter, 1969, p. 162).

As for the spill-over hypothesis, Schmitter indicates the following options open to a given actor in a given context:

1. spill-over, (i.e. to increase both the scope and level of his commitment concomitantly);
2. spill-around, (i.e. to increase only the scope);
3. buildup, (i.e. to agree to increase the decisional autonomy or capacity of joint institutions but deny them entrance into new issue areas);
4. retrench, (i.e. to increase the level of joint deliberation but withdraw the institutions from certain areas);
5. muddle-about, (i.e. to let the regional bureaucrats debate, suggest, and expostulate on a wider variety of issues but decrease their actual capacity to allocate values);
6. spill-back, (i.e. to retreat on both dimensions, possibly returning to the status quo ante);
7. encapsulate, (i.e. to respond to crisis by marginal modifications within the zone of indifference).[2]

NEO-FUNCTIONALISM

Haas formulated a theory that he called neofunctionalism. The neo-functionalists include Leon Lindberg and Joseph Nye, among others. Haas reformulated Mitrany's theory in three ways:

First, he tried the theory in actual application to regional groupings or existing international organizations. Neo-functionalism is a global functionalism revised and reduced to a regional scale. In view of the euphoria generated by the European integration process, Haas argues that neo-functionalism became "one of the most promising modes of analysis" in international relations (Haas, 1958, p. 3–4).

Second, Haas modified Mitrany's theory by attempting to integrate functionalism and general systems theory.[3] Finally, Haas tried to produce a set of hypotheses that could be tested in the light of empirical evidence to determine the actual impact of functionalism on international affairs. For example, Haas and Schmitter restate Mitrany's supposition that economic union will spill over into political integration (Haas and Schmitter, 1964).

In his study of the European Coal and Steel Community, Haas defined political integration as being the "process whereby political actors in several distinct national settings are persuaded to shift their loyalties, expectations and political activities toward a new center, whose institutions possess or demand jurisdiction over the pre-existing national states" (1958, p.16). Political union implies any arrangement under which existing nation-states cease to act as autonomous decision-making units with respect to an important range of policies. Political union can be said to exist when the politicized decision-making process has acquired legitimacy and authority (Haas and Schmitter, 1964, pp. 707, 709).

In addition, neo-functionalism emphatically espouses institutions that would lead to further integration. Neo-functionalists believe that international organizations, both governmental and nongovernmental, are the primary means of international cooperative activities. Haas argues that functional cooperation contributes to "consensus-building" and "institution-building." For example, Haas argues that congresses and conferences have brought specialized segments of the peoples of the world into contact with each other for the purpose of solving particular problems. Later some of these public conferences became institutionalized.

Haas contends that the functional theory of integration and organization has contributed to protection of human rights through international procedures and sanctions. By using a functional approach as an analytical tool, he examined the International Labor Organization (ILO) as an example of the international human rights protection machinery and concluded that a functional strategy of fostering the institutionalization of human rights has been vindicated (Haas, 1970). His work gives strong support for a would-be regional human rights protection arrangement in East Asia.

Neo-functionalists, in contrast to the earlier functionalism, argue that functional agencies do not sacrifice the sovereignty of nation-states but simply respond to practical needs. The agencies do not interfere with the nation-states' territory, population, and domestic jurisdiction. For that reason, neo-functionalism is a synthesis of federalism and functionalism.[4] The lessons of functionalist cooperation are linked to a utilitarian belief that national self-interests are maximized through cooperation. Haas argues that any cooperation that has occurred has been based not on calculations of the benefits for humanity, but rather on a convergence of separate interpretations of patterns of national interest. Accordingly, Haas questions Mitrany's insistence that there can be a gradual transfer of political loyalties to international organizations when global institutions become more successful in fulfilling functions formerly assumed by national governments.

Haas' investigation has indicated that high politics and low politics cannot be separated and isolated functional tasks tend to be autonomous and do not automatically "spill over" onto others. Haas has modified Mitrany's assertion that integration is maximized by the cooperative efforts of international experts and voluntary groups. Haas also repudiates Mitrany's globalism as both a goal and an explanation. Instead Haas argues that the smaller the group, the better are the chances for integration; universal participation is thus considered a hindrance to cooperation. The more homogeneous the group (in terms of belief systems, cultural background), the more likely the members will cooperate. He contends that closely knit, voluntary, and regional functional groups are more likely to achieve integration than are organizations that have representatives from across the globe.

By 1975, Haas admitted that neo-functional theories of regional integration were obsolescent in Western Europe because regional integration had by then been subordinated to overall interdependence. However, he also argued that the concepts, methods, and assumptions of functionalism continued to be applicable to many settings and processes in the rest of the world.[5]

Functionalism provides positive implications for international economic, social and political cooperation in East Asia. In fact, bilateral trade volumes between China and Japan, Japan and South Korea, South Korea and China have been increasing rapidly for the last two decades. When Kim Dae Jung, President of Korea, visited China in the fall of 1998, he stated that it was high time to have some "cooperative structure" in the region.

However, after a half century since the end of World War II, no significant cooperative arrangement has materialized in the region. Is this because of an antagonistic history and strong national rivalries in the region? Is it a result of Japan's refusal to offer war reparations that has contributed to the ill-feeling toward Japan and the Japanese people in neighboring countries?

Is it possible that cultural exchanges (e.g. learning others' languages, exchange students), communication, transportation and tourism—all of which have been steadily increasing in the region—could serve as functionalist "low politics" that could eventually spill over into "high politics" areas such as a human rights regime?

REGIONAL INTEGRATION

REGION

Regionalism derives its theoretical justification from certain unifying factors: geographic proximity, common historical traditions, cultural heritage, and economic and political mutuality. Regionalism has been called "a halfway house between the nation-state and a world not ready to become one."[6] Regionalization is "the movement of two or more societies toward greater integration or greater 'pooling' of their sovereignty" (Oman 1994, p. 21).

The region usually denotes a geographic area comprised of a number of independent states sharing common economic, social, and political values and goals (Yalem, 1979, p. 15). Regions are also defined as areas within which a higher degree of mutual dependence exists than relationships outside that area, where people are bound together by mutual dependence arising from common interests (Hawley, 1950, p. 260).

Russett, who does not specify priorities, defines region by five characteristic patterns: 1) social and cultural homogeneity; 2) sharing similar political attitudes or external behavior, as identified by the voting positions of governments in the United Nations; 3) political interdependence; 4) economic interdependence; 5) geographical proximity (Russett, 1979, p. 11).

Jacob and Tenue contend that there are ten integrative factors to make up a region:

1. geographical proximity;
2. homogeneity;
3. transactions, or interactions, among persons or groups;
4. knowledge of each other;
5. shared functional interests;
6. the character or motive patterns of a group;
7. the structural frame or system of power and decision-making;
8. the sovereignty-dependency status of the community;
9. governmental effectiveness;
10. previous integrative experiences.[7]

Cantori and Spiegel argue that international politics provides three analytical structures: the globe, the region, and the nation-state. They identify fifteen regions as "subordinate systems" (Cantori and Spiegel, 1970, p. 810) consisting of the core, periphery and intrusive sectors (i.e. the Middle East, West Europe, East Europe, USSR, North America, Latin America, East Asia, Southwest Pacific, Southeast Asia, South Asia, North Africa, West Africa, Southern Africa, Central Africa, and East Africa).
Their work gives strong support that East Asia is a distinctive and logical region for my study.

The core sector forms a central focus of international politics within a given region. The peripheral sector is alienated from the core sector to some degree by social, political, economic, or organizational factors. An intrusive sector consists of the politically significant participation of external powers in the international relations of the subordinate system. As for East Asia, Cantori and Spiegel identify the PRC as core and the Koreas,

Japan, Taiwan and Mongolia as periphery. The US, Portugal, the UK and Russia are the intrusive systems.

REGIONAL INTEGRATION

Regional integration is a complex process linking nations together through mutual involvement in collective decision-making mechanisms and institutions. The study of regional integration looks into how national units come to share part or all of their decisional authority with an emerging regional organization. According to Haas, the study of regional integration is concerned with explaining how and why states cease to be wholly sovereign, how and why they voluntarily mingle, merge, and mix with their neighbors so as to lose some of the attributes of sovereignty.[8]

There is no agreement among scholars as to what constitutes integration. In studies of regional integration, scholars have defined integration in terms of the process of shifting loyalties from a national setting to a larger entity, the establishment and maintenance of community, and the collective capacity to make decisions.

Karl Deutsch, a proponent of the transaction approach, speaks of integration as attainment within a territory of a sense of community, and of institutions and practices strong enough and widespread enough to assure dependable expectations of peaceful change among its population - a process leading to the creation of political communities defined in institutional and attitudinal terms.[9] Deutsch argues that integration produces "integrated" systems, "amalgamated" systems, or "integrated and amalgamated" systems.[10] Integration and amalgamation are measured by transaction flow (i.e. communication patterns) analysis. Transactions give indications of international contacts, communication flows and exchange, thus indicating the degree of social interaction among countries. Transnational interactions not controlled by central foreign-policy organs of governments are no longer ignored. They are regarded as being of crucial importance to the integration process.

Kaplan defines integration as "a process by which separate systems develop a common framework which allows for the common pursuit of some goals and common implementation of some policies" (Kaplan, 1957, p. 98). According to Lindberg, integration is the "process whereby a group of nations (or other political units) progressively takes on a collective capacity to make decisions which authoritatively allocates values for all their members." He defines political integration as the evolution over time of a collective decision-making system among nations (Lindberg, 1971, p.46). Nye defines integration as simply "forming parts into a whole or creating interdependence" (Nye, 1968, p. 858).

Puchara refers to integration as a "concordance system." This model is defined as an international system wherein actors find it possible to harmonize their interests, compromise their differences and reap mutual rewards from their interactions.[11] Puchara argues that transactions reflect regional integration. But he puts emphasis on the fact that transaction flows do not cause regional integration.[12] Caporaso points out that the concordance system is marked by a pragmatic bargaining style, a high degree of mutual sensitivity among actors, the presence of actors from several levels (subnational, national, transnational, and supranational), and a certain level of legitimacy for community institutions.[13]

Haas defines integration as "the process whereby political actors in several distinct national settings are persuaded to shift their loyalties, expectations and political activities toward a new center, whose institutions possess or demand jurisdiction over the preexisting national states."[14] According to Haas' work *The Uniting of Europe* (1957), the level of integration is indicated by: 1) political activities; 2) loyalties; and 3) new institutions possessing jurisdiction.

In order to ascertain the level of integration, Nye suggests measurement of integration in terms of economic integration (formation of a transnational economy), social integration (formation of a transnational society), and political integration (formation of a transnational political interdependence) (Nye, 1979). His argument provides an excellent clue for the study of regional integration in East Asia.

Economic Integration

Economic integration is defined as the abolition of discrimination between economic units belonging to different national states.[15] Balassa sets forth five categories of economic integration: free trade area, customs union, common market, economic union, and total economic integration.[16] In a free trade area, tariffs between the participating countries are abolished although each state determines its own economic relations with the rest of the world. A customs union involves establishing free trade association and having common policies toward trade with the rest of the world. A common market provides for common trade policies both among the members and with the rest of the world. A total economic integration such as in a nation-state, involves common monetary and fiscal policies, and a common currency. In addition, total economic integration requires the setting-up of a supra-national authority whose decisions are binding on the member states.

Balassa argues that a distinction should be made between integration and cooperation. The difference is qualitative as well as quantitative. Whereas cooperation includes actions aimed at lessening discrimination (e.g. international agreements on trade policies), the process of economic integration comprises measures suppressing discrimination (e.g. the removal of trade barriers).

Nye, however, points out that Balassa's categories have little relevance to planned economies such as PRC and North Korea and no adequate place for nontrade categories of economic interdependence between nations, which can sometimes be of considerable magnitude.[17] Nye proposes two types of economic integration: trade integration, namely, the proportion of intraregional exports to the total worldwide exports of the region; service integration, namely, expenditures on jointly administered services as a percent of the participating nations' gross national product (GNP).

Alker and Puchara contend, "the level of economic integration between nations can serve as a reliable indicator of their degree of political integration."[18] The question posed is: "Does economic integration of a group of nations automatically trigger political unity?"[19]

Social Integration

Social integration is defined as creation of a transnational society or the abolition of national impediments to the free flow of transactions (e.g. trade, mail, tourists). Social integration consists of two types: mass social integration and the social integration of special groups or elites (Nye, 1971, p. 32–36)

Political Integration

Political integration is the formation of transnational political interdependence and can be said to occur when the linkage consists of joint participation in regularized, ongoing decision-making.[20] It implies a relationship of community, a feeling of identity and self-awareness. Political integration involves a group of nations coming together to regularly make and implement binding public decisions by means of collective institutions and/or processes rather than by autonomous national means. According to Hayward, political integration is "adaptation and orientation of actors to a political structure."[21]

Nye argues that political integration is divided into four different types: 1) institutional integration; 2) policy integration; 3) attitudinal integration; and 4) the security community (Nye, 1968).

Regional integration theories provide various possibilities for East Asia. As Cantori and Spiegel identify East Asia as one of 15 subordinate systems, East Asia is a distinctive region based on geographic proximity, common historical traditions, and cultural heritage (Confucian heritage).

China is the core sector because the region has been under strong influence of the Chinese hegemonic cultural tradition. The peripheral sector is defined as "those states within a given region which are alienated from the core sector in some degree by social, political, economic, or organizational factors" and consists of Taiwan, North and South Koreas, Mongolia and Japan. East Asia is considered "coherent system" due to little communications and a high degree of conflict (e.g. DPRK and ROK and PRC and ROC). Yet it may move to "cohesive system" because of increasing level of social and economic communications (Cantori and Spiegel, 1970). For example, in recent years leaders of Japan, South Korea, China, Taiwan and Mongolia have visited countries in the region to promote economic, political and cultural tie.

The communication approach to regional integration suggests that the increase in trade, mail and tourist flow between nations create a closer community among the nations.[22] Intra-regional economic relationship in East Asia indicates that it has not reached the level of Balassa's definition of a free trade area. However, interdependent trade and foreign investment in the region have been increasing, especially since China's adoption of market economy, which may result in multilateral economic cooperation within the region.

INTERDEPENDENCE

The concept of interdependence provides a theoretical foundation for the establishment of regional human rights mechanism. Interdependence theorists point out today's world has become increasingly interdependent in many aspects. They argue that nation-states have largely become obsolete in solving the problems we face today.

The third wave of global democratization and growing civil society has been affecting East Asia. The phenomenon of interdependence has been taking place in human rights as well because all human rights are interdependent and indivisible and valid across cultural, economic and political division. Global and regional human rights treaties represent moral interdependence. Human rights takes into account different cultural, economic and political settings and priorities. However, internationally recognized human rights standards are applicable irrespective of political, economic, and cultural diversity.

The mechanisms are established for the impartial and effective implementation of human rights derived from global, regional, state and transnational sources of authority. Human rights are comprehensively conceived as encompassing economic, social and cultural rights, as well as civil and political rights, with a concern for both individual and collective understanding of rights. Convergence is taking place across cultures, which results in a "cross-fertilization" that reinforces the global consensus on human rights (An-Naim and Deng, 1990).

What happens in a country affects other countries because of the inter-dependent nature of the world in which we live today. East Asia has seen increasing economic interdependence. The interdependence theory chal-lenges China's insistence that human rights are essentially matters within the domestic jurisdiction of a sovereign country and adherence to the prin-ciple of non-interference in other countries' domestic affairs.

China today is in a stage of historic transition and experimentation. China began publishing a White Paper on Human Rights in 1991 to indi-cate that it is in compliance with international standards of human rights. China, however, still maintains economic development takes precedence over civil and political rights. It also claims that a repressive government is justified because it creates a stable environment conducive to economic development.

There is no agreement on what interdependence is or by what criteria it can be measured. However, proponents of interdependence agree that the state is often inadequate in solving many problems because of the interde-pendent (mutually dependent) nature of the contemporary world, which we call a "global village" and "world without borders." Governments have become less the masters of what occurs even within their own countries, even though they continue to claim sovereignty. The world has become increasingly interdependent - "a structural linkage of fates."[23]

All the peoples of the world have become inextricably bound up with all the other peoples of the world. The well-being of each depends, more or less, upon the well-being of all. Interdependence implies that nations are sensitive or vulnerable in significant ways to developments taking place beyond their borders.[24] Sensitivity involves mutual responsiveness of one nation to events occurring in another. Vulnerability refers to the measures of a government's inability to insulate itself from the effects of the events originating elsewhere.[25]

REALISTS AND IDEALISTS

According to the realist perspective, 1) nation-states are the most important actors in international politics; 2) politics is bifurcated into "domestic" and "international" spheres, each having distinctive characteristics and each subject to its own laws of behavior; 3) international relations is the "strug-gle for power." As an alternative to the realist model, Keohane and Nye propose the concept of "complex interdependence" (Keohane and Nye, 1977). They argue that in complex interdependence: 1) multiple channels connect societies; 2) there is absence of hierarchy on issues, that is, military security does not consistently dominate the agenda; 3) military force is irrelevant once complex interdependence prevails. In a recent article, Keohane and Nye argue that the information revolution has altered patterns of complex interdependence, since the channels of contact between societies have vastly increased (Keohane and Nye, 1998).

Their arguments are parallel to the traditional "liberal" claim that the growth of free trade and a mutually advantageous international division of labor will encourage global harmony and peace. However, the assumption that growing international interdependence will result in a more peaceful, integrated and cooperative world is problematic, because it is empirically ill-founded. One study concludes that "increasing levels of trade may be a highly divisive force... for international politics" and that "increasing trade in the international system is, by itself, unlikely to ease international tensions or promote greater international stability."[26] Another study argues that high levels of economic interdependence "can be either peace-inducing or war-inducing, depending on the expectations of future trade." Economic interdependence fosters peace only "when states expect that high trade levels will continue into the foreseeable future." If states do not expect high levels of interdependence to continue, war is likely to result.[27]

WHAT IS INTERDEPENDENCE?

Brown agrees with the contention of Keohane and Nye that the military's role in securing a nation's well-being and survival has become less important than strengthening international cooperation.[28] Based on the "only one earth" idea, he argues that a "threat to security may now arise less from the relationship of nation to nation and more from the relationship of man to nature." Brown examines interdependence from economic, ecological, resource, technological, and social aspects (Brown, 1972).

Young uses the concept "interdependence" to refer to "the extent to which events occurring within any given component unit of a world system affect events taking place in other component units of the system" (Young, 1969, p. 726). Mally, on the other hand, defines interdependence as a complex transnational phenomenon involving multisectoral patterns of interaction between nations and resulting in enhanced mutual sensitivity and vulnerability (Mally, 1976).

Mally argues that interdependence is, first, the product of the revolution in the field of communication that permits the instantaneous transmission of information to all parts of the planet.

Second, progress in transportation (systems of mass transportation) permits people to overcome distance (conquest of distance). The revolution in communications and transport technologies has facilitated the global interplay of cultures, values, ideals, knowledge, peoples, social networks, and social movements, thus, is eroding the boundaries between national markets and has resulted in undermining national economic autonomy.

Third, the revolution in science and technology has made people vulnerable to disturbance of the peace in any part of the world because we share a common body of scientific knowledge and science knows no frontiers (Mally, 1954). Mally identifies patterns of interdependence in the domains of security, ecology, economics, diplomacy, and sociocultural relations.

The theory of interdependence is based on a global outlook. However, the phenomenon of interdependence has been taking place at the regional level as well. Therefore, these writings provide ample suggestions for East Asian integration. Theorists of interdependence provide sufficient reasons why East Asian countries cannot be separate entities of themselves. Geographical proximity of the countries in the region provide mutual advantages. The degree of interdependence will increase because progress in transportation and communications make it easier for people to travel and to contact each other in the region.

Rosenau gives four characteristics of interdependence: complexity, the involvement of nongovernmental actors, fragmented governmental decision-making and the necessity of multilateral co-operation for management of issues (Rosenau, 1980). Reynolds and McKinlay identify interdependence from four aspects: institutionalization (IGOs, NGOs, Transnational Corporations [TNC], etc); transactions among states; global village (spaceship earth);[29] and linkage patterns (the blurring of the domestic-foreign policy distinction).[30]

According to Rosecrance and Stein, interdependence refers to "a relationship of interests such that if one nation's position changes, other states will be affected by that change" (Rosecrance and Stein, 1973, p. 2). They analyze interdependence by examining trade, investment, financial, and political sectors. Rosecrance et al. argue that interdependence is measured both by the flow of goods between states - horizontal interdependence, and the equalization of factor prices among states - vertical interdependence. They studied horizontal and vertical interdependence across six industrial states from 1890 to 1975.

These arguments provide an explanation as to why we need to have international cooperation in the various aspects of our lives including political, economic, cultural areas. International cooperation will certainly include promotion and protection of human rights. A regional human rights cooperative mechanism is an embodiment of international cooperation.

Interdependence theories provide far-reaching implications that cooperation between East Asian countries will inevitably increase. Functionalists argue that the cooperation will often result in institutionalization. The efforts to promote and protect human rights will need international cooperation because cooperative efforts are more efficient than separate ones in this increasingly interdependent nature of the world in which we live today, especially in view of geographical proximity of East Asian countries.

Ohmae argues that instantaneous movement of people, ideas, information, and capital across borders means that tastes and preferences of people begin to converge. According to Ohmae, nation-states were created to meet the needs of a much earlier historical period. Therefore, they do not have the will, the incentive, the tools to play an effective role in the borderless economy of today. They are dysfunctional as actors in a global economy because they are incapable of putting global logic first in their decisions.

In a borderless economy, nation-states are no longer meaningful units; nation-states are wearing away as economic actors. The units that do make sense Ohmae calls region-states. Region-states are natural economic zones drawn by the deft invisible hand of the global market (Ohmae, 1995). Ohmae's argument provides good guidelines for East Asian countries as to why it is imperative to pursue cooperative economic development, which may spillover other fields.

ECONOMIC INTERDEPENDENCE

The interdependent nature of the world is especially pronounced in the economic sphere. Economic interdependence gives ample implications for East Asia that may result in social or political regional arrangement.

Economic interdependence refers to the sensitivity of economic behavior in one country to developments in another (Tollison and Willett, 1973, p. 259). Some Marxist writers on imperialism, which they call the "highest stage of capitalism," have been aware of the internationalization of economic development, that is, economic interdependence (Magdoff, 1969; Emmanuel, 1972). They stress the sensitivity of economic behavior in one country to developments or policies originating outside its borders. As a result of the collapse of state socialism, the world has become a single capitalist market. The globalization of the capitalist economy has made the world economy more interpenetrating and interdependent than before. No nation-state can insulate itself from the global market mechanism, transnational movements of capital, and transnational flows of finance.

Wallerstein argues that there exists the capitalist world-economy, a globally integrated economic system in which all nation-states participate to some extent. It had its inception in 16th century Europe that has integrated a geographically vast set of production processes. This phenomenon Wallerstein calls a single international division of labor. The capitalist world-economy has created three structural positions through unequal exchange: core, periphery and semiperiphery (Wallerstein, 1979).

In this economically interdependent world, it is no longer possible to regard each country as having its own separate economy. For example, the most important attributes of sovereignty, control over the currency and control over foreign trade have been substantially diminished. Thus, the governments have lost control of financial flows.

The internationalization of production, finance, and exchanges erodes the capacity of the individual state to control its own economic future. The rise of an integrated world economy based on a complex multilateralism has become evident on a global scale. The value of world exports soared from $63 billion to $107 billion in 1958, $280 billion in 1970 and to more than $43.7 trillion in 1992.[31] An example of this international economic connection is described as:

> A study of the components of a European Ford Escort car assembled in either Britain or Germany, indicated that parts could come from as many as 15 different countries, including cylinder heads from Italy, heater hose from Austria, speedometers from Switzerland, brakes from France, fan belts from Denmark, tires from Belgium, and starters from Japan.

DEPENDENCY

As a flaw of interdependence, there is a phenomenon called dependency. According to the dependency theory, the present world economy grew out of the worldwide expansion of capitalism that perpetuates basic structures, namely, a global structure of asymmetrical and imbalanced interdependence. This situation results in the dependence of advanced capitalist states for their continued accumulation of capital and wealth upon the underdeveloped world and thus, upon the exploitation of the poor by the rich. Frank and Galtung seek to explain how the exchange relationships between the center and the periphery result in inequitable distribution of resources and hence in a perpetual international hierarchy.[32] The mechanism explaining international inequality is the operation of the Ricardian law of comparative advantage and international specialization.

Holsti argues that dependency can refer to a situation between any pair of states in which there are asymmetrical vulnerabilities (Holsti, 1978, p. 516), that is, the mutual dependence of industrialized and developing countries on raw materials and food or technology.

Thus, theorists interested in dependency ("dependencia") have stressed asymmetries of interdependent relationships, particularly between developed "center" countries and those of the underdeveloped "periphery"

(Frank, 1969; Galtung, 1971; Dos Santos, 1971; Wallerstein, 1974). The dependency theory implies that interdependence does not necessarily bring suitable relations among countries in East Asia because it may perpetuate have and have-not pattern and structure. Therefore, it may be a major task for the countries in the region to solve the problems stemming from dependency.

We have been observing the emergence of "an idealist" vision of a politically and economically interdependent world based on the crystallization of the entire world as a single place (Robertson, 1987, p. 38) because interdependence and transnationalism have eroded the capacity of the state to make domestic policy and to act independently in international relations, including human rights issue.

IGOs, NGOs, AND TNC

There has been a great increase in the number, membership and functions of IGOs and NGOs. The growth and network of IGOs and NGOs have created a network of international memberships, which foster the emergence of loyalties to a world community. The development of IGOs and INGOs is a manifestation and institutionalization of interdependence.

Another example of interdependence is the TNC. TNCs are world oriented and interdependent organizations, and they collaborate between headquarters and subsidiaries in decision-making, worldwide perspective, worldwide recruiting and interchange of personnel, and multidirectional communication among units of the corporation.[33] TNC is a positive force for the regional human rights mechanism because it is an impetus for interdependence and regional integration although TNC tends to widen economic inequity.

GLOBAL CIVIL SOCIETY AND NONGOVERNMENTAL ORGANIZATIONS (NGOS)

NGOs' activities will enhance the possibility of setting up a regional human rights mechanism in East Asia because their goals may be achieved by participating and contributing to the regional inter-governmental human rights mechanism. The development of regional integration has been taking place along with the globalization process. Globalization includes global social movements and global civic activism. The concept of global civil society suggests theoretical underpinning of activities of NGOs, which increasingly have become regional and global in their activities and membership (e.g. Medecin sans Frontiere).

GLOBALIZATION

Globalization is developing in every facet of life. It has been affecting lives of people throughout the world including East Asia. Globalization means that technological change has created a shrinking world. Globalization entails inexpensive mass transportation, the global communication system (radio broadcasting, coaxial cable, wireless broadcasting, earth satellites, fiber optic telephone connections, facsimile transmissions, telecommunications, television coverage and the Internet system - "information super high way"). This electronic revolution demonstrates global inter-connectedness in contemporary society.

Appadurai contends that global cultural flow has five dimensions:

a. ethnoscapes - tourists, immigrants, refugees, exiles, and guestworkers;
b. mediascapes - the distribution of the electronic capabilities to produce and disseminate information (newspaper, magazines, television, film);
c. technoscapes - global configuration of technology, multinational enterprises;
d. financscapes - global capital, currency markets, commodity speculations;
e. ideoscapes - ideologies such as democracy, rights, and freedom. (Featherstone, 1990, p. 296).

As for globalization of the economy, it can be seen in the globalization of manufacturing ("global factories"), marketing, production networks, and international division of labor. However, Korten warns that economic globalization deepens the dependence of localities on the detached global institutions that concentrate power and colonize local resources. The more globalized the economy, the greater the dependence of the local and the greater the power of central institutions (Korten, 1995, p. 269).

The globalization of economic activity is described as the "Mcdonaldization" of eating out and "Disneyfication" of entertainment (Spybey, 1996). The "Californiazation" of demand and supply, the "Toyotanization" of the production process (Ohmae, 1985, 1990). Spybey observes that a globalized world society in all its forms comes from the rise of the West and the implanting of Western institutions around the world (Spybey 1996, p. 71). He argues that it is a global spread of Western modernity.

The globalization effectively thwarts the territoriality of the nation-state and that borders have become increasingly meaningless, especially in economic terms. Globalization involves globalization of social institutions,

the globalization of culture (cultural homogenization), language hegemonies, clothing styles, global capitalist consumer cultures, the
"Americanization" of the world (Spybey, 1996).

We have witnessed the end of the Cold War and triumph of the capitalist world-economy (Wallerstein, 1989). According to Fukuyama,

> What we may be witnessing is not just the end of the Cold War, or the
> passing of postwar history, but the "end of history," as such: that is,
> the end point of mankind's ideological evolution and the universaliza-
> tion of Western liberal democracy as the final form of human govern-
> ment. (Fukuyama, 1989, p. 50)[34]

We have witnessed the "third wave of global democratic revolution"
(Huntington, 1991).[35] It is the globalization of democratic values and practice. Kim Dae Jung puts it, "Culture is not our destiny. Democracy is."[36]

We have been witnessing a gradual weakening of the "realist" vision
of the sovereign state system because of such factors as the globalization of
the free market, the acceleration of global communications, and an increasing non-state actors' participation in international affairs. Sovereignty is
disintegrating - "Sovereignty at Bay" (Vernon, 1971).

This is a positive phenomenon because the Westphalian model[37] of the
nation-state system over-emphasized sovereignty. Indeed, Luis Kutner
states:

> "Total sovereignty is to the state what egoism is to the individual - the
> last, holiest, most highly treasured source of all disaster." [38]

The state-centric realism of the UN Charter based on the principle of non-
intervention in domestic jurisdictions, especially in the field of human
rights, has become increasingly impertinent. There is growing awareness
that we are sharing a common world. It is the emergence of a global human
condition (Robertson, 1987, p. 23). Claude and Davis call it a "global society" where individuals and groups play significant roles.[39] The emergence
of a "global civil society"[40] has been undermining a "cult of state sovereignty."[41]

CIVIL SOCIETY

The flow of information on a global scale utilizing electronic revolution has
effectively eaten away at nation-state boundaries and has globalized individuals throughout the world. Those activists in NGOs advocate that we
should "think globally, act locally." Alberto Melucci calls this "planeta-
rization of action"[42] based on global consciousness and global human circumstances. Thus, national cultures, national economies and national

borders are dissolving. This development is positive because the greater the global whole, the more opportunities there are for the individual (Naisbitt, 1994).

The concept of civil society provides the theoretical framework the NGO movement. Civil society is distinguished not only from the "state of nature" but also from despotic rule. The notion of civil society is from Latin *civilis societas,* which refers to a "civilized" community sufficiently advanced to have its own legal codes - *jus civile.*

Weigle and Butterfield argue that there are four stages in the development of civil society;

1. defensive - private individuals and independent groups defend their autonomy vis-a-vis the state;
2. emergent - independent groups or movement seek limited goals in a wide public sphere;
3. mobilizational - independent groups or movements undermine the legitimacy of the state by offering alternative forms of governance; and
4. institutional - leaders enact laws guaranteeing autonomy of social action, leading to a contractual relationship between state and society (Weigle and Butterfield, 1992).

The idea of a civil society emerged in tandem with the capitalist modernity and bourgeois society, a market-driven economy based on private property, because civil society involves both freedom to buy and sell all kinds of goods as one sees fit (Young, 1997). Hence, private business is considered a force for political change by integrating civil society. Therefore, introduction of a market-oriented economy in China is likely to foster the development of a civil society. A global economy may be countervailing forces to tyrannical government and provides a place for a global civil society.

Unlike the revolution of 1917, the revolutions of 1989, "the Year of Truth"[43] in Eastern Europe, were not orchestrated by a tightly-knit band of professional ideologues but were effected by loosely organized social groups using the magnificent phrase "We, the People" (citizens' movements) such as the Civic Forum in Czechoslovakia, the Democratic Forum in Hungary, and the New Forum in East Germany. Among others, Poland, where "shock therapy" was needed to free the economy from central planning and state ownership, the independent social movement called Solidarity contributed to create a civil society under the oppressive conditions of the communist system.

Democracy needs civil society, a dense network of intermediate groups and voluntary associations independent of the state - a free press, independent universities, trade unions, banks, commercial firms, publishing houses, etc. Without civil society, democracy remains an empty shell (Ignatieff, 1995). Adam Ferguson, Adam Smith and David Hume called this new social formation a civil society to distinguish it from the tribal societies. Tribal societies are held together by ties of blood.

Voluntary associations perform many functions in a democracy. A network of associations institutionalizes problem-solving on questions of general interest. Walzer argues that civil society refers to the "space of uncoerced human association" (Walzer, 1991). In this regard, civil society is a community of free and equal citizens based on the recognition of fundamental human rights as manifested, for example, in the French Declaration of the Rights of Man and of the Citizens in 1789.

Civil society is composed of those spontaneously emerged associations, organizations, and movements that are attuned to how societal problems resonate in the private life spheres, so they can distill and transmit such reactions in amplified form to the public sphere. In civil society, division and diversity, checks and balances are of the essence. This is where sovereignty resides.

The magic word "citizen" referred not to one's subordination to the state but to one's membership in an authentic community. Civil society is regarded as a realm that is relatively autonomous of state control and, in particular, totalitarian control and allows individuals to associate with each other in complex networks. It is autonomous participation in the face of a state-directed society. Yet at times, there may be hybrid arrangements and state may nurture civil society.

On the contrary, totalitarianism is based on the ruins of the rights of man (Lefort, 1986, p. 246). Marx wrote that the state is the executive committee of the ruling bourgeoisie, and law is its chosen instrument of oppression. His contempt for bourgeois legality led toward a Leninist contempt for legality altogether. Civil society will undermine the foundation of state, especially in the case of single-party regimes (e.g. Eastern Europe). Civil society is built from "the bottom up, rather than the top down."

GLOBAL CIVIL SOCIETY

Whether the regional inter-governmental human rights regime functions well or not depends very much on whether there is active civil society participation in the system. Civil society need not be conceived as exclusively national in scope as coinciding with the boundaries of the nation-state because the civil society calls for the articulation of a set of universal human values - diversity, tolerance and pluralism. Civil society is increasingly becoming regional and global not only because groups are establishing strategic linkages across national borders, but also because of the composition and the nature of the issues around which NGOs converge.

Today human interaction is not contained within the territorial borders of the state. People communicate, collaborate, and build relationships across national boundaries. Global civil society is a domain where people voluntarily organize themselves to pursue various aims. They try to influence the beliefs and actions of people throughout the world concerning their particular issue area.

Christenson argues that global civil society is made up of individuals and groups in voluntary associations without regard to their identities as citizens of any particular country and outside the political and public dominion of the community of nations.[44] Global civil society is a realm of actors who engage in transnational politics that is characterized by a high degree of autonomy from the states. We see a growing number of transnational networks oriented around common issues and goals and a growing number of these networks are being organized around specific issues (e.g. AIDS, anti-nuclear, indigenous rights, environmental degradation) through extensive transnational alliances and networks of communication. Regional coalition and public-private networks recently have been formed in many parts of the globe to address these specific concerns and themes (e.g. the European Court of Human Rights, the Inter-American Commission and Court of Human Rights).

A function of global civil society has allowed nonstate actors to forge effective global alliances that are not subject to national governmental control. Global civil society is being considered as a functional response to the decreasing ability of governments to undertake a variety of welfare functions. The global civil society is based on the globalization of advanced communication technologies that facilitates exchange of information and opinion. Actors in civil society are forces for social and political changes in both domestic and global arenas.

According to Christenson, international law mediates between the political community of sovereign states and a newly emerged civil society. The emerging global rule of law is the beginning of world civil society. Global civil society is a system of what Gordenker and Weiss call "global governance"[45] and may replace a state centric system.

Global civil society is significant because transnational political networks have been established among actors who are challenging and changing from below the nation-state system (Lipschutz, 1996). Globalization-from-below represents global village realities, norms and values of the free market, the rule of law, human rights, effective participation of citizenry, accountability and transparency and the global public good.

The global civil society needs global citizenship (and vice versa) in this interdependent world. The time is ripe for global solidarity and citizenship (the planetary citizenship),[46] based on a global consciousness that we share the same planet and a common destiny - global networking, global citizen action, global citizen alliance and advocacy efforts of NGOs to influence the agenda and outcome.[47]

The growing significance of citizen participation in the public arena is based on the notion that the government is not the sole repository of all wisdom, concern, and capacity to act for the common good (Oliveira and Tandon 1994, p. 10). Voluntary associations are becoming a massive phenomenon worldwide. Participation is becoming a universal value. The future lies in the hands of an informed, inspired, committed, and engaged citizenry.[48] We are being pulled closer into one world. The worldwide emergence of people's organizations demands more and more say in shaping our own lives on behalf of every citizen.

NONGOVERNMENTAL ORGANIZATIONS (NGOS)

The growing number of NGOs' activities in recent years is evident in such countries as South Korea, Taiwan, Japan and Mongolia. This is a positive indication that in establishing a regional human rights regime, these groups can achieve their goals by actively participating in a would-be regional human rights arrangement. There are three categories of actors other than nation-state.

A. IGOs are defined as international organizations in which full legal membership is solely open to the states and decision-making authority lies with representatives from governments (e.g. the United Nations, the Organization of American States, the World Trade Organizations). There are approximately 300 IGOs worldwide.[49]

B. A TNC is a business enterprise organized in one society with activities abroad growing out of direct investment (e.g. Ford, Coca Cola, Nestle).[50] A TNC knows no national boundaries. TNCs are largely beyond national control. A global marketplace offers an arena where people can interact largely free from complete governmental intervention. A TNC has the ability to evade government attempts to control financial flows, to impose trade sanctions, or to regulate production. It should be noted that while TNC do expand competition and enhance world economic efficiency, they perpetuate and deepen global inequality (Kegley and Wittkopf, p. 270). There are approximately 38,500 TNCs worldwide.[51]

C. There are currently 4,830 active international NGOs (e.g. Amnesty International, the International Red Cross, Greenpeace) and 10,000 single-country NGOs (Freedom House, Sierra Club).[52] NGOs can be referred to as organizations which are not created by an agreement among governments and are usually operated on a nonprofit basis. According to the definition of the Heidelberg Max Planck Institute's Encyclopedia of Public

International Law (vol.9, 1986, p. 276), non-governmental organizations (NGOs) are:

> private organizations (associations, unions, institutes, groups) not established by a government or by intergovernmental agreement which are capable of playing a role in international affairs by virtue of their activities, and whose members enjoy independent voting rights. The members of an NGO may be individuals (private citizens) or corporate bodies.

Walker describes NGOs as "critical social movements" (Walker, 1988). In the post-war period, as an essential component of civil society, there has been an exponential growth in the number of NGOs on every continent - the "NGO revolution."[53] Rosenau calls NGOs "sovereign-free actors" (Rosenau, 1990), which operate independently of the state system and participate in global governance. Nonstate actors have remarkable freedom to operate as they see fit in their dealing with issues. Many NGOs are not tied to the territoriality of the state. As a result, they have established rich transnational networks.

Christenson argues that there has been a shift of power away from nation-states to corporations, international bodies, and NGOs of citizen groups.[54] The dominance of the sovereign state in global society has been undermined by voluntary associations who believe in the right to freedom of expression and association across borders to support decentralized institutions free from arbitrary state interference.

The NGOs operate across national boundaries and across the globe. Many NGOs have become global social movements by forming alliances, associations, and coalitions through complex patterns of global interaction. They have been seen as institutional expressions of the emergence of global civil society. Humanitarian and human rights organizations are the best models for the development of globalist campaign organizations. In this global society, it is necessary to transform institutions in national civil societies into ones with global thinking and global responsibility.

HUMAN RIGHTS NGOS

The growth of NGOs indicates participatory democracy and human rights NGOs have become an essential part of the worldwide human rights movement. In East Asian countries such as South Korea, Mongolia, Taiwan and Japan, human rights NGOs have been showing growing presence in recent years. These NGOs activities can and should lead to formation of regional inter-governmental human rights arrangement. Christenson points out that the two most powerful forces within this global civil society are transnational free markets and international human rights movements (Christenson, 1997).

Human rights NGOs facilitate democratization and build a "human rights culture." Yet human rights NGOs have to overcome problems related to their credibility, and impartiality, allegations of being politically motivated, and financial difficulties.

What is a human rights NGO? According to Wiseberg's definition, a human rights NGO is a private association that devotes significant resources to the promotion and protection of human rights. It is independent of both governmental and political groups and does not itself seek such power.[55] Examples of the human rights NGOs are:

> Amnesty International,[56] Article 19, the Anti-Slavery Society, Defense for Children International, the Andean Commission of Jurists, the International League for Human Rights,[57] the International Commission of Jurists,[58] Human Rights Watch, the Minority Rights Group, the International Committee of the Red Cross,[59] the International Human Rights Law Group, the Federation Internationale des Droits de l'Homme, Survival International, and The Decade of Human Rights Education, Inc.

Following nine areas are identified where NGOs have made significant contributions.

1. At the United Nations, NGOs play a crucial role providing for accurate, objective, up-to-date information and dissemination as well as implementation of U.N. decisions.[60] The UN human rights system would be virtually incapacitated in the absence of NGO briefs, petitions, documentary evidence, legal analysis, and written and oral interventions.[61]

The Economic and Social Council (ECOSOC) Resolution 1296 of 1968 enabled qualified NGOs to obtain one of three types of consultative status with the UN.[62] Consultative status offers NGOs official recognition by a governmental body and the right to attend meetings, make oral statements in their own names and circulate written statements. Some NGOs retain consultative status with such bodies as ECOSOC,[63] the International Labor Organization (ILO),[64] and the Educational, Scientific and Cultural Organization (UNESCO),[65] as well as regional organizations (e.g. the Council of Europe,[66] the Organization of American States [OAS],[67] and the Organization of African Unity [OAU][68]).

In addition, at the UN, NGOs have contributed considerably in establishing mechanisms, which address certain objectives (e.g. involuntary disappearances, summary executions, torture, and religious intolerance). Furthermore, NGOs have played an important role in identifying and defining new issues and areas requiring legislation.

2. NGOs monitor the behavior of the states and gather, evaluate and disseminate information, and expose human rights violations. Wiseberg notes "documentation is a precondition for stopping abuses and a prerequisite for effective action in the field of human rights."[69] Reports, studies, bulletins, newsletters, and press releases of NGOs are disseminated. NGOs provide information to their governments, the mass media, IGOs, opinion leaders, and community organizers.

3. NGOs help to draft international human rights norms in multilateral treaties and resolutions. NGOs were instrumental in the drafting of the Universal Declaration of Human Rights (1948).[70] Recent examples were the adoption of the U.N. Declaration on the Protection of All Persons from being Subjected to Torture and Other Cruel, Inhuman or Degrading Treatment or Punishment (assisted by Amnesty International),[71] and the Convention on the Rights of the Child.[72] Thus, NGOs participate closely in the drafting of new international human rights legislation - treaties, declarations, and guidelines - and make major inputs into the process.

4. Over the past four decades regional human rights regimes (e.g. the European and the Inter-American Commissions and Courts of Human Rights[73]) have established legal mechanisms that permit individuals, groups, and NGOs to file human rights complaints. NGOs provide legal aid such as legal defense, filing writs of habeas corpus, and amicus curiae briefs. NGOs represent and assist human rights victims in presenting communications.[74] For example, the U.N. Sub-Commission on the Prevention of Discrimination and Protection of Minorities states that communication may originate from:

> a person or group of persons who, it can be reasonably presumed, are victims of the violations..., any person or group of persons who have direct and reliable knowledge of those violations, or non-governmental organizations acting in good faith in accordance with recognized principles of human rights not resorting to politically motivated stands contrary to the provisions of the Charter of the United Nations and having direct and reliable knowledge of such violations.[75]

NGOs are in a better position than individuals to gather reliable information and to prepare the necessary legal documentation.

In addition, NGOs (e.g. Amnesty International, the International Commission of Jurists) have pioneered the practice of using eminent foreign lawyers or judges as observers at trials of individuals who have been charged with political offenses. A related practice utilized by the International Committee of the Red Cross inspects prisons and detention centers for political prisoners.

5. NGOs provide humanitarian assistance involving sending food, clothes, and material to the families of political prisoners, providing emer-

gency relief to refugees and internally displaced persons, providing shelter for the homeless, for street children, and battered women.[76]

6. When sovereign states fail to fulfill their responsibilities, the international community has a corresponding responsibilities to help the victims of failed states.[77] Governments rarely do make diplomatic interventions on issues relating to human rights. NGOs, on the other hand, directly or indirectly intervene in the situation. Hargrove argues that criticism of a government's human rights conduct is not an impermissible intervention.[78]

Direct intervention consists of the NGO directly apprising government officials of human rights violations. Indirect intervention involves mobilizing public opinion against human rights violators through NGOs' publications, news media, public meetings and seminars. The NGOs may send a fact-finding mission to the country, to interview alleged victims, lawyers, and government officials because fact-finding and analysis are critical conditions for effective action.[79] These works are very important because few IGOs' have real fact-finding capability. Most NGOs publicly report the results of their missions to facilitate what Welch calls the "mobilization of shame."[80]

7. NGOs have established an urgent action network, which is a tactic intended to permit an immediate response to a situation where there is a grave risk that someone will be tortured or killed. The idea was first developed by Amnesty International in 1976. Wiseberg reports that there are two dozen Amnesty- International-type urgent action networks (e.g. World Organization against Torture - SOS Torture, Physicians for Human Rights, and Survival International).[81]

8. HRE (human rights education) includes producing educational materials, participating in teacher training, networking with collaborating institutions, and undertaking technical assistance. Offering courses in human rights education to military and police has attracted attention.[82] Claude argues that NGOs view human rights education - formal, nonformal and informal - as a preventive strategy to diminish human rights violations and for HRE to succeed, the participation of human rights NGOs is critical at every stage of the implementation process.[83]

9. Human rights NGOs have tried to influence the human rights policies and diplomacy of various countries.[84] NGOs are often engaged in drafting legislative proposals, preparing position papers on pending legislation, and testifying before government committees. For example, in the United States, NGOs advocate and in addition have drafted legislation to deny U.S. economic and military assistance to governments that engage in large-scale violations of human rights. The Foreign Assistance Act, Section 502 B (1974) provides that:

> [T]he president should withhold security assistance from governments
> which engage in a consistent pattern of gross violations of internation-
> ally recognized human rights.[85]

STRENGTHS AND WEAKNESSES OF NGOS

NGOs have strengths where governments have weaknesses. Weissbrodt argues that NGOs are freer to criticize where criticism is due than are governments or international bodies.[86] Second, NGOs' strength stems from the objectivity of NGOs' activities. The legitimacy and credibility of a human rights organization rest in large part on its impartiality. Third, there has been a high degree of specialization and professionalization between and among the organizations.[87] As a consequence, the input of NGOs has been taken seriously by many government delegations.[88] Fourth, personnel of NGOs are often deemed to be highly motivated by humanitarian dedication. Finally, Morten Kjaerum of the Danish Center for Human Rights argues that the strengths of NGOs' lie in their capacity:

1. to articulate citizen demands through active participation and consciousness-raising;
2. to encourage diversity and the growth of different opinions;
3. to assist in integrating groups in civil society and within the political process;
4. to serve as early warning mechanisms (usually in conjunction with international networks);
5. to serve as buffers against both the state and the market structure.[89]

A weakness of NGOs is, first, that most NGOs are short on financial resources. As a result, they need to rely on the most cost-effective strategies possible. In order to alleviate the situation, Wiseberg advocates establishing a human rights fund to assist NGOs who are acutely in need of funding for their activities.[90] Second, for many NGOs UN bodies - either in Geneva or New York - are distant both geographically and psychologically (e.g. the cost of attending, the lack of information, requirement of "consultative status"). This hampers NGOs from utilizing the UN procedures effectively. This is the raison d'etre of regional human rights regime such as the proposed one in East Asia.

PROBLEMS NGOS FACE[91]

First, many governments deliberately hamper activities of NGOs and seek to isolate them and to undermine their effectiveness because they expose official wrong-doing and press for change.[92] For example, in China while basic freedoms of expression, association and assembly are recognized by law, they are strictly curtailed in practice although there are exceptions at the local level for self-help groups concerned with women's issue, health, and children, etc.[93] The government's action under the pretext of protecting national security is contrary to the provisions of international human rights laws.[94] In 1998 the UN adopted "Declaration on the Rights and Responsibilities of Individuals, Groups and Public Institutions to Promote and Protect Human Rights and Universally Recognized Fundamental Freedoms," known as the Declaration on Human Rights Defenders. This was the first formal recognition of the role of non-state actors in rights monitoring.

Second, for Third World NGOs,[95] funding by Western foundations, development agencies, churches and other donors is often critical. Many governments in the Third World have used legislation to make it illegal for NGOs to accept foreign funds. Moreover, obstacles have been placed on raising the funds internally.

Third, as I have stated earlier, the number of NGOs has increased dramatically. For example, more than 160 NGOs attended the session of the UN Human Rights Commission in 1993. Posner explains:

> [B]ecause so many governments and NGOs want to speak, NGOs are frequently allotted the least popular time, late at night, when the great majority of government representatives have gone home. As a result, the impact of months of research and information-gathering of NGOs' may be virtually nil.[96]

In order to solve the problem, Posner suggests holding a public hearing at which local, international NGOs and individual victims would present their cases.[97] At the same time, it is also necessary to establish effective uniform rules and procedures for NGO participation throughout the UN system.

Fourth, an ill-founded or politically motivated NGO statement can create a negative impression. Inappropriate intervention of NGOs at the Commission on Human Rights or the Sub-Commission has contributed to increased restrictions on the activities of NGOs at the UN. This constitutes a serious setback.

Finally, the active NGOs tend to be organizations that have their membership primarily in the industrialized countries. This has led to charges that the NGO community is unrepresentative of the world as a whole. Blaser explains why imbalance may be a problem:

1.   it leaves NGOs vulnerable to attacks from critics;
2.   it limits the access of NGOs to desired information;
3.   it reflects an inability to activate grass roots participation;
4.   it may result in NGOs activities taking on a missionary character;
5.   it may lead to biased conclusions.[98]

NGOs need worldwide structure. Therefore, more participation by NGOs based in the Third World has been encouraged.[99]

In summation, nine major fields where human rights NGOs have played a significant role have been identified. I have also examined NGOs' strengths, limitations and problems. NGOs have played a crucial role in advocacy, developing and disseminating human rights norms and influencing policy, legal, medical and humanitarian assistance, and moral condemnation. NGOs have involved all the regimes of human rights identified by Donnelly - declaratory, promotion, implementation, and enforcement.[100] Donnelly identifies international regimes as "systems of norms and decision-making procedures accepted by states as binding in a particular issue area." A declaratory regime involves international norms; a promotional regime involves international exchange of information and efforts to promote or assist the national implementation of international norms; an implementation regime involves weaker monitoring procedures and policy coordination, in which states make regular use of an international forum; an enforcement regime involves binding international decision-making and strong forms of international monitoring of national compliance with international norms.

Freedom of association is the crux of effective human rights promotion. The presence of NGOs represents the expression of the right to popular participation; participation itself is a basic human right. Therefore, the exponential increase of NGOs is a hopeful sign. The primary task of human rights NGOs is to seek to hold governments accountable to internationally defined human rights standards. The independent functioning of NGOs is a positive indicator of the vitality of a country's democratic institutions, rather than a threat to that society. The governments, therefore, should take effective measures to help ensure the free operation of such groups.[101]

The balance between NGOs and the state has been shifting - NGOs are becoming more influential as the nation-state declines. NGOs have been agents of the strengthening civil society; Some parts of civil society are committed to the development of participatory democracy. The task of NGOs is to build solidarity, among NGOs not only between North-South, but also between NGOs in the South.

According to Otto, the NGOs' presence is the "unfinished revolution of emergent international civil society."[102] NGOs embody "an emerging global watch" for the protection of human dignity at the dawn of a human rights century.[103]

THE IMPLICATIONS OF THEORETICAL FRAMEWORK FOR FORMULATION OF REGIONAL HUMAN RIGHTS REGIME IN EAST ASIA

What are the implications of the theoretical framework for the formulation of a regional human rights mechanism in East Asia? We live today in an interdependent world based on global cooperation (e.g. networking, collaboration, coalitions, and alliances). National cultures, economies and borders are dissolving. Functionalists call this web of interdependence "functional integration." Functional activities include a wide range of spheres involving social, cultural, economic and humanitarian concerns.

Since the end of World War II, functional integration among the countries in East Asia has been steadily growing mainly through bilateral trade relations. East Asia is closely tied into the world trading system. Recent evidence suggests that ties within the region are becoming more intensive than those with the rest of the world. For example, an intra-regional Asian trade increased from US $95 billion in 1980 to $273 billion in 1990, representing a 287 percent change. This rate is higher than the rate of growth of intra-regional trade in North America (246 percent) and in the European Community (233 percent) for the same period.[104] In addition, flows of capital, goods, services, investment, communications, tourism and cultural exchanges have also been growing rapidly among the countries in the region.

According to functionalist theory, the web of mutually dependent linkage may lead to political, social, economic and cultural institutional framework although in the case of East Asia, the relations between both North and South Korea and the PRC and Taiwan still remain precarious. Yet even in East Asia, geographical proximity, common cultural tradition and heritage, and technological advancement in communications and transportation provide the impetus for functional collaboration, which increases awareness that "we share a common destiny." Korean President Kim Dae-jung argued when he visited China in November 1998, "we must provide the framework for cooperation to turn the 21st century into a millennium of coexistence and coprosperity for Northeast Asia."[105] Regional integration may gradually transfer power from the sovereign state to new regional structures and arrangements.

Functional integration has been taking place not only in commerce and cultural exchange but in the field of human rights as well. For example, representatives of the Governments of China, North and South Korea, Japan and Mongolia met in December 1999 to explore strategies and components for the development and enhancement of national capacities for human rights education in the schools. Representatives of the UN regional and sub-regional organizations as well as NGOs such as the Asia-Pacific Resource Center for Human Rights Education, HURIGHTS Osaka, and the Asia-Pacific Network for International Education and Value Education also attended.[106]

Human rights NGOs, "sovereign-free-actors," (Rosenau 1990) are increasingly becoming regional and global because groups have been establishing strategic linkages across national borders. NGOs communicate, collaborate and build relationships across national boundaries through extensive transnational consultation, meetings, and exchange of information. NGOs are not tied to the territoriality of the state and have freedom to operate as they see fit in their dealing with issues. Human rights NGOs facilitate democratization and build a human rights culture. They promote regional integration in East Asia in order to achieve their organizational goals.

For some time, many Asian NGOs have expressed the need for an Asian Charter on Human Rights. This need began to be felt especially after some Asian governments advocated that human rights is a Western concept and has no relevance to Asia. The Asian Human Rights Charter: Our Common Humanity[107] was drafted by NGOs calling themselves the Asian Human Rights Commission (AHRC)[108] in cooperation with the International Affairs Office of the Christian Conference of Asia. The document was declared in Kwangju, South Korea in 1998 on the occasion of the 50th anniversary of the Universal Declaration of Human Rights. Kwangju was chosen symbolically for the affirmation of the Asian solidarity for all victims of human rights and to express the vindication of the rights of people and the aspirations of the peoples for democracy and human rights.

The Charter is the fruit of regional integration because thousands of people from various Asian countries participated in the debates during the three-year period of discussions on the document, especially regarding the most fundamental issues relating to the concept of human rights and the enforcement of human rights.   Three regional consultations had been held to discuss the proposed draft, which includes the South Asian Consultation in Colombo, Sri Lanka in January, 1995, the South-East Asian Consultation in Hong Kong in August 1995, and the East Asian Consultation in Hong Kong in January 1996. More than 200 NGOs took part in the drafting process and many other NGOs have endorsed the document. For example, the Taiwan Association of Human Rights expressed its support of the Charter by stating that:

> We firmly believe the reasons for the need for an Asian Charter of
> Human Rights. We agree with the principle of the universality and
> indivisibility of human rights. There is no difference on human rights
> between the Western and Eastern and North and South. We uncondi-
> tionally support the concept and practice of participatory democracy
> as the legitimate requirement of a government.[109]

The guiding principle of the drafted Asian Human Rights Charter is that
"human rights is an end in itself and not a means to an end."[110] As the sub-
title of the Charter "our common humanity" indicates, the Charter represents "moral interdependence." The Charter is a "consensus building"
effort at a time when of marketization and globalization of economies are
changing the balance between private and public, and between the state
and the international community.

Asian development is full of contradictions. There is massive poverty
in the midst of growing affluence in some sections. Asians have in recent
decades suffered from various forms of conflict, and violence and human
rights abuses. There is massive displacement of communities and an
increasing number of refugees.

The Charter states that governments have arrogated enormous powers
to themselves that have often resulted in authoritarianism, corruption and
nepotism. The Charter rejects "Asian values" and cultural relativism arguments and strongly affirms universality and the indivisibility of human
rights. The document states: "we believe that rights are universal, every
person being entitled to them by virtue of being a human being." The
Charter is modeled after the African Charter on Human and Peoples'
Rights and includes such rights as:

1.   the responsibility for the protection of human rights;
2.   sustainable development and the protection of the environ-
     ment;
3.   the right to life;
4.   the rights to peace, democracy, development and social jus-
     tice;
5.   the right to cultural identity;
6.   freedom of conscience;
7.   rights to vulnerable groups, women, children, disabled per-
     sons, workers and students.

Thus, the Charter encompasses rights of first generation (civil and political) and of second generation (economic, social and cultural rights) as well
as of third generation (right to peace, democracy and development).

As for an enforcement mechanism, the Charter states that:

there should be an inter-state convention on human rights, formulated in regional forums with the collaboration of national and regional NGOs. The Convention must address the realities of Asia. At the same time it must be fully consistent with international norms and standards. An independent commission or a court must be established to enforce the Convention. Access to the commission or the court must be open to NGOs and other organizations.

The Charter is intended to be used as an educational document and has been translated into many Asian languages. It will be used as a basis to develop solidarity for the promotion and protection of human rights in Asia because the Charter is considered a common standard of achievement for peoples and nations in the region.

Using innovative language, the Charter responds to some of the negative consequences of economic globalization and the non-state power of multi-national corporations by stating that a new inter-state organization should "cover violations of rights by groups and corporations in addition to state institutions." The Charter demonstrates civic activism played by global civil society, loosely organized voluntary associations independent of the state who demand accountability and transparency in governance. The Charter is a manifestation of the internationalization of human rights[111] and reflects the impact of globalization on human rights matters. The Charter is an important landmark for the East Asian people, based on regional solidarity, consciousness, and responsibility.

The Charter is a positive step toward regional human rights "institution-building" in East Asia because an enforcement mechanism can be built upon the Charter. The effectiveness of regional machinery is that it can reflect regional particularities (e.g. needs, priorities, conditions).

Chapter III

The Impact of Globalization on Human Rights

IN CHAPTER III, I INVESTIGATE THE ISSUE OF THE UNIVERSALITY OF human rights as opposed to cultural relativism. I examine cultural relativism based on African, Confucian, and Islamic traditions. My contention is that a global culture of human rights has been spreading because of the common culture of modernity based on the global wave of democratization. The Asian Human Rights Charter is a reflection of this global trend and it embodies the universality of human rights, even though the people who participated in the drafting process of the Charter were primarily from Confucian cultures and traditions. I investigate whether the so-called Asian concept of human rights, based on cultural relativism, is a valid argument.

The cross-cultural and inter-civilizational human rights norms have been increasingly accepted in a pluralistic contemporary world. Convergence on human rights has been taking place across cultures, which we call the universality of human rights. The concept of human rights can and should apply for all human beings in every human society equally and in equal measure by virtue of their humanity.

THE UNIVERSALITY OF HUMAN RIGHTS

People display enormous diversity in customs, languages, religions, moral norms, values, and political practices. In the article "Clash of Civilizations?", Huntington identifies eight major civilizations—Western, Confucian, Japanese, Islamic, Hindu, Slavic-Orthodox, Latin American and African.[1] The world is also divided by levels of economic development and ideologies into either first, second, and third worlds or a North-South framework.[2] This enormous civilizational diversity has led to a situation where ideas on human rights seem to lack a commonly shared philosophical foundation upon which to promote a uniform interpretation of rights in the international community.

The debate between universality versus cultural relativism is one of the major issues in study of human rights. The cause of this debate is that the modern concept of human rights stems from largely the liberal tradition of Western thought,[3] especially the Lockean theory of natural rights that constitutes an indispensable source of contemporary ideas of human rights.[4] According to the European concept, human rights are composed of principles and rules made available to the individual with the essential aim of enabling him to defend himself against the state.

For instance, the idea of natural rights reflects a view of man as natural, autonomous, and private. This derives from Protestantism. The U.S. Constitution states that:

> "We hold these truths to be self-evident, that all men are created equal, that they are endowed by their Creator with certain unalienable rights, that among these are life, liberty and the pursuit of happiness... to secure these rights governments are instituted among men, deriving just power from the consent of the governed; that whenever any form of government becomes destructive of these ends it is the right of the people to alter or abolish it and to institute a new government."

Because of this Western origin of human rights (e.g. the Habeas Corpus Act [1679], the English Bill of Rights [1689], the American Declaration of Independence [1776], the French Declaration of the Rights of Man and the Citizen [1789]), An-Naim contends that the concept of human rights is inherently alien to the non-Western tradition of third world countries to which it is now being extended.[5] He argues that a blanket application of Western principles to non-western conditions is unjustifiable.

Onuma observes critically on the universality of human rights that "in the discourse of universalism and cultural particularity, there is an implied assumption of the West signifying the universal and Asia signifying the particular. But universality is actually the Western approach in disguise."[6] Does universality embody the "cultural imperialism" of the "decadent West", and does cultural relativism represent what Bull calls "the revolt against the West" by non-Western states?[7] Should the West have more respect for other values and cultures?[8]

I shall begin with a brief investigation of African,[9] Confucian (East Asia)[10] and Islamic[11] traditions and human rights by highlighting those features of the three cultures relating to the role of individual in an effort to trace the roots of cultural relativism. Then, I will examine and assess the debate between cultural relativism and the universality of human rights. I will elucidate the evolution of the concept of the universality of human rights.

HUMAN RIGHTS IN AFRICA, EAST ASIA AND ISLAM

AFRICA

The African Charter on Human and Peoples' Rights emphasizes the rights of collectivities such as "peoples."[12] In Africa, the concept of human rights is based on the fact that "the group is more important than the individual, decisions are made by consensus rather than by competition."[13]

Second, rights are inseparable from the idea of duty because the African family is buttressed by powerful ideologies that stress loyalty to kinfolk and performance of duty (rather than assertion of rights).[14] Article 29 of the African Charter stresses the individual's duty; to serve his national community; to preserve and strengthen social and national solidarity, as well as the national independence and the territorial integrity of his country and positive African cultural values; and to contribute to the promotion and achievement of African unity. Third, as for women, they have lacked all formal legally recognized rights throughout the four centuries of the colonial era.[15]

Cohen observes that in Africa colonial rule destroyed traditional institutions that had constrained power and protected people, and introduced into Africa security police, prisons, and the practice of preventive detention. Colonial rule was replaced with authoritarian governments. As a result, Africans have had no real experience of living under democratic rule.[16]

After independence the African governments became members of the United Nations and accepted its principles, including the Universal Declaration of Human Rights. African governments' concentration on economic development and nation building has led to centralization of power in the hands of the state. M'Baye sums up human rights situations in Africa by saying that "governments have sacrificed rights and freedoms for the sake of economic development and political stability."[17]

EAST ASIA

People in East Asia (Taiwan, Japan, China and the Koreas) are still instilled with Confucian values and habits. Confucianism has been so powerful and so pronounced that it has virtually ruled people's lives in East Asia. Confucius stresses submission to the hierarchical and patriarchal authority and the proper place for each person within the hierarchy. Confucius also emphasizes preservation of group harmony and discourages individualism.[18] No man lives independently of other people or of his community. This idea is directly in contrast to Mill's notion that the "individual is sovereign."[19]

Confucian societies are structured around duties, not rights. Lee Manwoo points out that East Asian society as a whole has preoccupied itself not with individual rights but with duties.[20] The ruler had a duty towards Heaven rather than to the well-being of the people (the Mandate of Heaven). The well-being of the community (family bondage, communal peace, social harmony, etc) takes priority over that of the individual and conformity is stressed at the expense of individual expression[21] ("Confucian communitarianism," de Bary, 1998); In this context the family is considered the building brick of society.[22]

In Confucian tradition rights are granted, not inherent but granted by government to serve societal purposes.[23] The ideal is not individual liberty, but order and harmony, not individual independence but cooperation, not the freedom of individual conscience but conformity to society. Confucius argues that to be effective, law must comply with the moral order inherent in society. He encourages the virtues of filiality, loyalty and social compassion. In Confucian society, the preferred mode of conflict resolution has been nonadversarial and nonjudicial. This legacy has become the foundation of what Hsiung calls the "Oriental consensual model"[24] and has often resulted in despotism. According to "Asian Values," (Asian concept of human rights, espoused by some leaders in the region), Asia has a unique set of values that provides a different understanding of human rights.[25] The "Asian Values," of which the principal philosophical foundation is the Confucian heritage, prescribe that, first, duties and discipline are more important than political liberty and civil rights; second, the collective good takes priority over an individual's rights; third, economic development must precede the advance of political and civil rights because political authoritarianism is helpful for economic growth.

Thus, social and economic rights are more important than civil and political rights. This is sometimes called the "Lee thesis" (based on a contention of Lee Kuan Yew, the influential ex-Prime Minister of Singapore). Lee Kuan Yew stresses that Western-style democracy is not applicable to East Asia and defends "soft" authoritarianism by arguing that:

> "As Prime Minister of Singapore, my first task was to lift my country out of the degradation that poverty, ignorance, and disease had wrought. Since it was dire poverty that made for such a low priority given to human life, all other things became secondary."[26]

Tremewan, however, observes that Singapore holds its population in a political straitjacket.[27] It has been argued that rights are not luxuries to be enjoyed only after a certain level of economic development has been achieved. In fact, there is no relationship between economic growth, the level of economic development, and overall protection of human rights.

Amartya Sen warns against the "Asian Values" contention by offering a penetrating observation that "no substantial famine has ever occurred in any country with a democratic form of government and a relatively free press."[28]
In the meantime, Sen recognizes human rights elements in Asian traditions that the treatment of elderly members of the family (such as aged parents) is more supportive in Asian countries.

Asian values also hold that rights are a matter of national sovereignty;[29] Ding defends China's human rights policy by arguing that no universal human rights override the laws of various countries.[30]

ISLAM

Islam is the faith of nearly one-fifth of the world's population. There are neither monolithic Islamic cultural standards nor a single, definitive interpretation of Islamic rights principles. The term Islam means both "submission" and "peace." According to Monshipouri, Islam is a set of convictions, values, ideals, symbols, doctrines, institutions, and practice (Monshipouri, 1998, p. 1). On the interpretation, the purpose of the state in Islam is to enforce the principles of the Sharia (Islamic religious law). Abdullahi Ahmed El Naiem points out that Sharia does not recognize universal suffrage, organized political opposition, independence of the judiciary, separation of powers, or the rights of women.[31]

Islamic authority stems from the Koran (general ethical principles), Sunna (the practice of the prophet Muhammad) and Sharia.[32]

Said explains that:

> the essential characteristic of human rights in Islam is that they constitute obligations connected with the Divine. Human rights exist only in relation to human obligations. Individuals possess certain obligations toward God, fellow humans and nature, all of which are defined by Sharia. When individuals meet these obligations they acquire certain rights and freedoms.[33]

In Islam the community comes before the individual because it is thought that the human personality is realized by action for the good of the collectivity through self-abnegation.[34] Second, in Islam rights are subordinated to, and determined by duties because moral obligations to other persons and peoples take precedence over individual human rights. Donnelly comments, "in Islam what matters is duty rather than rights."[35]

Khalid lists the following rights contemplated in the Koran:

1.   Right to protection of life;
2.   Right to justice;
3.   Right to equality;
4.   Duty to obey what is lawful, and right to disobey what is unlawful;
5.   Right to participate in public life;
6.   Right to freedom;
7.   Right to freedom of conviction;
8.   Right to freedom of expression;
9.   Right of protection against persecution on the ground of difference;
10. Right to protection of honor and good name;
11. Right to privacy;
12. Economic rights;
13. Right to property;
14. Right to adequate remuneration and compensation.[36]

Islam does not include the equal treatment of women[37] and the freedom to change religion.[38] The general rule of Sharia is that men are the guardians of women and as such have the license to discipline them to the extent of beating them "lightly" if they fear the women will become unruly. Whereas a man is entitled to marry up to four wives and divorce them at will, a woman is restricted to one husband and can only seek a judicial divorce on very limited and restricted grounds. Women receive only half a share of the man's inheritance, and less monetary compensation for criminal bodily harm (diya). Women are incompetent to testify in serious criminal cases; it takes two women to make a single witness. Muslim women may not hold any office involving exercise of authority over Muslim men.

Similarly, unbelievers are not allowed to live within an Islamic state except with a special permit of self-conduct (aman). Consequently non-Muslims are denied any public office, which would involve exercising such authority.[39] Consequently, Islamic culture has been a breeding ground for authoritarian/patriarchal regimes.[40]

CULTURAL RELATIVISM

Cultural relativism is defined as that culture is the so; e of the validity of moral rights and rules. The conceptual analysis of cultural relativism is provided by Nickel, who argues that cultural relativism means that all moral values, including human rights, are "culturally embedded" and thus are relative to the cultural context.[41]

Crocker argues that moral relativism consists of three doctrines: (i) social descriptive relativism (i.e. cultural relativism) claims that different cultures, societies, or classes have significantly different positive social morality; (ii) social normative relativism (prescriptive relativism) prescribes to that one should follow the moral rules of one's group, since morality is relative; (iii) metaethical relativism (skeptical relativism) argues that moral judgments cannot be resolved rationally and both sides to the conflict are equally correct or justified.[42]

Donnelly distinguishes three types of cultural relativism—radical, strong and weak. The differences between these relativist positions are that culture is either the sole, principal or maybe an important source of the validity of moral rights or rule.[43] Teson also proposes three types of relativism - descriptive, metaethical and normative - in order to analyze the moral status of relativism. For example, descriptive relativism asserts that different societies have different perceptions of right and wrong.[44]

According to cultural relativism, in view of the existence of diverse cultures, there is no universal culture therefore, no culture, tradition, ideology or religion can speak for all humankind.[45] Thus, there exist no universal and transboundary legal or moral standards. Every society or culture recognizes certain values, mores, norms, and operational principles by which it seeks to approximate the ideas of human dignity.[46]

Each country's human rights conditions are circumscribed by its historical, social, economic, and cultural conditions, and human rights reflect a country's stage of historical development. Non-relativists or universalists argue that the Universal Declaration of Human Rights constitutes a common core of values to which all peoples and nations should aspire. However, what these rights mean in practice will differ from nation to nation and from culture to culture.

Even if a body of substantive human rights norms does exist, its application varies substantially from culture to culture. For example, the European Court of Human Rights has developed the concept of the "margin of appreciation" when examining national legislation for compatibility with the European Convention of Human Rights, which enables the Court to permit a diversity of approaches within Europe.

In this context, relativists argue that certain human values such as equal protection or political participation are inappropriate in certain cultural or political contexts. For that reason, current international human rights standards are insensitive to or incompatible with various cultural, political, and social conditions. Mahbubani argues that the West has no right to give moral lectures to Asia.[47] This line of argument may be used, however, for self-serving excuses for some governments' violations of human rights.

Western societies consider human rights to be individualistic, adversarial, just, and inalienable in contrast to social welfare, collective rights, consensual dispute resolution, economic development, and state interests in

Asian, African and Islamic traditions. These have resulted in the contention that the concept of human rights is alien to non-Western cultures. Therefore, the contention has been made that the meaning and application of human rights should be dependent upon regional and national conditions. The Third World leaders may think that the human rights movement involves one more attempt by ethnocentric Europeans and Americans to impose their values on the rest of the world. They feel deeply about the importance of preserving their own traditions and cultures.

In addition, the diversity of cultural traditions, political structures, and levels of economic development make it difficult to define a single distinctive and coherent human rights regime that can encompass vast regions.

These arguments lead to the notion that different societies have and should have different perceptions of right and wrong; "What is right or good for one individual or society is not right or good for another, even if the situations involved are similar."[48] Then, they conclude: there is no one universally valid standard of human rights. In this context, human rights violations may have been condoned because they happen to be tolerated or sanctioned by the cultural tradition of the society or the community in question (e.g. female genital mutilation, child labor, and flogging).

Furthermore, cultural relativists argues, human nature is to a considerable extent culturally determined, and if human rights are based on human nature, human rights themselves are culturally relative.[49] The "Statement on Human Rights" prepared by the American Anthropological Association stated in 1947, in part:

1.   The individual realizes his personality through his culture. Hence respect for individual differences entails a respect for cultural differences.
2.   Standards and values are relative to the culture from which they derive.

The relativist position was strongly expressed in the Bangkok Government Declaration, which affirms a state-centric perspective based on respect for national sovereignty, and territorial integrity and noninterference in the internal affairs of states. The Declaration provides, in part:

> Human rights must be considered in the context of the dynamic and evolving process of international norm-setting, bearing in mind the significance of national and regional particularities and various historical, cultural and religious backgrounds.

The strength of the relativists' argument stems from the fact that descriptive relativism captures much truth: there is diversity in norms.

Their view reflects realities of contemporary international society. They demand that the concept of human rights should be modified by local cultural conditions. The universalist position sometimes lacks local cultural sensitivity and destroys cultural diversity. The cultural relativity provides a legal ground for self-determination.[50] It is an affirmation of "a right to be different."[51] Another feature of cultural relativism is that it inconsistently may advocate tolerance and call for respect for other cultures. Its cultural egalitarianism might reduce ethnocentrism in a multi-cultural world.[52] But tolerance is a universally valid norm and it does not follow logically from diversity of values. Yet the negative aspect of relativism is that to uphold cultural pluralism is to argue that every culture is equally valid and that no external values should be allowed to influence them. Thus, oppressive governments have used the principle of nonintervention in the internal affairs of sovereign states as an defense of their human rights violations.

Relativists attack the universalist position that the seemingly neutral title of international human rights law in fact favors widening and deepening the legitimacy of Western conceptions of human rights; the objections have ranged from accusations of "Western bias" to "cultural imperialism." Human rights is a "Western construct with limited applicability."[53] Third World views on international human rights differ widely.[54] Vincent makes the point that the international law of human rights is an export of the West to the rest of the world.[55] In this respect, the Universal Declaration of Human Rights is the imposition of an alien value system - the universalization of Western values and aspirations.[56]

UNIVERSALITY OF HUMAN RIGHTS

The universalist position argues against the various forms of normative and metaethical relativism and affirms the existence of legitimate cross-cultural standards for evaluating human rights practices — even though some cultures may not yet accept them.

Li argues that there are three ways in which a value can be either universal or non-universal - origin, validity and implementation.[57] Cranston affirms the "universality of validity" of human rights by arguing that a human right by definition is something which all men, everywhere, at all times ought to have, something of which no one may be deprived.[58]

As for the validity of human rights, even if rights conceptions originated in the West (elements may have originated in the East), universalists claim that there is a core of values that is valid for culture. All individuals solely by virtue of being human, that is, solely by virtue of potential ability to exercise rational choice, have moral rights which no society or state should deny. According to Shue, a moral right provides:

1. the rational basis for a justified demand;
2. the actual enjoyment of a substance;
3. social guarantees against standard threats.[59]

Likewise, for most of us, Donnelly argues, morality is inherently universalistic and egalitarian.[60] All societies have underlying conceptions of human dignity and social justice.

Furthermore, Li argues that an intercultural discourse has been taking place among people with different cultural assumptions, which has resulted in verifying the universal validity of human rights. Onuma argues that the raison d'etre of human rights must be grounded in a globally-legitimate intercivilizational perspective.[61] There is a reasonable cross-cultural consensus on many of the values that today we seek to protect through human rights (e.g. life, protection from arbitrary rule, prohibition of inhuman and degrading treatment, slavery, genocide, and extrajudicial execution). This indicates the existence of the inherent validity of basic moral precepts even though some groups may not agree and may hold beliefs incompatible with human rights.

Individuals are entitled to basic rights (security, liberty and subsistence[62]) regardless of contingent factors such as their cultural surroundings or the norms dominant in their societies. Basic rights represent "everyone's minimal reasonable demands upon the rest of humanity."[63] Human rights apply for all human beings in every human society equally and in equal measure by virtue of their humanity; for every human being, regardless of gender or race, class or status, wealth or poverty, occupation, talent, merit, religion, ideology, or other commitment; in every society, regardless of geography, or history, culture or ideology, political or economic system, or stage of development. One argument appeals to a human nature in which rights are independent of time, place, culture, ideology, or value systems. Human rights are claims made on society by individuals or groups on the basis of their humanity. They apply regardless of race, color, sex, or other distinctions and may not be withdrawn or denied by governments.

Korea's Foreign Minister Han Sung-joo stresses that human rights cannot be altered according to circumstances.[64] For that reason, the concept that human rights are alien to Asian culture is being challenged by Asian people themselves.[65] It is the institutional implementation of human rights that differs between Asia and the West, not the concepts themselves.[66]

As for the universality of the implementation of human rights a large number of international human rights agreements are in force today. They have been ratified by a substantial majority of the international community of states. The Universal Declaration of Human Rights, "Magna Carta of Mankind",[67] (1948) proclaims that the Declaration is "a common standard of achievement for all peoples and all nations."[68] It has been argued that the Declaration has become part of international customary law binding on all states without their express consent. The UN Charter (Article 1) stresses "respect for human rights and fundamental freedoms for all without distinction as to race, sex, language, religion." The Vienna Declaration and Programme of Action of 1993[69] stresses that the "universal nature of these rights and freedoms is beyond question." (paragraph 1) and states that:

> [A]ll human rights are universal, indivisible, and interdependent and interrelated. The international community must treat human rights globally in a fair and equal manner, on the same footing, and with the same emphasis.

Kofi Annan, UN General-Secretary, states that:

> Human rights are African rights. They are also Asian rights, they are European rights. They are American rights. They belong to no government, they are limited to no continent, for they are fundamental to humankind itself.[70]

While the codification efforts, which Donnelly calls "the convergence of cross-cultural human values,"[71] have been successful, the opposite is true with regard to implementation (e.g. the International Court of Human Rights[72]).

As I have indicated so far, Africa, East Asia and Islam have distinctive traditions and outlooks on the concept of human rights. Current "internationally recognized human rights" may not be sufficiently universal because they lack legitimacy in major cultural traditions. The full idea of human rights is certainly Western-based. This is the root cause of the impediment to realizing universality of human rights.

However, even if there may not be a universal foundation in human nature, natural law, or existing normative beliefs for a concept of human rights, a global consensus could emerge because, as An-Naim argues, cultures are constantly changing and evolving internally.[73] For example, the 1993 Bangkok NGO Declaration states, in part, that "We can learn from different cultures in a pluralistic perspective and draw lessons from the humanity of these cultures to deepen respect for human rights. There is emerging a new understanding of universalism... Universal human rights standards are rooted in many cultures."

In this context, Bielefeldt advocates that a serious international discourse on human rights through self-critical reevaluation is necessary to create a cross-cultural "overlapping consensus,"[74] which John Rawls defines this way:

> Different groups, countries, religious communities, civilizations, while holding incompatible fundamental views on theology, metaphysics, human nature, etc., would come to an agreement on certain norms that ought to govern human behavior. Each would have its own way of justifying this from out of its profound background conception. We would agree on the norms, while disagreeing on why they were the right norms. And we would be content to live in this consensus, undisturbed by the difference of profound underlying belief.[75]

The world has become increasingly interdependent.[76] Interdependence implies that nations are sensitive or vulnerable in significant ways to developments taking place beyond their borders. Thus, governments become less the masters of what occurs within their countries, even though they continue to claim sovereignty.[77]

The concept of a right has been removed from the domain of domestic jurisdiction and has become a matter of treaty obligation. A state is thus obligated to incorporate international standards into its domestic system. The concern for human rights nullifies the principle of non-interference in domestic affairs. Rather, breaches of human rights, especially gross breaches, are increasingly removed from domestic jurisdiction and placed in international judicial processes, such as international criminal court.

Ghai argues that the national and international movement of rights is itself a product of globalization.[70] Convergence is taking place across cultures, which results in a "cross-fertilization" that reinforces the global consensus on human rights.[79] It promotes cosmopolitanism and respect for diversity. Taylor suggests an "unforced international consensus" that is defined as

> Agreement on 'norms, but a profound sense of difference, of unfamiliarity, in the ideals, the notions of human excellence, the rhetorical tropes and reference points by which these norms become objects of deep commitment for us.[80]

I disagree with Marfording's argument that the universality versus cultural relativism debate has reached an impasse.[81] Human rights is an evolving conception, expressing imperfectly the aspirations of many, if not all, peoples.[82] It is my strong contention that human rights standards have been in a process of becoming universal because of modernization, which is a coherent process that produces a certain uniformity of economic and political institutions across different regions and cultures.[83] Accordingly, in the last decade a majority of governments have either participated in the formulation process or subsequently ratified the relevant international human rights instruments.[84] Thus, despite its largely Western origin, the concept of human rights has finally been in a process of becoming universally valid.

Moreover, it should be noted that universal human rights do not impose one thick cultural standard, rather one moral and legal standard of minimum protection necessary for human dignity.[85]

Meanwhile, as Donoho argues, I must caution that a certain degree of cultural and political sensitivity with respect to implementation (not validity) is necessary in the interim to achieve human rights values in a diverse, pluralistic world. Human rights can be harmful if universalism is used to deny all aspects of diversity.[86] To be denied are aspects of local culture that violate core rights.

Pluralism is not merely healthy but necessary to any successful international human rights system.[87] But pluralism must be constrained by universal rights and religious tolerance and freedom is one the rights. Based on an eclectic, cross-cultural approach[88] to universal human rights, Schwartz contends that:

> [E]very culture will have its distinctive ways of formulating and supporting human rights. Every society can learn from other societies more effective ways to implement human rights. While honoring the diversity of cultures, we can also build toward common principles that all can support.[89]

We are living at one of those junctures of history when a unique new culture is in the making.[90] A global culture of human rights is an emerging world order, in Forsythe's phrase the "internationalization of human rights.[91] Onuma advocates an "intercivilizational approach to human rights" because it would liberate the human rights discourse from domination by Westcentrism; and second, it would expand and improve commitment to all human rights on a global scale.[92]

Universal human rights are possible because of the emerging common culture of modernity[93] and the global wave of democratization;[94] Modernization involves industrialization, urbanization, increasing levels of education, literacy, wealth and social mobilization. Human rights are universal values to be defended and promoted. Human rights are a pillar of the UN Charter to which all states are bound. The Vienna Declaration provides that while the significance of national and regional particularities and various historical, cultural and religious backgrounds must be borne in mind, it is the duty of states, regardless of their political, economic and cultural systems, to promote and protect all human rights and fundamental freedoms.

Kofi Annan, General Secretary of the UN, provides a penetrating remark: "it was never the people who complained of the universality of human rights, nor did the people consider human rights as a Western imposition. It was often their leaders who did so."[95]

The global repudiation of normative and metaethical relativism and growing global acceptance of universality is a positive sign for establishing a regional human rights regime in East Asia. People in Asia are beginning to understand that it is necessary to have an implementation mechanism, albeit one with Asian traits, based on universality of human rights in the region.

INCREASING THE NUMBER OF INTERNATIONAL HUMAN RIGHTS TREATIES AND EXPANDING UNITED NATIONS HUMAN RIGHTS MECHANISMS

The acceptance of universality of human rights has resulted in codification of a large number of international human rights treaties, which have been signed and ratified by a majority of the international community. As a result, human rights laws occupy a major domain of international law today. Human rights promotion and protection mechanisms at the UN have been expanding rapidly to enforce international human rights standards and principles. According to functionalist analysis, this indicates the functional strategy of "consensus building." This globalization of human rights is a positive impetus for setting up a regional mechanism in East Asia.

International human rights standards and principles have been dramatically developed, especially since the end of the World War II, to promote and protect human rights in the world. The nucleus of international human rights treaties, in addition to the human rights provisions of the UN Charter, the International Bill of Rights, consists of the Universal Declaration of Human Rights (1948);[96] the International Covenant on Economic, Social and Cultural Rights (1966);[97] the International Covenant on Civil and Political Rights (1966);[98] and the Optional Protocols to the Covenant on Civil and Political Rights.[99]

In 1948 the UN General Assembly adopted the Universal Declaration of Human Rights. The Universal Declaration is the first comprehensive human rights instrument and is ranked with the Magna Carta, the American Declaration of Independence, and the French Declaration of the Rights of Man and the Citizen. The Declaration, "a minimum response to the convergence of cross-cultural human values,"[100] is not a treaty, therefore, has no binding power but has a moral value. It serves as "a common standard of achievement for all peoples and all nations."

French jurist Karel Vasak developed the notion of "three generations of human rights"; the first generation of civil and political rights (liberte), the second generation of economic, social and cultural rights (egalite), and the third generation of solidarity rights (fraternite) (e.g. the right to development, to peace, to democracy, to a healthy environment).[101]

In 1948 the UN adopted the Genocide Convention. The Genocide Convention declares that genocide is a "crime under international law." The Convention defines genocide as the commission of acts "with intent to destroy, in whole or in part, a national, ethnic, racial or religious group (Art II)." The Convention does not have an implementation system. A dispute between state parties relating to the Convention may be brought to the International Court of Justice. The Tribunal does not have jurisdiction to try individuals for genocide.

In 1965 the UN adopted the International Convention on the Elimination of All Forms of Racial Discrimination (CERD). The Convention prohibits "racial discrimination" which is defined as "any distinction, exclusion, restriction or preference based on race, color, descent, or national or ethnic origin" (Art. 1). The state parties to the Convention have a legal obligation to eliminate racial discrimination in their territory by any person, group or organization.

In 1966 the UN General Assembly adopted the Covenants on Civil and Political Rights (ICCPR) and on Economic, Social and Cultural Rights (ICESCR). The Covenants created binding legal obligations for the state parties to them. Each Covenant establishes a distinct international enforcement system designed to insure that the state parties comply with their obligations. Each state party to the Covenants undertakes to respect and to ensure to all individuals within its territory and subject to its jurisdiction the rights recognized in the Covenant, without distinction of any kind.

Whereas the obligations which a state party assumes by ratifying the Civil and Political Rights require immediate implementation, the Covenant on Economic, Social and Cultural Rights obligates state parties to achieve "progressively the full realization" of the rights enumerated in the Covenant. The ICESCR Covenant does not establish any inter-state or individual complaint system. It only requires the state parties to submit reports on the measures, which they have adopted to realize the recognized rights.

In 1979 the UN adopted the Convention on the Elimination of All Forms of Discrimination Against Women (CEDAW). That discrimination is defined as "any distinction, exclusion, or restriction made on the basis of sex." Article 5 of the Convention provides that State Parties shall take all appropriate measures:

(a) To modify the social and cultural patterns of conduct of men and women, with a view to achieving the elimination of prejudices and customary and all other practices which are based on the idea of the inferiority or the superiority of either of the sexes or on stereotyped roles for men and women.

The Convention is the first international treaty dealing with the rights of women in a global manner including provisions for a reporting system and review machinery. The Convention requires state parties to submit periodic reports relating to "the legislative, judicial, administrative or other measures they have adopted to give effect to the provisions of the Convention" (Art 18 [1]).

In 1984 the UN adopted the Convention Against Torture and Other Cruel, Inhuman or Degrading Treatment. This Convention is designed to prevent and punish torture, which is defined as "any act by which severe pain or suffering, whether physical or mental, is intentionally inflicted on a person" for the purpose of obtaining from him or a third person information or a confession (Art. 1[1]). The Torture Convention establishes a reporting system (Art. 19) as well as an optional inter-state complaint (Art. 21) and individual petition system (Art. 22).

Other relevant instruments preceding this Convention are: the Standard Minimum Rules for the Treatment of Prisoners (1955), the Code of Conduct for Law Enforcement Officers (1979), and the Principles of Medical Ethics (1982). In 1982 the United Nations established a Voluntary Fund for Victims of Torture.[102]

In 1986 the Declaration of the Right to Development was adopted.[103] The Declaration states that the right to development is an integral part of human rights and fundamental freedoms and aims at constant improvement of the well-being of the entire population, free and meaningful participation, and fair distribution of benefits. The Declaration postulates equality of opportunity as the main principle applicable to both nations and individuals.

In 1989 the UN adopted the Convention on the Rights of the Child (CRC). The Convention is the proposition that children are entitled to human rights in their own capacity.

In summation, as of May 2002, the number of countries who have ratified the major human rights covenants are as follows:

Table 1. Ratification Status of Major Human Rights Instruments [As of May 2002]

CESCR	CCPR	OPT 1	OPT 2	*Genocide*	CERD	CEDAW	CAT	CRC
145	148	103	47	125	162	168	128	191

In addition to the above major human rights conventions, the following human rights instruments have been adopted at the UN.

1949	The Convention on the Suppression of Traffic in Persons
1951	The Convention on the Status of Refugees
1952	The Convention on the Political Status of Women
1956	The Supplementary Convention on the Abolition of Slavery
1957	The Convention on the Nationality of Married Women
1957	The Abolition of Forced Labor Convention
1958	The Discrimination (Employment and Occupation) Convention
1960	The Convention Against Discrimination in Education
1965	The Convention on Consent to Marriage, Minimum Age for Marriage and Registration of Marriages
1969	The Declaration on Social Progress and Development
1971	The Declaration on the Rights of Mentally Retarded Persons
1973	The International Convention on the Suppression and Punishment of Apartheid
1974	The Universal Declaration on the Eradication of Hunger and Malnutrition
1974	The Declaration on the Protection of Women and Children in Emergency and Armed Conflict
1975	The Declaration on the Rights of Disabled Persons
1978	The Declaration on Race and Racial Prejudice
1979	The Declaration on the Elimination of All Forms of Discrimination against Women
1981	The Declaration on the Elimination of All Forms of Intolerance and of Discrimination Based on Religion or Belief
1991	The International Convention on the Protection of the Rights of All Migrant Workers and Members of Their Families
1992	The Declaration on the Protection of All Persons from Enforced Disappearance

These international human rights treaties occupy a significant portion of international law today. These conventions connote an expanding human rights culture. As members of the international community the countries in East Asia have been influenced by this enlightenment. These treaties are the foundations for "internationally recognized human rights" upon which proposed East Asian human rights protection mechanisms would be based.

REGIONAL INSTRUMENTS[104]

In Europe, the Council of Europe was established in 1949 by a group of ten states, which, as of 1995, expanded to include 34 states. The Council of Europe organized one of the most advanced human rights protection mechanisms.[105] The Council supported the European Convention for the Protection of Human Rights and Fundamental Freedoms, which covers mainly civil and political rights, and was signed in 1950, as well as the European Social Charter, which recognizes economic and social rights, and was signed in 1961. In 1987 the European Convention for the Prevention of Torture and Inhuman or Degrading Treatment or Punishment was also adopted by the Council of Europe. The Convention established a Committee for the Prevention of Torture (CPT).[106]

In 1948 the Organization of American States (OAS) was established and as of 1995 the OAS has 35 member states. The OAS adopted the American Declaration of the Rights and Duties of Man in 1948. The Declaration proclaims a list of twenty-seven rights and ten duties. The catalog of rights embraces civil and political as well as economic, social and cultural rights. The American Convention of Human Rights was opened for signature in 1969. In addition, the Inter-American Convention to Prevent and Punish Torture, the Inter-American Convention on the Forced Disappearance of Persons, and the Inter-American Convention on the Prevention, Punishment and Eradication of Violence Against Women were signed.[107]

In 1963 the Organization of African Unity (OAU) was established and in 1981 the African Charter on Human and Peoples' Rights was adopted. As of 1995, forty-nine African states subscribed to the Charter. First, the Charter claims not only rights but also duties. Second, it codifies individual as well as peoples' rights. Third, it protects civil and political rights as well as economic, social and cultural rights.

In 1975 at Helsinki, in the Final Act of the Conference on Security and Cooperation in Europe, 35 countries - all the sovereign states of Eastern and Western Europe with the single exception of Albania, as well as the United States and Canada, made a commitment to respect human rights. In 1994 the Council of the League of Arab States adopted the Arab Charter on Human Rights.

THE UNITED NATIONS HUMAN RIGHTS MECHANISMS

Let us examine the UN human rights mechanisms, which is the pragmatic and concrete expression of functional integration and interdependence. The expansion of UN mechanisms has contributed to globalization of human rights culture. However, as I will point out in due course, one of the drawbacks of the UN mechanisms are its weak enforcement. This is because the UN is comprised of nation-states. Accordingly under the UN mechanism, ultimate responsibility for human rights enforcement lies in the hands of nation-states. One raison d'etre of regional human rights regimes is its strong implementation mechanism compared to the UN arrangements. This is one reason the East Asian regional human rights protection mechanism is justified and will be found useful. In 1997 Kofi Annan, Secretary-General, organized the work of the United Nations into five substantive fields - peace and security, economic and social affairs, development cooperation, humanitarian affairs and human rights. The UN employs a "two-track" approach in relation to human rights enforcement machinery, namely, the Charter-based organs (e.g. the Commission on Human Rights) and the treaty-based organs (e.g. the Human Rights Committee). According to Alston, the evolution of the United Nations human rights mechanism has gone through different phases of activity, that is, standard-setting (1947–54), promotion (1955–66), and protection (since 1967) (Alston, 1992).

The United Nations human rights structure is a triptych of which one of the panels, the central panel is the Universal Declaration of Human Rights, while the two side panels could be formed by the various conventions and covenants on the one hand and the implementation measures on the other, the latter being the least developed.[108]

Boven observes that although the UN has developed a comprehensive set of international norms for the promotion and protection of human rights, its system of actual implementation and supervision is still rudimentary."[109] Another criticism is made that the UN has given a high priority to peace and security and given a low priority to human rights.[110] In fact, human rights get less than two percent of the UN budget.[111]

The United Nations human rights mechanism utilizes the following three methods to enforce protection of human rights.

The Reporting Procedure

The reporting procedures envisage a system of international supervision, which obliges state parties to report on their implementation and enables supervisory bodies to evaluate their performance.[112] The reporting procedures enable human rights bodies to determine national laws and practices which conform to the international standards, and to suggest necessary changes. In this way governments submit their human rights records to international supervision. Reports are assessments of the situations of human rights by the government itself, a form of self-evaluation. Therefore, the weakness of the reporting system is dependent, to a large extent, upon the good faith of the states concerned. Tamasevski points out that an alarming number of overdue reports was noted by the General Assembly as early as 1985.[113] Bayefsky summarizes the reporting system problems as follows:

> In large numbers governments fail to produce timely reports, do not engage in reform activities in the course of producing reports, author inadequate reports, send uninformed representatives to the examination of reports by the treaty bodies, fail to respond to questions during the examinations, discourage greater media attention of the examination of reports, fail to disseminate reports and results of the examination within the state, elect non- independent/government employees to treaty body membership.[114]

However, the positive aspect of reporting procedure is that it indicates the acceptance by governments concerned of the international community's right to scrutinize the observance of human rights (Tamasevski, 1993, p. 163).

Inter-State Procedures[115]

A state party can claim that another state party is not fulfilling its obligations under the relevant treaty. The applicant state does not have to demonstrate any special interest in or relationship to the victim of the violation or in its subject matter. Inter-state complaints are not subject to the admissibility requirements prescribed for private petitions other than the obligation to exhaust domestic remedies. That some inter-state complaints have been politically motivated cannot be denied. Some cases, however, were compelled by humanitarian considerations.[116]

Individual Communications[117]

An individual's interests are supposed to be protected by the state of which he is a national, and the individual has been considered to have no *locus standi* before international tribunes. However, individuals belonging to a state increasingly have in various ways come in contact with a foreign state in time of peace as well as of war.

Various historical events have contributed to establish the individual as a subject of international law. For example, the Charter of the International Military Tribunals at Nuremberg and Tokyo rejected the view that states are the only subjects of international law and established the principle that the obligations of international law bind individuals directly, regardless of the law of their state and of any contrary order received from their superiors. The Tribunal states as follows:

> "Crimes against international law are committed by men not by abstract entities, and only by punishing individuals who commit such crimes can the provisions of international law be enforced."[118]

In 1948 the U.N. General Assembly declared that the right of petition is an essential human right.[119] These historical events lead us to the conclusion that a rigid doctrine of absolute national sovereignty is incompatible with the concepts of fundamental human rights and duties.

The denial of human rights in one country has consequences that affect the affairs and interests of other countries. Only through an international mutuality of responsibility can individual liberty be preserved. Today it is widely held that a consideration of individual complaints would justify intervention in matters that are essentially within the domestic jurisdiction of states.

THE UNITED NATIONS COMMISSION ON HUMAN RIGHTS

The Commission on Human Rights was established in 1946 as a subsidiary organ of ECOSOC. The 53 Commission members represent member states of the UN on the basis of "equitable geographical distribution and the representation of the different forms of civilization and the principal legal systems."[120] Because the Commission is made up of governmental representatives, it is considered a highly political body.

Matthews and Pratt argue that the history of the Commission has been normative (1946–1954), promotional (1954–1966), and protection (1966–present) (Matthews and Pratt, 1988, p. 82). The main achievements of the Commission have been in standard setting, supervision and monitoring, and publicity. The Commission has played a critical role, especially in international human rights standard-setting, including drafting the Universal Declaration of Human Rights as one of its first acts. In recent years, the Commission has increasingly turned its attention to the promotion of economic, social and cultural rights, including the right to development.

Resolution 1235 (XLII) Procedure[121]

The Resolution was adopted in 1967. It authorizes the Commission and its Sub-Commission on Prevention of Discrimination and Protection of Minorities to examine information relevant to "gross violations of human rights and fundamental freedoms." The 1235 procedure can be initiated by a member state, or group of states, or by the Sub-Commission.

The procedure is considered to be effective because the mere mention of a situation might embarrass a country ("mobilization of shame"), generate media coverage, or influence another country's foreign policy. Alston, however, points out that between 1975 and 1979 a succession of horror stories was presented to the Commission (e.g. Idi Amin's atrocities in Uganda, Pol Pot's genocidal regime in Democratic Kampuchea, the systematic disappearances and the widespread terror in Argentina and Uruguay, and the brutality of the military regime in Brazil). However, all these cases were ignored in the 1235 context (Alston, 1992, p. 159).

Resolution 1503 (XLVIII) Procedure[122]

Resolution 1503 was adopted by ECOSOC in 1970 and authorized the Commission and the Sub-Commission to examine the communications received by the UN, which "appear to reveal a consistent pattern of gross and reliably attested violations of human rights and fundamental freedoms."

Communications are examined by the Working Group on Situations, which makes recommendations as to how situations should be dealt with. The recommendations are then examined by the full Commission. The 1503 procedure is confidential until the Commission makes recommendations to the ECOSOC. The process is often criticized because of its painful slowness and vulnerability to political influence at many junctures. Amnesty International characterizes the confidentiality as not an instrument for promoting and protecting and exposing large-scale violations of human rights, but rather for concealing their occurrence.

Iain Guest observes, "confidentiality has offered a useful refuge for repressive regimes."[123] Alston points out that the 1503 procedure is not called a "petition-redress" procedure since it does not offer any redress to individual victims.[124] He also points out that alleged violations of economic, social and cultural rights have never been examined and the Commission has responded to violations of only a limited range of civil and political rights. According to Nowak, resolution 1503 has played an important role for the development of protection mechanisms. Yet it has lost much of its importance and no longer responds to the present needs and is often misused by governments and should, therefore, be slowly abolished.[125]

The Commission may at times establish a thematic mechanism (i.e. Working Group and Special Rapporteur) as opposed to country- linked supervisory activities. The thematic mechanism may use such methods as: 1) a request to governments for information on specific cases; 2) an urgent request that a government take immediate action to rectify a case;[126] and 3) on-site visits for a more intensive examination of a case. Member states to the UN are obligated to co-operate in good faith with the thematic procedures.

WORKING GROUP

The Commission has established the following Ad Hoc Working Groups of Experts: the Working Group on Enforced and Involuntary Disappearances, the Working Group on Indigenous Populations, and the Working Group on Arbitrary Detention, among others. The members of a Working Group act in an individual capacity.

SPECIAL RAPPORTEUR

A thematic rapporteur acts on his or her own initiative to address individual complaints, and investigates situations of widespread abuse and reports to the Commission. Special rapporteurs submit annual reports to the Commission on Human Rights. Special rapporteurs have dealt with such issues as torture, summary or arbitrary executions, religious intolerance, sale of children, racism, freedom of expression, internally displaced persons and mercenaries. Kamminga points out that the thematic procedures lack a firm legal framework, which has made the procedures vulnerable to outside pressure. However, the advantage of this has been that it provides a space to develop activities in a flexible way through trial and error.[127]

The Sub-Commission on the Promotion and Protection of Human Rights

This is the main subsidiary organ of the Commission on Human Rights. The Sub-Commission is composed of 26 experts who act in their personal capacity. Because the Sub-Commission is a subsidiary organ of the Commission on Human Rights composed of governmental representatives, the Sub-Commission has been dependent upon the "political will" of the governments concerned.[128]

The subsidiary Working Groups of the Sub-Commission have been working on such themes as indigenous populations, contemporary forms of slavery, indigenous populations, minorities, administration of justice and transnational corporations. The Sub-Commission can also appoint a special rapporteur.

The Commission on the Status of Women

The Commission is the leading United Nations policy-making body concerned with women's rights and issues. The Commission prepares recommendations and reports to the ECOSOC on the promotion of women's rights. In 1982 the Commission established an individual complaint procedure. Reanda argues that the problem the Commission has been facing is that the question of equality for women has never become a priority issue for governments on the same level as racism and economic development.[129]

The Commission was responsible for the International Women's Year in 1975 and the subsequent Women's Decade, which were "to intensify action to promote equality between men and women and to increase women's participation in national and international development." The Commission organized the World Conferences on Women being held in Mexico City (1975), Copenhagen (1980), Nairobi (1985) and Beijing (1990). The conferences were credited with laying the foundations for an international women's movement (e.g. the Mexico Declaration and Plan of Action, and the Copenhagen Programme of Action).

The Commission on Crime Prevention and Criminal Justice

This is the main United Nations policy-making body on criminal justice. It develops and monitors the United Nations program on crime prevention.

The United Nations High Commissioner for Human Rights

The High Commissioner for Human Rights was established in 1993 to coordinate the human rights work at the U.N. The mandates of the High Commissioner cover six areas, namely,

1. promotion and protection of human rights throughout the world;
2. reinforcement of international cooperation in the field of human rights;
3. the establishment of a dialogue with Governments with a view to ensuring respect for human rights;
4. the coordination of efforts made in this area by the different United Nations organs;
5. adaptation of the United Nations machinery in this area to current and future needs; and
6. the supervision of the Center for Human Rights.

The High Commissioner would bring both moral and political stature to UN bodies seeking to ameliorate human rights abuses and ensure accountability.[130]

The Office of the High Commissioner for Human Rights (OHCHR)[131] is located in Geneva with a liaison office at the New York headquarters, and serves as the focal point of the United Nations in the field of human rights, provides secretariat and substantive services to the United Nations organs concerned with human rights, including the General Assembly and ECOSOC and their subsidiary bodies. It also carries out research, administers the advisory services and technical assistance on human rights, coordinates with NGOs, and collects and disseminates information. The Office maintains a 24–hour fax "hot line" for reporting alleged human rights violations. Each year, it receives nearly 200,000 communications reporting violations.

The Human Rights Committee

The Committee was established under the International Covenant on Civil and Political Rights and is described as "the most important UN's human rights body."[132] The Committee's task is, first, to examine state reports, which are required to be submitted to the Committee every five years by member states. Second, the Committee hears inter-state complaints.[133] Third, the Committee considers individual communications, alleging violations of the Covenant by a state party.[134] The individual must have exhausted all available domestic remedies. The role of the Committee is considered to be a promoter, monitor and supervisory body.

The Committee on the Elimination of Racial Discrimination (CERD)

State parties to the International Convention on the Elimination of All Forms of Racial Discrimination (CERD) submit reports every two years to the Committee. The Committee makes annual reports to the General Assembly. The Committee also receives inter-state complaints and individual petitions.

The Committee Against Torture (CAT)

The Committee receives states' reports, inter-state complaints and hears individual communications. If the Committee receives "reliable evidence" that torture is being systematically practiced in the territory of a state party, it may invite the state in question to examine the evidence. The Committee will transmit the findings of the inquiry to the state, together with comments and suggestions.

The Committee on the Elimination of All Forms of Discrimination Against Women (CEDAW)

The Committee oversees the implementation of the Convention by examining state reports and submitting annual reports to the General Assembly. Jacobson points out that many states have been tardy in their submission of reports.[135] The Committee does not have authority to receive individual petitions or inter-state complaints under the Convention.

The Committee on Economic, Social and Cultural Rights (CESCR)

The primary function of the Committee is to monitor the implementation of the Covenant by the state parties so that economic, social and cultural rights are effectively secured. The state parties are required to submit periodic reports outlining the legislative, judicial and other measures, which have been taken to ensure the enjoyment of the rights contained in the Covenant. The problem stems from the fact that the Committee holds a single annual session of three weeks' duration for the consideration of state reports. Secondly, the breadth of subjects covered by the Covenant, combined with the lack of case law, means that significant importance has to be placed upon the Committee's "creative" or "interpretative" functions (Craven, 1995).

The Committee on the Rights of the Child

State parties are required to submit regular reports to the Committee on the measures they have taken to put the Convention into effect and on progress in the enjoyment of children's rights in their territories (Art. 44). There is no procedure for individual complaints. The Committee submits reports every two years to the General Assembly.

In conclusion, the six treaty bodies together have a membership of 97. A state party to all six treaties must submit six different reports to each Committee over a period of four to five years. In order to lessen the administrative burden for some states and make the UN mechanisms more cost effective, it has been suggested to have consolidated Committees, namely, the Committee on State Reports and the Committee on Communications and have single consolidated reporting.[136]

SPECIALIZED AGENCIES

The specialized agencies of the United Nations are functional intergovernmental organizations affiliated with the UN.

International Labor Organization (ILO)

The ILO was created in 1919 and has been in the vanguard of efforts to ensure the international protection of human rights.[137] The ILO is composed of a unique tripartite structure representing governments, workers, and employers. The primary focus of ILO Conventions (e.g. the 1944 Declaration of Philadelphia) is in the field of labor and social justice (e.g. freedom of association, the right to organize trade unions, freedom from forced labor, freedom from discrimination in employment and equal remuneration) and the ILO utilizes such methods of compliance as reporting systems, complaint procedures, the Commission of Inquiry (guarantor of impartiality and objectivity), and direct contacts with government representatives.

The ILO has no procedure for receiving individual complaints. In addition, Leary points out that human rights NGOs have no easy means of participating in ILO activities.[138] In sum, Cox observes that:

> The ILO emerged from World War II as a small staff with a high sense of commitment to building a new world order. The staff members were united by their efforts to survive the debacle of the League of Nations, by their conviction that they had a viewpoint on the issues of social policy (Cox and Jacobson, 1974).

The average number of ratification for the Asian countries is nineteen. As for East Asian countries, as of December 1998 PRC has ratified 19 ILO Conventions, Japan 42 Conventions, ROK 12 Conventions, Mongolia 12 Conventions.[139]

The United Nations Educational, Scientific and Cultural Organization (UNESCO)

The first article of the UNESCO Constitution adopted in 1945 provides that the purpose of the organization is:

> "to contribute to peace and security by promoting collaboration among the nations through education, science and culture in order to further universal respect for justice, for the rule of law and for the human rights and fundamental freedoms which are affirmed by the Charter of the United Nations."

In 1978 UNESCO adopted a decision by which it established a procedure to handle communications alleging violations of human rights. Weissbrodt and Farley point out that one of the strengths of the UNESCO procedure is its wide accessibility to individuals and NGOs.[140] However, Marks points out that one of the drawbacks of the UNESCO procedure is its lack of strong investigatory mechanism.[141]

The following rights are covered by the procedure:

1. The right to education including the right of parents and guardians to ensure the religious and moral education of their children in conformity with their own convictions;
2. The right to share in scientific advancement and its benefits;
3. The right freely to participate in the cultural life of the community;

4.   The right to hold opinions and to freedom of expression, including freedom to seek, receive, and impart information and ideas of all kinds;
5.   The right to freedom of thought, conscience, and religion;
6.   The right to protection of interests resulting from any scientific, literary, or artistic production;
7.   The right to freedom of association including the right to form and join trade unions;
8.   The right to every child, without discrimination, to such measures of protection as are required by his status as a minor;
9.   The right of members of minority groups to enjoy their own culture, to profess and practice their own religion, or to use their own language.

In addition to the rights specified above, the procedure also deals with "massive, systematic or flagrant violations of human rights and fundamental freedoms." The Executive Board's Committee on Conventions and Recommendations makes a decision on the merits. The Committee tries to reach a "friendly solution to promote human rights." Under this procedure the Director-General has a role in seeking to strengthen the action of UNESCO in promoting human rights.

UNESCO adopted the Convention against Discrimination in Education in 1960. The purpose of the Convention is to eliminate and prevent all discrimination and promote equal opportunity and treatment in education.

THE WORLD CONFERENCE ON HUMAN RIGHTS

The UN General Assembly designated 1968 as an International Year for Human Rights and in the same year an International Conference on Human Rights was held in Teheran. The goal of the Conference was to review the progress made in the 20 years since the adoption of the Universal Declaration, to identify obstacles to further progress, and to formulate a program for the future. The proclamation issued stated that "the primary aim of the United Nations in the sphere of human rights is the achievement of each individual of the maximum freedom and dignity" but acknowledged that "the widening gap between the economically developed and the developing countries impedes the realization of human rights in the international community."

The Second World Conference on Human Rights was held at Vienna in 1993. 171 states and approximately 1,500 NGOs participated in the Conference. The objectives of the Conference were:

1. To review and assess progress made in the field of human rights, since the adoption of the Universal Declaration in 1948;
2. To identify obstacles and ways in which they may be overcome;
3. To examine the link between development and the enjoyment of economic, social, cultural, civil and political rights;
4. To evaluate the effectiveness of the UN mechanisms;
5. To recommend ways to ensure adequate financial and other sources for UN human rights activities.

The Conference adopted the Vienna Declaration and Programme of Action, which stressed the principles of universality as well as indivisibility, interdependence and interrelatedness of human rights[142]and urged the universal ratification of human rights treaties. It should be noted that the Universal Declaration of Human Rights was adopted with 48 states voting in favor of adoption, while the Vienna Declaration was adopted with 171 states' participation.

In conclusion, I have presented a brief overview on the development of the UN human rights mechanisms since World War II. As I pointed out earlier, the UN mechanisms lack strong enforcement procedures. This leads to legitimacy and justification of regional human rights mechanisms, including the one proposed in East Asia. It should be noted that the global mechanisms and regional mechanisms are mutually supporting and complementary.

HUMAN RIGHTS DIPLOMACY OF THE U.S., MAJOR COUNTRIES, AND INTERNATIONAL LENDING INSTITUTIONS

Human rights diplomacy and development aid policy of the US, other developed countries, and international lending institutions have contributed to put human rights in a prominent place in international relations. Their policies have put pressure on human rights violating countries to comply with internationally recognized human rights standards. East Asian countries such as China have been feeling pressure from human rights diplomacy on the part of the US, the sole remaining superpower, to recognize that human rights have become the legitimate concern of the international community.

In this section, I will trace human rights diplomacy and the development aid policy of the US, major developed countries, and international lending institutions to demonstrate that human rights diplomacy and development aid policy are the catalyst for establishing a regional human rights regime in East Asia.

Article 2 (7) of the United Nations Charter provides that:

> Nothing contained in the present Charter shall authorize the United Nations to intervene in matters which are essentially within the domestic jurisdiction.[143]

However, the U.N. Charter requires the member states "to pledge themselves to take joint and separate action in cooperation with the Organization (Art.56)" in order "to promote universal respect for and observance of human rights and fundamental freedoms [Art.55(c)]." In this context, it has been widely accepted that no UN member state can claim that human rights as such are a matter within its domestic jurisdiction. In fact, it has been recognized that how a state treats its own subjects is now the legitimate concern of international law; especially serious violations of human rights are a matter of concern to the international community as a whole.

The argument has been made that there is "a right to intervene"[144] when human rights are at stake. Eminent international lawyer H. Lauterpacht stated in the 1950s that:

> "When a state renders itself guilty of cruelties against and persecution of its nationals in such a way as to deny their fundamental human rights and to shock the conscience of mankind, intervention in the interest of humanity is legally permissible."[145]

Moving from permissibility to obligation, Murphy argues that the international community has a duty to intervene under customary international law to punish those states or individuals that commit "crimes against humanity" recognized by civilized nations.[146]

Today there are few states that consider it inadmissible for another government to express concern about human rights issues in general; however, many accept that governments must sometimes express concern about the oppressive human rights situation in particular states. There is evidence that policies have been significantly altered because of hostile comment from elsewhere. In human rights diplomacy, there are bilateral and multilateral efforts to deal with existing situations. Bilateral human rights diplomacy remains an important means for the promotion of human rights, though multilateral measures by like-minded states also should be undertaken against human rights violators. Mills supports human rights diplomacy by arguing that today it is necessary to reinvent conceptualization of sovereignty. He advocates "The New Sovereignty," which is based on the concept of individuals as humans rather than citizens of states, and as citizens of an emerging global community.[147]

THE UNITED STATES

President Roosevelt outlined the "Four Freedoms" in his January 1941 State of the Union Message:

> "We look forward to a world founded upon four essential freedoms, freedom of speech and expression, freedom of worship, freedom from want, and freedom from fear of aggression, and these freedoms are to prevail everywhere in the world."

In this message, he made clear that: 1) human rights everywhere would be an American concern; 2) the rights to be served are both civil, political, economic, and social; and 3) international peace and security is itself a human right.

In 1952 the California Court of Appeals in the Sei Fujii v. State case, held that the human rights provisions of the U.N. Charter were binding treaty obligations which superseded inconsistent state legislation by virtue of the supremacy clause.[148] Article VI of the U.S. Constitution provides that "this Constitution ... shall be the supreme Law of the Land." This provision has been interpreted to mean that federal statutes and the treaties to which the US is a party have the same normative rank under the Constitution. In the event of a conflict between a federal statute and a self-executing treaty provision, the latter prevails as far as the domestic law of the US is concerned. However, no treaty can override or conflict with the Constitution. The Constitution is paramount.

The Bricker Amendment was introduced between 1952 and 1957. The aims of the Amendment were: first, to make all international agreements non-self-executing under US law; second, to make international agreements subject under US law to those restraints of the Constitution that limit all powers of the federal government.[149]

In 1961 the Foreign Assistance Act was adopted and Section 502B of the Act states that:

> The United States shall, in accordance with its international obligations as set forth in the Charter of the United Nations...promote and encourage increased respect for human rights and fundamental freedoms throughout the world... Accordingly, a principal goal of the foreign policy of the United States shall be to promote the increased observance of internationally recognized human rights by all countries.

In 1967 and 1970 the United States joined the overwhelming votes for the ECOSOC Resolution 1235 and Resolution 1503 respectively.

Meanwhile, in the early 1970's, the Congress of the U.S. began a thorough assessment of international human rights issues and their foreign policy implications. In 1973, Donald Fraser, chair of the Subcommittee on International Organizations and Movements of the House Committee on Foreign Affairs, began extensive hearings on the subject. The hearings resulted, for example, in designating human rights officers in each of the State Department's five geographic bureaus and in creating an Office of Humanitarian Affairs.[150]

Section 32 of the Foreign Assistance Act of 1973 and Section 46 of the Foreign Assistance Act of 1974 expressed the view that the President should reduce or terminate economic, military or security assistance in cases of a "consistent pattern of gross violations of internationally recognized human rights."[151]

In 1975 the Final Act of the Conference on Security and Cooperation in Europe was signed in Helsinki by 33 Western and Eastern European States as well as the United States and Canada. All of the signatories agreed to respect the human rights set forth in the document, thereby abandoning the argument that external scrutiny was an improper interference in their domestic affairs. The International Development and Food Assistance Act of 1975 became the first human rights legislation to adopt mandatory language, prohibiting aid to any government which grossly and consistently violates internationally recognized rights, unless such assistance will directly benefit the needy people of that country.

In 1975 Congress adopted Section 116 of the Foreign Assistance Act. The pertinent part of Section 116 reads:

> No assistance may be provided to the government of any country which engages in a consistent pattern of gross violations of internationally recognized human rights, including torture or cruel, inhuman, or degrading treatment or punishment, prolonged detention without charges, or other flagrant denial of the right to life, liberty and the security of person, unless such assistance will directly benefit the needy people in such country.

The International Security Assistance and Arms Export Control Act of 1976 specifies in part that "a principal goal of the foreign policy of the United States is to promote the increased observance of internationally recognized human rights by all countries." The Act also provides that "no security assistance may be provided to any country the government of which engages in a consistent pattern of gross violations of internationally recognized human rights."

The Act requires the Secretary of State to submit to Congress a statement on the status of human rights in the countries concerned; and Secretary is mandated to express an opinion as to whether US aid should be continued.[152]

Meanwhile, a proponent of "realpolitik," Kissinger advocated "quiet diplomacy" by arguing that US foreign policy must reflect fundamental national purposes, and the basic challenge of foreign policy is the perennial tension between morality and pragmatism.[153]

In 1976 Jimmy Carter was elected and in his inaugural address he stated that:

> "Because we are free we can never be indifferent to the fate of freedom elsewhere. Our commitment to human rights must be absolute."

Speaking before the United Nations, Mr. Carter stated, "no member of the United Nations can claim that mistreatment of its citizens is solely its own business ... All the signatories of the United Nations Charter have pledged themselves to observe and to respect basic human rights."[154] He further stated, "in formulating security assistance programs, we will continue our efforts to promote and advance respect for human rights in recipient countries."[155]

Secretary of State Cyrus Vance articulated what the Carter Administration meant by human rights:

1. The right to be free from governmental violation of the integrity of the person: torture, cruel, inhuman, or degrading treatment or punishment, arbitrary arrest or imprisonment, denial of a fair, public trial, invasion of the home;
2. The right to the fulfillment of such vital needs as food, shelter, health care, and education;
3. The right to enjoy civil and political liberties: freedom of thought, religion, assembly, speech, press, movement both within and outside one's own country, and freedom to take part in government.[156]

Under Carter, human rights concerns became more institutionalized and accepted as a high priority interest of the administration. For example, the State Department established a Bureau of Human Rights and Humanitarian Affairs in 1977, and established the first Country Reports requiring, for each country proposed for security assistance, that an annual report on human rights practices be submitted to Congress.[157]

The Harkin Amendment of 1976 required the American representatives at the Inter-American Development Bank, the African Development Fund and other international lending institutions to vote against loans to governments who engage "in a consistent pattern of gross violations of internationally recognized human rights."

The 1976 Amendment to Section 502B of the Foreign Assistance Act of 1961 states:

1. the promotion of internationally recognized human rights as a principal goal of U.S. foreign policy;
2. no security assistance is to be provided for any country whose government engages in a consistent pattern of gross violations of internationally recognized human rights;
3. international security assistance programs are so formulated as to promote and advance human rights.

In 1984, USAID, the agency of the US State Department responsible for official development assistance, recommended the guideline for policy determination as to development aid, that includes strengthening awareness of civil and political rights, of a legal order based on the rule of law, promotion of free and democratic election systems, development of democratic principles and institutions which promote human rights, establishment of human rights NGOs and better access for women and ethnic groups to justice and the political process.

Thus, since the end of World War II, the US has gradually improved human rights provisions of pertinent foreign policy legislation. It has been pointed out, however, that the problem of the US human rights policy is the selective application of human rights criteria in the punitive approach.[158] The US has overlooked the poor human rights record of friendly repressive authoritarian regimes provided that they were opposed to the totalitarian states of communism,[159] in Kirkpatrick's term "moderate autocrats friendly to American interests with less friendly autocrats of extreme persuasion."[160] The lack of consistency of the US human rights policy has resulted in being criticized as a "double standard." However, two years earlier Moynihan defended this by saying that human rights is a political component of American foreign policy, not a humanitarian program.[161]

Furthermore, historically, the US has had ideological limitations towards human rights by focusing solely on civil and political rights and overlooking economic, social and cultural rights.[162] Third, the U.S. has an extremely poor record, when it comes to the ratification of human rights treaties, be they universal or regional in character.[163]

In conclusion, the Lawyers Committee for Human Rights advocate that it should be in the US national interest for human rights issues to be afforded a higher priority and given greater attention in the foreign policy decision-making process.[164]

NETHERLANDS

In Netherlands, the criteria for development aid originally included human rights in 1975 and were further developed in the ensuing years. The Netherlands considers human rights an important component of development assistance and appraises civil and political and economic, social and cultural rights situations of receiving countries based on three criteria:

1. a pluralist, representative democracy supported by human rights;
2. a market economy organized and regulated by an active government;
3. public services and a safety net for the promotion of equal opportunities as a guarantee against poverty.[165]

Thus, the relevance of the human rights policy of the recipient government is explicitly recognized as an aid criterion because the Netherlands considers democracy, good governance and respect for human rights are essential for the achievement of international order and conflict management. The Permanent Commission on Human Rights gives advice to the Foreign Minister on development aid. The Netherlands considers human rights as a matter of realizing "internationally recognized universal values and norms" (Rehof & Gulmann, 1989). The Netherlands and Norway, followed by Sweden and Denmark, have been in competition for many years over who gives the largest percentage of GNP for development aid.

Table 2: The Percentage of GNP to Foreign Aid of Major Countries

Denmark	Norway	Netherlands	France	Canada	Germany	Japan	USA
1.04	0.85	0.81	0.48	0.32	0.33	0.20	0.12

Net Official Development Assistance (US$ millions)

Denmark	Norway	Netherlands	France	Canada	Germany	Japan	USA
1,772	1,311	3,246	7,451	1,795	7,601	9,439	9,377

[Sources: Human Development Report, 1998]

The main criteria for the allocation of aid are: aid needs (that is, the priority for the poorest countries); the socio-economic policy pursued by the recipient government; and respect for human rights. Contrary to the punitive American approach, Dutch development aid aims to create conditions for the realization of human rights because the Dutch policy affirms that development assistance ought to be guided by the needs of the people, rather than by the conduct of their government.[166]

NORWAY

Norway initiated its official development aid (ODA) in 1952 and published the first White Paper "Norway and the Protection of International Human Rights" in 1977. The Ministry of Foreign Affairs began publishing "Annual Report on Norway's Efforts to Promote Human Rights." In 1998 the government presented a Bill on the incorporation of the three human rights conventions into Norwegian law, namely, the European Convention on Human Rights, the UN Covenants on Civil and Political Rights (CCPR) and Economic, Social and Cultural Rights (CESCR).

The Norwegian Agency for Development Corporation (NORAD) and the Norwegian Institute for Human Rights cooperate to implement projects relating to human rights and democracy (e.g. the China Project). Norway protested against human rights violations in international fora and in bilateral contacts with such countries as Burma, China and Turkey. The Ministry of International Development and Human Rights evaluates the human rights situations in the recipient countries of Norwegian development assistance and publishes an Annual Human Rights Review. Kjekhus stresses that using aid to strive for improvements in human rights is not exporting myopic Eurocentric values.[167]

CANADA

Canada considers development aid as a vital instrument of foreign policy and is overseen by the Canadian International Development Agency (CIDA). The purpose of such aid is to:

> "support sustainable development in developing countries in order to reduce poverty and to contribute to a more secure, equitable and prosperous world."

The priorities of development aid are given to basic human needs, women in development, infrastructure services, human rights, democracy, good governance, private sector development and environment. As for human rights, development aid policy is "to increase respect for human rights to promote democracy and better governance and to strengthen civil society."

By 1979, linking aid with human rights became accepted Canadian foreign policy. Criteria for granting aid include assessment of the recipient's policies to promote human rights because Canadian aid policy is based on the premise that "respect for human rights is one of the most important conditions for a true development process."[168]

Development aid is considered essential in contributing to an improved respect for human rights in developing countries. Canada was the first donor whose aid policy required recipient governments to adhere to international human rights treaties and implement their human rights obligations, that is, the ratification of human rights treaties and/or the incorporation of international human rights standards into national law.

The policy stresses that human rights criteria must be applied in a universal, consistent and transparent manner. Gross, systematic and continuous violations of human rights are recognized as an obstacle to Canadian aid.[169]

GERMANY

The development policy of Germany is overseen by the Ministry for Economic Cooperation and Development. The aims of the development policy of Germany are to:

1. promote social justice all over the world, alleviate poverty, and support respect for human rights and democratic principles;
2. contribute to the peaceful resolution and management of conflicts;
3. protect the environment and limit population growth; and
4. help to shape economic development in our partner countries.

The guiding principle of their development policy is to contribute to globally sustainable development, that is, productive economic growth, social justice and ecological sustainability. The criteria which influences development cooperation are:

1. respect for human rights;
2. the rule of law and the certainty of the law;
3. introduction of a social market economy; and
4. the development commitment of the partner government (e.g. consideration of excessive arms expenditure).

The development cooperation is carried out through the European Union, the European Development Fund, the World Bank and the UN. One of the characteristics of the development policy of Germany is that development cooperation is carried out by NGOs, who have many years of experience in cooperation with their partners abroad because some of NGOs have considerable expertise in the areas of education, poverty alleviation, environment and development, human rights, emergency relief, crisis prevention and conflict resolution.

JAPAN

Japan has been the largest aid donor in the world since 1989. Japanese foreign aid is equivalent to approximately one fifth of all worldwide foreign aid. The Japanese Official Development Aid (ODA) Charter was first adopted in 1991 and the 1992 ODA Charter attempted to blend a diversity of objectives, ranging from environmental concerns and women in development, to democratization and attention to military spending.

Japan has considered ODA as an important tool of diplomacy, especially in Asia. For example, in 1993, approximately two-thirds of ODA was given to Asian countries such as Indonesia, China, India, the Philippines, and Thailand.

The basic rationales of the ODA Charter are a) humanitarianism, and b) interdependence, among others. The Charter states, in part, that:

> Full attention should be paid to the efforts for promoting democratization and introduction of a market-oriented economy, and the situation regarding the securing of basic human rights and freedoms in the recipient country.[170]

In spite of this provision, Japan lacks strict implementation of the ODA policy (e.g. China and Burma).[171] Japanese aid has been intended to serve its own mercantilist interests, by promoting Japanese exports and securing imports of natural resources.[172] Japanese foreign aid is a legitimate arm of industrial policy for Japan's model of guided capitalism.

The ODA policy has been formulated as a result of consensus-building between the following governmental bodies:

1. Ministry of Foreign Affairs (MOFA)
2. Japan International Co-operation Agency (JICA)
    (Foreign policy related economic co-operation, including grant aid and technical assistance)
3. Ministry of Finance (MOF)
    (Public finance and international monetary policy)
4. Ministry of International Trade and Industry (MITI)
    (Economic co-operation related to trade)
5. Economic Planning Agency (EPA)
6. the Overseas Economic Co-operation Fund (OECF)
    (Formulation of basic policies on economic co-operation, including loan aid)

Yasutomo argues that Japan's bureaucratic policy process makes it impossible to develop a comprehensive aid philosophy. ODA has a role to play as a diplomatic tool that combines Japan's national strengths—finance, technology, knowledge, and human resources (Yasutomo, 1995, p. 26). Lehmann sums up Japanese foreign aid that Japan's aid is business for Japanese business[173] although Japan has had opportunities to improve human rights situations of recipient countries. Critics argue that ODA requires Diet oversight, consideration of recipient people's interests, and greater transparency and centralization of the aid policy apparatus and process.

WORLD BANK

The Bank is a specialized agency of the United Nations, and the specialized agencies are the main pillars of the UN, which ought to promote universal respect for and observance of human rights. The World Bank is a group of four multilateral financial institutions: 1) the International Bank for Reconstruction and Development (IBRD); 2) the International Development Association (IDA); 3) the International Finance Corporation (IFC); and 4) the Multilateral Investment Guarantee Agency (MIGA).[174]

The World Bank is the largest single source of lending for development, with significant influence on the political and economic fate of Third World countries. The Bank applies its own constitutional rules, contained in its Articles of Agreement and follows its own policies. The Bank's role encompasses three different functions: lending, policy advice and co-ordination of development aid.

The World Bank's development aid reflects the following contemporary trends:

1. the normative global appeal of human rights and democratic governance;
2. an erosion of the principles of sovereignty and non-intervention;
3. the demonstrative effect of bilateral donors linking human rights and foreign aid;
4. the addition of human rights and democracy to the charter of the European Bank for Reconstruction and Development.[175]

The "conditionality of aid" is viewed as a legitimate intervention by aid donors in the domestic affairs of borrowing countries to maintain the sustainable development of recipient countries. The conditionality of the World Bank is based on the concept of "good governance" that entails accountability of the government, rule of law, an independent and effective judiciary, transparency of decision-making and freedom of information, institutional pluralism and freedom of association and participation.

The World Bank also insists on the release of political prisoners, the establishment of national and independent human rights commissions, access by international human rights monitors, action to improve government accountability and transparency, dismantling of legislation circumscribing the role of NGOs, freedom of the press and of association.[176] However, it has been pointed out that in practice the World Bank hardly ever addresses civil and political rights in its development aid mandate except in rare circumstances, because civil and political rights are considered political interference[177] and the Bank should be "neutral" politically.

As for NGOs, the World Bank recognizes the expanding role and influence of NGOs, as well as benefits NGO involvement brings to its operations. Capacity building for NGOs is encouraged. The World Bank maintains a consultative committee comprising World Bank staff and NGO representatives.

Gillies suggests five guiding principles to international donors such as the World Bank;

1.   State sovereignty is not sacrosanct. True sovereignty resides in the will of the people. As the Universal Declaration of Human Rights puts it: "The will of the people shall be the basis of the authority of government [Art. 21(3)]."

2.   Respect for fundamental human rights is a *sine qua non* of legitimate governance.

3.   State sovereignty is abused and loses its legitimacy when it seeks to shield gross violations of human rights or grievous and deliberate human suffering.

4.   The principle of non-intervention cannot be used to prohibit legitimate international action to protect human rights.

5.   The international community has a duty to act for the relief of human suffering and to end the gross violation of human rights.[178]

ASIAN DEVELOPMENT BANK (ADB)

ADB, a multilateral development finance institution, was established in 1966. The purpose of ADB is, among others, to:

(i)   extend loans and equity investments;
(ii)   provide technical assistance and advisory services;

ADB, located in Manila, Philippines, currently has 58 members including ROK, Japan, ROC, PRC and Mongolia.

ADB's work with regard to human rights is that lately ADB has been working on harmonization of laws in the region. The project involves codification, unification and standard setting of trade, commerce, banking and financial transaction. The models for harmonization are the Hague Conference on Private International Law (UNCITRAL) and the Uniform Commercial Code (UCC) in the US. The development of legal regime in the region contributes to underpin market-driven economic development. The consistent legal system and institutions are indispensable for economic development because market exchange cannot be affected in the absence of a reasonable expectation that market agreement will be performed and enforced. ADB's efforts in this field would consequently create environment to set up a regional human rights protection mechanism.

Secondly, the Bank's 1987 policy paper "The Bank's Cooperation with Non-Governmental Organization" established a broad framework for cooperation between the Bank and NGOs. NGOs have been sources of information on local conditions and implementing agencies. The emergence of NGOs is becoming apparent in a number of countries in Asia and there has been steadily increasing NGO involvement in Bank operations in a variety of fields. As NGO capacity develops, it is likely that new occasions for such cooperation will emerge. This Bank's work indicates a good example of cooperation between IGO and NGOs. It also indicates NGOs' participation in regional governance and contribution to regional integration.

HUMANITARIAN INTERVENTION

Humanitarian intervention is considered international enforcement of human rights and thus contributes to growing globalization of human rights. Henkin defines humanitarian intervention as "coercive intervention by states, singly or collectively, through economic sanctions or by use of military force, in response to widespread deprivation of internationally recognized human rights."[179] Vincent contends that the doctrine of humanitarian intervention obliges a response from outsiders if a state by its conduct shocks the "conscience of mankind."[180]

The legal basis for collective intervention is based on Article 1 of the UN, which provides that:

> To maintain international peace and security, and to that end to take effective collective measures for the prevention and removal of threats to the peace, and for suppression of acts of aggression or other breaches of the peace, and to bring about by peaceful means... adjustments or settlements of international disputes or situations that might lead to a breach of the peace.

However, it is important to note that military intervention must be a measure of last resort. The Article 2(4) of the UN Charter states that:

> All members shall refrain in their international relations from the threat or use of force against the territorial integrity or political independence of any state, or in any other manner inconsistent with the purposes of the United Nations.

The principal sources of humanitarian intervention law are the four Geneva Conventions of 1949 and the two 1977 Additional Protocols to those treaties. The four Geneva Conventions are:
1.   The Geneva Convention for the Amelioration of the Condition of the Wounded and Sick in Armed Forces in the Field;
2.   The Geneva Convention for the Amelioration of the Condition of Wounded, Sick and Shipwrecked Members of Armed Forces at Sea;
3.   The Geneva Convention Relative to the Treatment of Prisoners of War; and
4.   The Geneva Convention Relative to the Protection of Civilian Persons in Time of War.

These Conventions were formed considering that the First World War was responsible for 10 million deaths, the Second for 50 million; this included 26 million combatants and 24 million civilians.[181] To ensure that the state parties comply with their obligations, the Geneva Conventions provide for a system of supervision that is administered by Protecting Powers. Each state party to the Convention has the right to designate a neutral country to serve as its Protecting Power. The role of Protecting Power may also be performed by the International Red Cross or another comparable impartial humanitarian organization (Art. 10 of Geneva Convention I, II and III and Art. 11 of Geneva Convention IV). Protocol I of 1977 provides for an International Fact-Finding Commission for competence to inquire into grave breaches of the Geneva Conventions (Article 85 of Protocol I of 1977). The Conventions do not, however, establish a mandatory system for the arbitration or adjudication of disputes.

POSTSCRIPT

What I have attempted to set forth in this chapter is that the globalization of human rights has increasingly crossed cultures since the dawn of the human rights century. The steady convergence of cross-cultural human values has resulted in the global consensus on human rights that is called the universality of human rights. Human rights, many now believe, apply to all human beings in every human society, equally, by virtue of their humanity.

The overwhelming majority of states and organizations in the international community has accepted the universality of human rights. The ratification of international human rights treaties by a large number of countries indicates precisely the globalization of human rights.

Moreover, as indicated in this chapter, international human rights standards have been codified in rapid succession since World War II, beginning with the Universal Declaration of Human Rights in 1948. The codification efforts have not only taken place at the global level but also at regional and national levels. The treaty system constitutes the cornerstone of human rights endeavors and represents the globalization of human rights.

At the UN, human rights endeavors have gone through three different phases- standard-setting, promotion, and currently the protection stage. In the process the UN has created and developed numerous mechanisms and procedures within the UN structure to promote and protect human rights (e.g. Working Group, Special Rapporteur, a High Commissioner for Human Rights, etc). At the same time, the UN has devised and employed various methods such as reporting procedures, inter-state procedures and individual communications to enforce protection of human rights.

The UN human rights mechanism has been in a process of evolution. As I point out in this chapter, each mechanism and procedure has strengths and weaknesses. The overall shortcoming of the UN mechanism is that it depends to a great extent upon the good will of member states. It will be necessary to develop the procedures based on the concept of individuals as citizen of an emerging global community rather than merely as citizens of a state.

In addition, globalization of human rights has also been achieved by human rights diplomacy and the development aid policy of the US, major countries and international lending institutions. Democracy, good governance, and respect for human rights are essential for maintaining international peace and security. Human rights diplomacy is an expression of the internationalization of human rights. Based on global consciousness and responsibility, humanitarian intervention and proposal for a permanent international criminal court are good examples of the globalization of human rights. These trends represent a likely step toward establishing a regional human rights regime in East Asia.

Chapter IV

Prospects for a Regional Human Rights Regime in East Asia

ASSESSMENT OF OTHER REGIONAL HUMAN RIGHTS REGIMES AND NGOS CONTRIBUTIONS TO THE REGIMES.

THIS SECTION EXAMINES COMPARATIVE LEGAL ARRANGEMENTS, INSTITUTIONAL frameworks and procedures of the three regional human rights mechanisms that now exist, to learn how these mechanisms have been functioning. Have they been functioning effectively? What are the institutional characteristics and strengths and limitations of each regional human rights regime?[1] What has been the role of NGOs in these three regimes? How relevant is the experience of these three regimes to the human rights regime in East Asia?

Presently there are three regional human rights implementation mechanisms in operation, namely, the European, Inter-American and African systems. The three regional regimes differ in the breadth and depth of the rights they recognize. Leary asserts that the most effective human rights implementation systems are regional arrangements because governments are more likely to agree to regional machinery for supervision where cultural, legal and intellectual traditions are similar.[2] Cultural relativists[3] argue that the content of rights must be compatible with (universalists argue that human rights must be applied with sensitivity to) a society's cultural, political, and social circumstances in order to be accepted and effectively realized.

EUROPE

Legal Arrangements

The European human rights system, the most developed system for the regional protection of human rights, has its legal origins in two treaties: The European Convention on Human Rights of 1950[4] and the European

Social Charter of 1961.[5] The Convention emphasizes civil and political rights,[6] whereas the Charter guarantees economic and social rights.[7]

The Convention is the first comprehensive treaty to establish the international complaint procedure and the international court for the protection of human rights matters. However, the flaw of the Convention is that it contains no provisions relating to self-determination and to the rights of minority groups, children, refugees and aliens.[8] For the Social Charter there is no judicial supervision. Nowak criticizes the Charter as being "subject to a totally inefficient reporting procedure."[9]

How the European system came into being is explained by Robertson as "a natural reaction against the Nazi," and a "defense against all forms of totalitarianism."[10] The Convention is "a common ideological framework to consolidate unity among Western democracies in the face of the Communist threat."[11] Leaders of Europe believed that as long as human rights are respected, democracy is secure and the danger of dictatorship and war is remote. The strength of the European system is derived from the requirement that only countries that adhere to a pluralistic democracy and the rule of law can be members of the Council of Europe[12] and signers of the Convention. The European system for the protection of human rights put approximately some 550 million people under the system's jurisdiction.

The European Convention establishes two institutions: the European Commission of Human Rights and the Court of Human Rights. It should be noted that the merger of the Commission and Court has been debated for sometime in order to make the procedure more efficient and, in fact, the Commission ceased to exist in November 1998.[13] The Convention also confers some supervisory functions on the Committee of Ministers (governmental representatives) of the Council of Europe.[14]

The European Court of Human Rights

The Court consists of a number of judges equal to the members of states of the Council of Europe. However, the cases are heard by chamber of the Court consisting of seven judges.[15] The judges of the Court are elected to a nine year term by the Consultative Assembly of the Council of Europe. No two judges may be nationals of the same state. Judges will sit in an individual capacity and enjoy complete independence.

First, the Court receives inter-state communications.[16] Some of the cases which the European Commission has dealt with are as follows:

> Ireland v. the United Kingdom relating to the situation in Northern Ireland in 1971 and 1972; Denmark, Netherlands, Norway and Sweden v. Greece in 1967,1968 and 1970 concerning the Greek government's alleged violations of Art. 3, 4, 6, 8, 9, 10, 11, 13, and 14 and Art. 3 of the Protocol No. 1.

The inter-state complaint can be a valuable weapon for dealing with massive violations of human rights. However, it has been argued that an inter-state complaint has been brought only if and when the complaining state has political reasons of its own. It has been doubted that a state could be willing to take up in an international forum a matter that did not concern its own citizens and thereby risk endangering its friendly relations with the state against which the complaint was directed.[17]

Second, the Court receives applications lodged by any person, NGOs, group of individuals claiming to be the victim of a violation of the rights set forth in the Convention.[18] The Committee undertakes an examination of the petition including on-site investigation, hearing witnesses and experts. The state concerned must furnish all necessary facilities.

Admissibility

The individual petition must meet the following admissibility conditions:

1. All domestic remedies must be exhausted;[19]
2. The petition should not be substantially the same as a matter which has already been examined by the Commission or has already been submitted to another procedure of international investigation or settlement;
3. The petition should not be manifestly ill-founded,[20] or an abuse of the right of petition.[21]

If the complaints are considered admissible, the Court examines the allegations, seeks information from the government concerned and undertakes a thorough investigation of the facts.[22]

Individuals have no standing to refer a case to the Court.[23] The Court decides whether or not the facts found constitute a violation of the Convention. The Court awards just satisfaction to an injured party. In addition, the Court renders advisory opinions on legal questions concerning the interpretation of the Convention.

The Committee of Ministers of the Council of Europe

The Committee of Ministers is the executive organ of the Council of Europe. The members of the Committee are the Ministers of Foreign Affairs of the member states. Its members serve as government representatives. The Committee of Ministers is responsible for supervising the execution of the Court's judgment. Decisions of the Committee are binding upon the state parties.

NGOs' Involvements

In the European system, human rights NGOs do not have the right, independently, to lodge an application with the Commission unless they themselves are victims of infringements of the Convention. In 1954 the Committee of Ministers adopted guidelines for granting consultative status to a group of NGOs. Presently over 350 NGOs have been granted the consultative status.[24] Some of the significant contributions NGOs have made to the European human rights system are the following:

1. The European Torture Convention was prepared jointly by the International Commission of Jurists and Swiss Committee Against Torture.
2. NGOs help applicants to complete the application and provide legal assistance before the Court (e.g. the National Council for Liberties, Justice, the National Association for Mental Health, the Advice on Individual Rights in European Center).
3. NGOs provide legal advice to the victims, assist them in formulating applications and in finding adequate arguments, and suggest competent lawyers capable of representing the victims.
4. NGOs may take part in proceedings by third party intervention (the amicus curiae brief). (e.g. Justice, INTERIGHTS, British/Irish Rights Watch, and the Northern Ireland Standing Advisory Commission for Human Rights).
5. NGOs propagate knowledge on the European Convention, especially Central and Eastern Europe (e.g. the Helsinki Committee in Romania).

Concluding Remarks

The European system is receptive to processing human rights grievances. However, because of this, the existing system is unable to deal with the greatly increased number of cases.[25] This has placed severe strains on the entire system - "victim of its own success," which have resulted in the procedures becoming extremely time-consuming.[26] For example, in 1993, it took, on average, five years and eight months for a case to be finally decided. The national courts usually take equivalent periods of time to decide a case. This is a breach of the right to a hearing "within a reasonable time." The European procedure is also extremely selective - less than five percent of all cases are considered on the merits.[27] In spite of this flaw, it has been argued that the European system has provided the most effective remedy for individual violations compared to other mechanisms.

THE AMERICAS

In the Americas, the legal basis of human rights is the Charter of the Organization of American States (1948),[28] the American Declaration of the Rights and Duties of Man (1948)[29] and the American Convention on Human Rights (1978).[30] The OAS is a regional organization whose purpose is to achieve peace and justice and promote solidarity of people in Latin America and the United States. The Charter of the OAS affirms, among others, the following principles:

1. the effective exercise of representative democracy;
2. act of aggression against one state means aggression against all;
3. economic cooperation is essential to the welfare and prosperity of the peoples of the hemisphere;
4. the fundamental rights of the individual without distinction as to race, nationality, creed or sex

The Declaration of Rights and Duties of Man is the first comprehensive statement of human rights in the history of the Western Hemisphere. The American Convention is longer than most international human rights instruments and recognizes rights not contained in the European Convention, which include the rights of the child, the right to nationality, and the right to asylum. Unlike the European Convention, the American Convention stresses duties.[31] The Convention establishes two organs to safeguard its implementation: the Commission and the Court of Human Rights.

The Inter-American Commission on Human Rights

The Commission is composed of seven nationals of member states elected in their personal capacity. The term of the Commission members is four years. They may be reelected. The functions of the Commission include:

1. promoting human rights in all OAS member states;
2. assisting in the drafting of human rights documents;
3. advising member states of the OAS;
4. preparing country reports;
5. mediating disputes over serious human rights problems;
6. handling individual complaints;

7.   participating in the handling of cases and advisory opinions before the Court.

Like its European counterpart, the Commission examines either individual petitions or inter-state communications. The Commission receives approximately 500 individual complaints a year. The individual petitions must meet admissibility requirements. The Commission, on average, carries out a few on-site investigations a year. The Inter-American Commission has not received any inter-state complaint to date. The Commission attempts a friendly settlement.

The Inter-American Commission is described as the "sole guarantor of human rights in a continent plagued with gross, systematic violations."[32] However, the flaw of the Inter-American Commission is that it faces financial limitations - the Commission receives less than two percent of the OAS budget.[33] Medina observes that this situation does not make the Commission rank the handling of individual petitions very high.[34]

The Inter-American Court of Human Rights

The Court consists of seven judges elected in their personal capacity. The judges are elected for a term of six years and may be reelected. The Court is located in Costa Rica.[35] The Court has adjudicatory jurisdiction. The state parties and the Commission may submit contentious cases to the Court. Individuals lack *locus standi*, although complaint lodged by the individuals may be taken to the Court either by the Commission or a state party. Judgments of the Court are binding on the parties and not subject to appeal. The Court also has advisory jurisdiction, which empowers the Court to interpret the Convention and other human rights instruments at the request of OAS member states and various OAS organs.[36]

NGOs' activities

Active NGOs who contribute to the Inter-American system include Human Rights Watch/America, Amnesty International, the International Human Rights Law Group, the Lawyers Committee for Human Rights, Washington Office on Latin America and Center for Justice and International Law. These NGO activities involve collecting information, visiting countries, disseminating information, intervening cases directly and indirectly.

For example, the Center for Justice and International Law (CEJIL) was established in 1991 to "achieve the full implementation of international human rights norms in the member states of OAS." CEJIL's works consist of legal defense, consulting, training and publications. CEJIL's cases involve, for example, forced disappearances, extrajudicial executions, due process violations, conditions of detention, freedom of expression, and inhumane treatment. CEJIL conducts workshops throughout out Latin America and publishes *The Gazette* every two months to provide information regarding their activities.[37]

Concluding Remarks

In the Americas, large scale poverty persist; and the regional system has had to deal with hostile governments, a weak or corrupt domestic judiciary as well as gross, flagrant and systematic human rights violations involving torture, disappearances, arbitrary killings, and incommunicado detention. Tom Farer describes the situations of Latin America that:

> it is an enduring culture of impunity for public security agencies, weak judicial systems, a tradition of broad executive discretion in the exercise of power and a continuing tendency of elites to dismiss nongovernmental human rights activists as "Leftists."[38]

AFRICA

The Organization of African Unity (OAU) was created in 1963. The OAU is a regional inter-governmental organization which was primarily dedicated to the eradication of colonialism and unity of African states. According to the Charter of OAU, its purposes include promoting solidarity among the independent African countries, safeguarding their independence, sovereignty, and territorial integrity, and fighting against neo-colonialism in all forms. The OAU is state-centric organization based on the principles of territorial integrity and non-interference in the internal affairs of other states. It has a membership of 52 states.

The African Charter on Human and Peoples' Rights[39] reflects the African concept of human rights; for example, the Charter codifies individual as well as peoples' rights[40] and proclaims not only rights but also duties.[41] Keba M'baye argues that the African concept of man is not that of the isolated individual, but of an integral member of a group animated by a spirit of solidarity - rights are to be exercised with "due regard to the rights of others, collective security, morality and common interest."[42] However, the Charter has been criticized by some who say that the excessive duties imposed on individuals entrench the oppressive family structure and compete with the exploitation and marginalization of women.[43]

The Charter also protects the third generation of solidarity rights, with particular emphasis on the right to development.[44] The shortcoming of the Charter are its "claw back" clauses that confine the Charter's protections to rights as they are defined in national law.[45]

The African Commission on Human and Peoples' Rights

The Commission consists of eleven members[46] who are elected for a six-year term. The Commission's functions are largely promotional. The Commission undertakes fact-finding, seeks to achieve amicable settlements, prepares reports, and makes recommendations.[47]

The African Commission also examines state reports, which state parties are required to submit to the Commission every two years.[48] However, first, the majority of state parties have not submitted their reports and the Commission has been powerless to force compliance. Second, the Commission deals with inter-state complaints, which the Commission has not received to date; third, the Commission receives communications from individuals, groups of individuals, and NGOs. The African Commission has similar admissibility requirements for individual communications.[49] The Commission may conduct on-site investigation. The Commission does not provide for enforceable remedies.

The Commission has suffered from a chronic lack of staff, resources and services necessary for its effective functioning.[50] Steiner and Alston describes the African system as the "least developed or effective and the most controversial regional human rights regimes."[51]

The African Court on Human and Peoples' Rights

The African system does not provide for a court of human rights. The explanation has been given that African customs and traditions favor mediation, conciliation, and consensus over the adversarial and adjudicative procedures common to Western legal systems. However, the initiative has been taken to establish an African Court on Human and Peoples' Rights.[52] The Protocol suggests that the Court would complement the Commission and thus make the African system more effective. The Court is composed of eleven judges elected in their personal capacity and serve six-year term.[53] The Commission may exercise both contentious as well as advisory jurisdiction. The African Commission, state parties, and African intergovernmental organizations (IGOs) can bring cases to the Court. Yet individuals and NGOs cannot bring a suit against a state. Mutua argues that this limitation renders the Court virtually meaningless because the Court is not meant to be an institution for the protection of the rights of states or OAU organs.[54]

NGOs' participation

NGOs have been in a position to act as a conduit of access and information between the African Commission and the people at large. They may submit communications to the African Commission on behalf of individuals or groups and thus assist people who might otherwise not know how to approach the regional African system of human rights protection. The Commission allows NGOs to act as lawyers in the proceedings of cases and communications brought before it.

The Commission grants observer status to NGOs[55], who have the opportunity to sit in on public sessions of the Commission and of its subsidiary bodies, and may propose suggestions for the Commission's agenda. They submit a report to the Commission every two years on their human rights activities. These reports provide an alternative view to the official reports submitted by states.

NGOs also serve the Commission in a consultative capacity at the invitation of the Commission. NGOs are thus in a position to offer invaluable input to the proceedings of the Commission. According to the Rules of Procedures of the Commission, NGOs can participate in the open sessions of the Commission. Some of the NGOs that are granted observer status with the African Commission on Human and Peoples' Rights include:

> African Association of International Law (Kenya), the Arab Lawyers Union (Egypt), the African Journalists Union (Egypt), the African Center for Democracy and Human Rights Studies (The Gambia), Civil Liberties Organization (Nigeria), Institute Arabe des Droits de l'Homme (Tunisia), Human Rights Africa (Nigeria), Constitutional Rights Project (Nigeria), L'Association des Jurists Africaine (Senegal).[56]

Concluding Remarks

One of the characteristics of the African system compared to other regional mechanisms is that the African system is based on strict state-centric perspectives such as the principle of respect for national sovereignty, territorial integrity, and noninterference in the internal affairs of another state and give great authority to the Assembly of Heads of State and Government. The African Commission is subordinate to the OAU Assembly of Heads of State and Governments, to which it reports. Therefore, it has been argued that the Commission is at the mercy of states, for example, habitual tardiness in reporting.

COMPARATIVE OBSERVATIONS ON REGIONAL HUMAN RIGHTS REGIMES

Europe and the Americas have significant historical and legal affinity. In two regions, a two-tier system - the division of labor between the Commission and the Court - has been established. The mandates and functions of the Commissions are similar.[57]

One of the significant differences is that the European system does not permit access to non-victim representatives, whereas the American Convention grants the right to file private petitions not only to victims of violations but also "any person or group of persons, or any non-governmental entity." The African Commission does not deal with individual cases of human rights like the counterparts in Europe and Americas. The case must reveal the "existence of a series of serious or massive violations of human and peoples' rights."

The Inter-American Commissions has power to carry out an investigation on the spot, and the state concerned must furnish to the Commission all necessary facilities. The Commissions hold hearings, receive written submissions, and examine witnesses. The Commissions try to reach a friendly settlement.[58] If a friendly settlement is obtained, it is published. If the Inter-American Commission fails to achieve a friendly settlement, it prepares a confidential report and recommendations and submits cases to the Inter-American Court of Human Rights.

The African system limits itself to diplomatic settlement of cases involving human rights violations, whereas the European and American systems have advanced beyond diplomatic settlement to judicial arbitration of human rights violations.

In Europe and the Americas, the Courts are similar in jurisdiction and function, but they differ in composition.[59] These Courts exercise both an adjudicatory and an advisory jurisdiction. In the Americas the case may be referred to the Court by the Commission, or a state party to the Convention. Individuals cannot participate in proceedings before the Court in both systems. The judgments of the Courts are final and binding. In the European system, the Committee of Ministers supervises the execution of the Court's judgments, whereas the OAS General Assembly supervises of the Court in the American system. The difference between the two Courts relates to their power to render advisory opinions. The European Court has limited advisory jurisdiction,[60] while the advisory jurisdiction of the Inter-American Court, by contrasts, extends not only to the interpretation of the Convention but also to other treaties concerning the protection of human rights in the Americas.

The European system utilizes a mandatory inter-state complaint and optional individual petition procedure, whereas the American utilizes an optional inter-state complaint and a mandatory individual petition procedure. It is important that the American system should place inter-state complaints on a mandatory footing like individual petitions in order to make the system more competent. The African system opts for a mandatory approach in both instances.

The three regional human rights systems share the same limitation namely that the primary responsibility for implementation rests with the sovereign states themselves because the implementation machinery provided for come into play only when domestic remedies have been exhausted. In addition, the right of an individual to file a complaint with the Commission against a state party is conditioned on that state having previously recognized the right of individual petition. The criticism has been made that this procedure has prevented swift reaction to violations.

In each respective region, political and economic realities are markedly different. For example, the European system has been concerned with such questions as to what is the precise content of the right to a fair trial and what are the implications of the right to freedom of expression, and so forth, and has rarely faced antagonistic governments. Therefore, the problems confronting the Inter-American Commission are far greater than those of the European system. Moreover, it must be noted that the American system has achieved very little in relation to economic, social and cultural rights.

CONCLUDING OBSERVATIONS

Examination of the three regional human rights regimes in terms of their institutional frameworks and procedures made it possible to draw lessons with regard to the possibility for a human rights regime in East Asia. On the basis of materials presented, one can conclude that the experience of the three existing regional human rights regimes is relevant to East Asia at least the following:

1. A regional system of enforcement has proven to be useful because it is more readily accepted and accessible than a universal system. This is so in part because regional machinery has to be set up by a group of like-minded countries that are in geographic proximity and share a common cultural and historical heritage. Sharing a cultural and historical heritage make it easier to establish and operate a supranational legal framework. In addition, experience has demonstrated that regional machinery can effectively reflect the region's needs, priorities and conditions when compared to global machinery.

East Asia does not yet have a functioning regional human rights organization, in large part because East Asian realities are markedly different from other regions. For example, strong Confucian traditions and the fact that the popular participation of democracy and human rights are relatively new to the people in this region have meant that leaders have had to move slowly when considering human rights issues. However, as will be discussed below, the growth of human rights concern among NGOs in East Asia, and their increasing ability to work together, may signal possibilities for previous inhibitions to be eventually overcome.

2. Three regional mechanisms have proven that regional human rights regimes can supplant global human rights arrangements. Experiences in other parts of the world, as discussed above, makes clear that regional and global mechanisms are not necessarily contradictory and can coexist. Sometimes, in fact, they can be mutually reinforcing. An effective regional human rights regime can result in a productive division of labor and in which a healthy pluralism, particularly in the diverse world we live.

3. The raison d'etre of regional human rights regimes, as outlined above, is the premise that human rights do not belong to matters essentially within the domestic jurisdiction of any state. In fact, human rights have become a legitimate international concern. Regional mechanisms are instrument through which concerted efforts for the promotion and protection of human rights can be constructive and beneficial in this increasingly interdependent world to which all nations belong.

4. The development of regional human rights regimes is a reflection of the globalization (internationalization) of human rights in an increasing number of countries. Moreover, accession to international human rights instruments has taken place in spite of enormous cultural, historical and religious divergences among and within nation-states. For example, the Convention on the Rights of the Child (CRC) has been ratified by 191 countries. This is an excellent example of universal respect for and observance of human rights, which requires acceptance of the universality of human rights and renunciation of cultural relativism. It also supports the notion that human rights are applicable irrespective of differences of culture, religion, sex, creed, and nationality.

5. The institutional strengths and limitations that might promote the birth and development of a regional human rights organization for East Asia are similar in some respects to those found in other parts of the world. Individual and inter-state communications are essential for human rights protection mechanisms. The experiences of other regional mechanisms indicate that inter-state communication may not be utilized as much as individual communication. Yet a regional organization would provide an international humanitarian forum to safeguard human rights. Periodical reporting procedures by such an organization would be useful because they would offer an opportunity for international scrutiny and critical self-evaluation of human rights situations. For the regime to be effective, reporting procedure would have to be accompanied by stringent measures so as to implement human rights agreed international standards.

6. As the previous discussion made clear, regional political organizations such as the Council of Europe, OAS and OAU are a prerequisite for a human rights RIGO because political organization of the type found in a RIGO is the sole provider of enforcement measures. In East Asia, increasing interdependence—due to development in communications, transporta-

tion, technology and economic ties—may create a regional cooperative framework growing out of the work of existing NGOs.

7. Finally, progress in democratization and consolidation of democracy in the region may facilitate the creation of conditions leading to a supranational framework for the protection of human rights, if civil societies are allowed to grow, regional human rights treaties expressing common standards and principles, in collaboration with national and regional NGOs, could be expected to emerge in countries concerned. In this context, the 1998 Asian Human Rights Charter, drafted by regional NGOs, is a significant milestone.

ASSESSMENT OF CURRENT HUMAN RIGHTS SITUATIONS IN EAST ASIA

My aim in this chapter is to test, with empirical evidence, the efficacy of some of the generalizations elucidated previously, by examining the human rights situation in each of the East Asian nations. To begin with, it might be useful to lay out some of the basic dimensions of the six East Asian nations, in the manner of Tables 3, 4, and 5.

Table 3: Population, GDP and Religion/Creed of East Asian Nations

	Pop. (millions)	GDP Per Capita (US dollars)	Religion/Creed
DPRK	22	1,000	Communism/Confucianism
ROK	47	13,300	Confucianism
Japan	126	23,400	Confucianism/Buddhism
ROC	22	16,000	Confucianism/Buddhism
PRC	1,273	3,800	Communism/Confucianism
Mongolia	2	2,320	Buddhism

[Source: World Almanac, 2002]

As indicated in Table 3 above, the People's Republic of China is by far the largest country in the region, but also clearly the poorest. The PRC and the Democratic People's Republic of Korea are the only communist countries in the region, but they share a Confucian past with all of the other countries except Mongolia. There is a tremendous gap in terms of economic well being, with Japan, Taiwan (Republic of China) and South Korea (ROK) being among the wealthiest countries of Asia while the DPRK, PRC and Mongolia are among the poorest countries in the world. As will be indicated in the pages that follow, each of these variables has an impact on the propensity of leaders and organizations in the various nations to work for or countenance a regional human rights organization.

Table 4: Adherence of East Asian countries to International Human Rights Instruments (As of May 2002)

	CESCR	CCPR	OPT	OPT2	CERD	CEDAW	CAT	CRC
DPRK	Yes	Yes	*	*	Yes	*	*	Yes
ROK	Yes	Yes	Yes	*	Yes	Yes	Yes	Yes
Japan	Yes	Yes	*	*	Yes	Yes	*	Yes
ROC	*	*	*	*	*	*	*	*
PRC	Yes	s	*	*	Yes	Yes	Yes	Yes
Mongolia	Yes	Yes	Yes	*	Yes	Yes	Yes	Yes

* indicates that the country has not ratified the instrument.

s indicates that the country has signed the instrument but not ratified.

Table 5: Ratification of International Human Rights Instruments in Chronological Order

	DPRK	ROK	Japan	PRC	Mongolia
1969	*	*	*	*	CERD
1974	*	*	*	*	CESCR
	*	*	*	*	CCPR
1978	*	CERD	*	*	*
1979	*	*	CESCR *	*	
	*	*	CCPR	*	*
1980	*	*	*	CEDAW	CEDAW
1981	CESCR	*	*	CERD	*
	CCPR	*	*	*	*
1984	*	CEDAW	*	*	*
1985	*	*	CEDAW	*	*
1988	*	*	*	CAT	*
1990	CRC	CESCR	*	*	CRC
	*	CCPR	*	*	*
	*	OPT	*	*	*
1991	*	*	*	*	OPT
1992	*	*	*	CRC	*
1994	*	*	CRC	*	*
1995	*	CAT	CERD *	*	

CESCR - The International Covenant on Economic, Social and Cultural Rights, which is monitored by the Committee on Economic, Social and Cultural Rights;

CCPR - The International Covenant on Civil and Political Rights), which is monitored by the Human Rights Committee;

OPT - The Optional Protocol to the International Covenant on Civil and Political Rights, which is supervised by the Human Rights Committee;

OPT2 - The Second Optional Protocol to the International Covenant on Civil and Political Rights aimed at the abolition of the death penalty;

CERD - The International Covenant on the Elimination of All Forms of Racial Discrimination, which is monitored by the Committee on the Elimination of Racial Discrimination

CEDAW - The Convention on the Elimination of All Forms of Discrimination against Women, which is monitored by the Committee on the Elimination of Discrimination against Women;

CAT - The Convention against Torture and Other Cruel, Inhuman or Degrading Treatment or Punishment (CAT), which is monitored by the Committee against Torture;

CRC - The Convention on the Rights of the Child, which is monitored by the Committee on the Rights of the Child.

In view of establishing a regional human rights mechanism, ratification of international human rights treaties is a critical factor. First, as the above table indicates, in East Asia only South Korea and Mongolia have ratified the Optional Protocol to the International Covenant on Civil and Political Rights. Therefore, people in these two countries alone can communicate to the UN Human Rights Committee. Second, it should be noted that none of the East Asia countries has ratified the Second Optional Protocol to the International Covenant on Civil and Political Rights, which aims to abolish the death penalty. Third, since Taiwan lost its UN membership in 1971, 20 million people in Taiwan have no direct access to the UN human rights protection mechanism. Fourth, one of the crucial conditions to have a regional human rights regime is whether the countries in the region have established the rule of law. It must be noted that North Korea and China are still under dictatorial communist rule and Freedom House included these countries in the 16 worst rated countries in their 1997–1998 survey.[61]

THE DEMOCRATIC PEOPLE'S REPUBLIC OF KOREA (DPRK)

The government of North Korea is presently the most isolated society in the world because of its leadership's deliberate policy of "self-imposed isolation," which has brought extreme misery to a population of 22 million people. The DPRK is under a single-party led by (the Korean Workers' Party [KWP]). The decisions and orders of the KWP are in effect superior to the constitution. The leader, Kim Jong Il, embraces an intense personality cult. The state directs all significant economic activity and controls all news that enters and leaves the DPRK.

Individual rights remain totally subordinated to collectivism although article 53 of the 1972 Constitution guarantees freedom of speech, the press, association, assembly and demonstration, in reality, the state freely control its citizens. North Koreans are required to observe "the socialist norm of life and the socialist rules of conduct." Article 49 states that "rights and duties of citizens are based on the collectivist principle of one for all and all for one." Individual responsibilities take precedents over rights. Thus, the DPRK continues to deny its citizens the most fundamental human rights.

There are no known organizations other than those created by the government. Free elections do not exist in North Korea. The government strictly curtails the rights of freedom of expression and association. However, the leadership argues that the country is a "people's paradise" and human rights problems do not exist in North Korea. North Korea argues that the demand by the international community to improve human rights is an infringement on its sovereignty and constitutes interference in its internal affairs.

The politics of the DPRK blatantly disregards the "democratic entitlement"[62] of people and is a violation of Art. 21 of the Universal Declaration of Human Rights, which states that:

> the will of the people shall be the basis of the authority of government; this will be expressed in periodic and genuine elections which shall be by universal and equal suffrage and shall be held by secret vote.

It has been argued that a democratic society operating under a market economy has a strong predisposition towards peace. Empirical data suggest that no liberal democracies have ever fought against each other in the past 150 years.[63] Therefore, a totalitarian state like the DPRK is a threat to international peace and security.

In North Korea there is no such thing as civil society. A proposed regional human rights mechanism would put pressure on North Korea to comply with internationally recognized human rights standards. The same would be true for a proposal to establish an ad-hoc Tribunal in North Korea, or appoint a special rapporteur at the UN.[64] As regards this issue, efforts to create a regional human rights organization in East Asia have not been supported by the DPRK.

THE REPUBLIC OF KOREA (ROK)

In contrast to North Korea, the people of the ROK have the right to elect their own government. Korean society has been historically ruled by Confucian ethical code which emphasizes "reciprocal-duty consciousness" instead of "individual-rights consciousness."[65] The conservative Confucian ethos has left women subordinate to men. The National Assembly enacted an Equal Employment Opportunity (EEO) law in 1988, but the law has had only limited practical effect. The average female worker's wages are approximately 40 percent less than those of their male counterparts.

While South Korea is a racially homogeneous country with no ethnic minorities of significant size, discrimination does occur particularly against Amer-Asian children and foreign workers, most of which come from China, the Philippines, Bangladesh, Nepal, and Pakistan. Moreover, a National Security Law mandates harsh punishments for "any person who has organized an association or group for the purpose of disturbing the state." As a result, almost 400 people, most of them prisoners of conscience, were sentenced to prison terms in 1998.[66]

Despite its shortcoming in the human rights area, the ROK has been seen emerging as a multifaceted society with vibrant civic organizations. The influence of civic organizations has been particularly noticeable as a vehicle for active citizen participation. President Kim Dae-jung has met with representatives of various civic organizations and asked for their cooperation. Some active NGOs include The People's Solidarity for Participatory Democracy, the Citizens' Coalition for Economic Justice, the Korea Women's Association United, Green Korea United, the Korea Women's Association for Democracy and Sisterhood, the Korea Action Federation for Environment, and the Association of Families of Political Prisoners.

According to recent opinion polls, more than 70 percent of the people of South Korea consider NGOs favorably and NGOs reflect the "moral high ground" of Korean society. According to the *NGO Weekly* and *the Citizen Tribune* there are currently about 12,000 civic groups in Korea, representing a 12 percent increase in two years.[67] The presence of an active civil society indicates positively that South Korea is a potential candidate for participation in the regional human rights mechanism.

JAPAN

Japan's free market economy has the world's second largest gross national product. However, Japan is a "human rights deficient" country in many ways. The Constitution states:

"All of the people are equal under the law and there shall be no discrimination in political, economic, or social relations because of race,
creed, sex, social status, or family origin."

Nevertheless, Koreans,[68] the Burakumin (descendants of feudal-era outcasts),[69] women,[70] the Ainu (Japan's indigenous people), and other alien
residents experience varying degrees of discrimination.[71]

During World War II approximately 200,000 women, mostly Koreans,
were forcibly recruited to serve as sexual slaves, or "comfort women," to
the Japanese Army.[72] In addition, approximately 200,000 Koreans and
240,000 Taiwanese were forcibly conscripted into the Japanese Army.[73]
These people have received no adequate compensation. Japan's refusal of
compensation is a root cause of lingering ill feeling of people in neighboring countries. The would-be regional human rights mechanism in East
Asia could provide a venue for war victims to receive reparation.

Global economic integration and interdependence has resulted in the
increasing number of foreigners residing in Japan and thus
the "internationalization" of Japanese society. For the last decade Japan
has seen explosive growth of NGOs and reportedly there are approximately 1,005 registered NGOs in Japan[74] and Japanese NGO Center for
International Cooperation's (JANIC) Directory of Non-Governmental
Organizations in Japan lists NGOs in Japan and it indicates that seventy
six percent of NGOs have programs in Asia. They involve refugee issues,
economic development, environment, human rights, and civic education.
Japanese media coverage of NGOs has increased dramatically. For example, the Asia-Pacific Human Rights Information Center (HURIGHTS
Osaka), began its operation in December 1994. It has the following goals:

1. to promote human rights in the Asia-Pacific region;
2. to convey Asia-Pacific perspectives on human rights to the
   international community;
3. to ensure that human rights principles are included in
   Japanese international cooperative activities; and
4. to raise human rights awareness among the people in Japan
   to meet its growing internationalization.

In spite of its economic power, Japan has been "passive" in international
human rights diplomacy. Yet increasingly vocal civil society indicates positive sign for regional integration.

REPUBLIC OF CHINA (ROC)

Taiwan has an export-oriented, free-market economy. Citizens enjoy a high
standard of living, freedoms and political rights. When the PRC was

admitted to the UN in 1971, ROC was expelled from the UN and its specialized agencies like the ILO. Therefore, people of the ROC do not have access to any human rights protection mechanisms available at the UN. A would-be regional human rights mechanism in Asia can rectify this situation. There is a trend to increased use of the death penalty in Taiwan. In 1998 32 people were executed in Taiwan.

According to Hsiao, civil society in Taiwan originated from such social movements as the consumer, anti-pollution, and conservation organization, and from organizations devoted to women's issues, aborigine human rights, as well as those of students, church, labor, farmers, teachers, the handicapped and disadvantaged, veterans, political victims, and mainlanders.[75] In the field of human rights, the Chinese Association for Human Rights (CAHR) began its operation in 1979. CAHR not only has focused on human rights advocacy, the refugee issue, and human rights in the PRC, but has developed information networks with more than one hundred human rights NGOs in more than ten Asia Pacific countries. The well-developed rule of law and vibrant civil society indicate that Taiwan can fulfill conditions for a proposed regional human rights arrangement.

PEOPLE'S REPUBLIC OF CHINA (PRC)

The PRC is the most populous country in the world. The PRC is a one-party state, in which the Chinese Communist Party (CCP) monopolizes decision-making authority.[76] Citizens lack the means legally to change their government, nor can they freely choose officials who govern them. There are no independent indigenous Chinese organizations that publicly monitor human rights conditions in China.

Socialist Legality

In China the idea of socialist legality has been promoted. According to this idea, the class nature of law is stressed. Thus, law is an instrument of domination and oppression by the bourgeois class. As a result, the following principles have been denounced as bourgeois: judicial independence, equality before the law, the presumption of innocence on the part of the accused, and the value of human rights, among others.[77]

Collective and Individual Rights

In China, individual rights are always subordinate to the needs of society.[78] Rights are, thus, collective as opposed to individual, and they are therefore always subjected to the collective interest. Article 51 of the 1982 Constitution provides that "the exercise by citizens of the People's Republic of China of their freedoms and rights may not infringe upon the interests of the state, of society and of the collective."

Neier observes that in an authoritarian state like China, the norm is hardly "consensus-seeking" but rather "consensus-imposing."[79]
According to Svensson, today's authoritarian regime use the common good, as defined by themselves, as a pretext to clamp down on individual dissent (Svensson, 1996, p. 43), which often results in dynastic politics, nepotism, cronyism, the lack of transparency and accountability.

Human Rights and State Sovereignty

China is opposed to interfering in other countries' internal affairs on the pretext of human rights.[80] China does not accept the principle that human rights are universal. For example, China considers the "right to subsistence" as a basic right for the exercise of any other rights (Shue, 1980). However, this attitude has been softening. For example, China began rights talks with the European Union, England, Norway, Japan and Canada. China allowed a UN delegation to interview detainees at prisons and labor camps and is negotiating with the International Committee of the Red Cross on similar visits.[81] Since 1991 the State Council began publishing a White Paper on *Human Rights in China.*

In 1988 China ratified the Torture Convention. Under the Torture Convention, states "shall take effective legislative, administrative, judicial measures to prevent torture; victims of torture should have access to competent authorities, to redress, and to fair and adequate compensation. Nevertheless, torture and other forms of cruel, inhuman and degrading treatment and punishment still prevail in China.[82] Torture and mistreatment of detainees are due, in part, to the government's hostile attitude towards political prisoners and the absence of a presumption of innocence in Chinese law.

Individual Chinese are arrested and detained for long periods of time without access to lawyers, friends, or families. Warrants for detention are required by law but seldom produced. Political prisoners are detained pursuant to the 1957 Decision of the State Council of the PRC on the Question of Re-education Through Labor, which provides for detention without trial of people considered to have "anti-socialist views."[83]

Article 35 of the 1982 Constitution reads: "Citizens of the People's Republic of China enjoy freedom of speech, of the press, of assembly, of association, of procession and of demonstration. " The Constitution seems to bear no relation to reality in China. The Chinese government also denies the freedom of opinion and expression through censorship and the arrest of dissidents and through control of the media, and the publication of printed material and textbooks used in colleges and universities.

Article 36 of the 1982 Constitution provides that "citizens of [PRC] enjoy freedom of religious belief." However, Tibetan Buddhism has been subjected to intensive repression. China argues that certain religious practice must be suppressed in the interests of public order.

Civil Society in China

There are so-called "GONGOS" - government-organized non-government organizations. GONGOS (shetuan) are formed voluntarily for common objectives and do not depend on government funding. Government regulations stipulate that shetuan must not harm the interest of the state and must be sponsored and accountable to a government agency, which serves as its parent organization.[84] GONGOs include the All China Women's Federation, the China Federation of Disabled Persons, and the China Society for Human Rights Studies.

In 1979 the Chinese Human Rights Alliance adopted the Chinese Declaration of Human Rights,[85] which stipulates, among others, that:

1. The citizens demand freedom of expression and the release of all political prisoners;
2. The citizens demand that Chinese society be genuinely built on the foundation of democracy;
3. The citizens demand that China be a multi-party country;
4. The citizens demand that general elections be held to choose state and local leaders by direct balloting;
5. The citizens demand that the following information be made public: state budget, gross national income, military expenditures, size of armed forces, etc.
6. The National People's Congress shall be open to the public.
7. The state ownership of means of production shall be gradually abolished.
8. We are the "citizens of the world" and as such, we demand the opening of the borders, cultural exchanges, the freedom to travel abroad.

MONGOLIAN REPUBLIC

In 1924 the single-party Leninist Socialist Republic of Mongolia was established with intimate ties to the Soviet Union. However, as a result of the 1990 free election, Mongolia became a multiparty, parliamentary democracy. Rapid marketization has been in progress. Yet most large economic entities remain under state control. Mongolia remains a very poor country.

Yet Mongolian democracy allows for a vigorous free press and a vibrant civil society. Major human rights problems are poor prison conditions, official harassment of some religious groups, and violence against women. For example, in 1998 approximately 200 prisoners died in custody due to largely inadequate management (Country Report on Human Rights 1999).

Mongolia has been one of the few countries in East Asia that has been actively participating in the UN initiatives for a regional human rights arrangement and has a good record of ratification of human rights instruments.

ASSESSMENT OF PAST ATTEMPTS TO SET UP REGIONAL HUMAN RIGHTS MECHANISMS IN ASIA

Since World War II various attempts at various levels have been made to establish regional human rights mechanisms in Asia. The initiatives for setting up regional human rights mechanisms have been taken mainly by the United Nations and regional NGOs.

UN INITIATIVES

A seminar on "National, Local and Regional Arrangements for the Promotion and Protection of Human Rights in the Asian Region" was organized by the UN and was held in Colombo, Sri Lanka in 1982. Representatives of 19 countries, regional organizations, NGOs and UN agencies attended the Seminar. The East Asian countries participating were China, Mongolia and the Republic of Korea.
In spite of the UN's initiatives, the Seminar concluded that "the necessary political will, a prerequisite for evolving intergovernmental collaboration for the promotion of human rights, does not at present exist in the region."

THE 1990 MANILA WORKSHOP

The first Asia-Pacific Human Rights Workshop was organized by the UN Center for Human Rights and was held in Manila in May 1990. The Workshop was attended by representatives of 23 countries including China, Japan and Mongolia. The Workshop reviewed the role that he Universal Declaration of Human Rights had played; the efforts of the international community to realize those rights; and consideration of regional and national institutions for the promotion and protection of human rights. Three experts of regional mechanisms in Africa, the Americas, and Europe made presentations on respective arrangements. The debate was held on the advantages of establishing a regional institution for the promotion and protection of human rights, its function, complementary role vis-a-vis the UN system, investigative role, individual complaints process, and remedies to the victims of human rights violations.

THE 1993 JAKARTA WORKSHOP

The 2nd UN Workshop for the Asia-Pacific Region on Human Rights Issues was held in Jakarta in January 1993 primarily to discuss regional arrangements for the promotion and protection of human rights. The Workshop was attended by representatives of 28 states including China, Japan, the Democratic People's Republic of Korea, the Republic of Korea, and Mongolia.

The central objectives of the Jakarta workshop were as follows:

   a.   To increase awareness among countries of the region of international human rights standards and procedures and of the role of the states in implementing human rights norms;
   b.   To inform participants of the mechanisms which are available to assist states in fulfilling their obligations under the various international human rights instruments;
   c.   To promote bilateral cooperation in the field of human rights between countries of the region;
   d.   To foster the development of national human rights institutions in the region;
   e.   To provide a forum for the establishment of regional human rights arrangements;
   f.   To facilitate dialogue between Asia-Pacific nations on the upcoming World Conference on Human Rights.

The majority of the delegates expressed willingness to work towards the development of a human rights system at the regional or sub-regional level. The workshop identified key obstacles to the establishment of a regional system: the geographical complexity, different levels of development and cultural diversity, the lack of a unifying tradition and the absence of mutual understanding between governments.

THE 1994 SEOUL WORKSHOP

The 3rd UN Workshop for the Asian and Pacific Region on Human Rights Issues was held in Seoul in July 1994. The representatives of 29 countries in the region participated in the workshop, including China, Japan, Mongolia, and the Republic of Korea.

The three central objectives of the workshop were:

1. To explore possibilities for the establishment of regional arrangements for the promotion and protection of human rights;
2. To review progress in the development of national institutions for the promotion and protection of human rights in the region;
3. To examine national action for promoting and protecting human rights, the development of strategies for human rights education in the Asian and Pacific region; and means to encourage ratification of human rights treaties by countries in the region.

The proposal was made to convene workshops on a regular basis, which would facilitate the exchange of ideas and information regarding matters of common interest in the field of human rights. This attempt would serve to broaden the common understanding of human rights issues among nations of the region.

The workshop discussed the desirability of each country in the region drawing up a national action plan for the promotion and protection of human rights and developing strategies for human rights education. The Chairman of the workshop in his concluding remark pointed out that regional cooperation should, where appropriate, begin through sub-regional initiatives.

THE 1996 KATHMANDU WORKSHOP

The 4th Workshop was held in Kathmandu in February 1996. The objective of the workshop was the establishment of an effective regional human rights mechanism. The representatives of 30 states and 9 NGOs in the region attended. The East Asian countries participating were China, the Democratic People's Republic of Korea, Japan and the Republic of Korea.

The workshop reached the following "common principles" regarding the establishment of a regional human rights arrangement.

1. Any regional arrangement would need to be based on the needs, priorities, and conditions prevailing in the region;
2. The roles, functions and tasks of regional arrangements should be identified by the governments of the region;
3. The diversities and complexities of the region would require extensive consultations among countries in the region;
4. The workshop welcomes the NGOs' constructive participation in the process of development of regional arrangements;

5.   A process should be initiated on a step-by-step basis with the sharing of information and experiences and the building up of national capacities to promote and protect human rights.

THE 1997 AMMAN WORKSHOP

The 5th workshop was held in Amman, Jordan in January 1997. The workshop was attended by representatives of 31 countries, including China, the Democratic Republic of Korea, Japan, Mongolia, and the Republic of Korea.

The following two key issues were agreed upon at the Amman workshop:

a.   The development of a regional technical cooperation programme for the purpose of strengthening national and regional human rights capacities through the sharing of expertise, experiences and practices;
b.   A process for designing the regional programme and future preparatory work in the area of developing a regional arrangement through the establishment of a working group.

The Amman workshop reaffirmed the aspiration for the establishment of regional arrangements in the Asia-Pacific region adopted at the Kathmandu workshop (1996) and reiterated that any such arrangement must emerge from the needs and priorities set by governments of the region.

First, the workshop endorsed the "step-by-step" approach, sharing information, the building up of national capacities, and the establishment of confidence-building measures. Second, ratification of international human rights instruments was crucial in this process. Third, the workshop urged the governments to create independent national human rights institutions. The workshop recommended the creation of the Asia-Pacific Forum of National Human Rights Institutions, which supports all independent and autonomous national institutions in the region. Fourth, the workshop recognized the importance of national human rights institutions and the civil society in various step towards regional arrangements. Fifth, the workshop reaffirmed that all human rights, civil and political, economic, social and cultural, including the right to self-determination and the right to development, are universal, interdependent and indivisible.

THE 1998 TEHERAN WORKSHOP

The 6th Workshop was held in Tehran in February 1998. The workshop was attended by representatives of 36 countries including China, North

Korea, South Korea, Japan and Mongolia in addition to NGOs such as Amnesty International, the World Muslim Congress, and the Asia-Pacific Human Rights NGOs Facilitating Team. The workshop stressed that any regional arrangement for Asia and Pacific should be based on priorities and needs identified by the region and through incorporating "step-by-step" and "building-blocks" approach involving extensive consultation among the governments concerned; and it is necessary to keep in mind the richness of cultural, historical and religious diversities within the region in considering regional arrangements.

There was consensus that technical cooperation aimed at national capacity building should be the foundation for any further move towards the establishment of a regional human rights arrangement. The workshop adopted a Framework for Regional Technical Cooperation in the Asia-Pacific area to develop, inter alia:

a. national plans of actions and the strengthening of national capacities;
b. human rights education;[86]
c. national institutions for the promotion and protection of human rights;
d. strategies for the realization of the right to development and economic, social and cultural rights.[87]

THE 1999 NEW DELHI WORKSHOP

The 7th workshop was held in New Delhi in February 1999. The workshop reaffirmed the universality, indivisibility, interdependence, and inter-relatedness of all human rights and recognized that democracy, development and respect for human rights and fundamental freedom are interdependent and mutually reinforcing. The workshop was committed to enhancing regional cooperation and to promoting universal respect for human rights by step-by-step and building-blocks approach.

The workshop reaffirmed strengthening the national capacity for the promotion and protection of human rights and called for technical cooperation activities in all areas of human rights as an essential element of a promotional approach. The workshop affirmed the development of regional cooperation through the building of national capacities and an exchange of experiences within the region based on regional technical cooperation with the support of the UN Voluntary Fund for Technical Cooperation in the Field of Human Rights. The workshop decided that an annual regional workshop should be called for an in-depth discussion pertaining to the four areas identified by the Framework for Regional Technical Cooperation.

THE ASIA-PACIFIC REGIONAL WORKSHOP OF NATIONAL HUMAN RIGHTS INSTITUTIONS

The first Asia-Pacific Regional Workshop of National Human Rights Institutions was held in Darwin, Australia in 1996. The workshop produced the Larrakia Declaration, which states, "at the international level, regional cooperation is essential to ensure the effective promotion and protection of human rights." The workshop set up the Asia-Pacific Forum of National Institutions.

The second workshop was held in New Delhi in 1997. Australia, India, Indonesia, the Philippines, New Zealand, Sri Lanka, Mongolia have so far set up such a national human rights commissions.[88] The possible functions of national human rights commission are:

1. to act as a source of human rights information for the government and people of the country;
2. to assist in educating the public and promoting awareness of and respect for human rights;
3. to advise on any questions regarding human rights matters referred to them by the government;
4. to keep under review the status of legislation, judicial decisions for the promotion of human rights, and to submit reports on these matters to the appropriate authorities;
5. to promote conformity of national laws and practices with international human rights standards;
6. to encourage ratification and implementation of international standards. [89]

It should be noted that the national human rights institutions have a unique status because they are located somewhere between the sphere of government and that of civil society. They are established and funded by the government but are expected to function in an independent and autonomous manner. The UN Human Rights Commission considers that national human rights institutions constitute one of the most important building blocks necessary for the establishment of regional human rights arrangements in the Asia Pacific region.

NGOS INITIATIVES

In March 1993 the Asia Pacific NGO Conference on Human Rights was held in Bangkok. Some 240 participants and from 110 NGOs from about 26 countries attended the Conference. The Conference adopted the Bangkok NGO Declaration on Human Rights.[90] The Conference stressed that the advocacy of human rights cannot be considered to be an encroachment upon national sovereignty. NGOs urged the UN to allocate at least 5 percent of the UN budget to human rights work and to establish a Permanent International Court on Human Rights.

The Sub-Group on Regional Charter/Mechanism agreed to set up a regional commission on conditions that:

1. It should be mandated to apply without reservation the International Bill of Human Rights, CEDAW, the Convention Against Torture, the Declaration of the Right to Development and other relevant instruments;
2. Member states of the Commission must ratify the above international human rights instruments prior to their membership in the Commission;
3. The right of individual and NGOs to petition the Commission must be guaranteed;
4. Such petition should not utilize concurrently the various UN mechanisms for the protection of human rights;
5. No member of the Commission should not be hold official position in government and member should be appointed in consultation with NGOs;
6. The meeting of the commission and its deliberation should be open to the public. There should be separate court on human rights with the power to adjudicate complaints, and make binding judgments, including compensation, and the court should have the power to enforce its decisions through appropriate measures;
7. The commission should have full investigative power;
8. A separate body should be set up to adjudicate complaints;
9. Governments must be required to disseminate information on the commission and how it operates.

The NGOs considered the possibility of setting up an NGO-led machinery for the region in the absence of an intergovernmental mechanism.

In 1995 the Expert Meeting organized by the Asia-Pacific Human Rights Information Center (HURIGHTS Osaka) was held. Yamazaki proposed three-step program be adopted.[91] The first step is to set up sub-regional NGO machinery dedicated human rights information handling, research and education. The second step is to have an inter-governmental Asia-Pacific Forum for the Promotion of Human Rights. The third step is to set up sub-regional or regional human rights machinery.

In conclusion, the problems identified by the Meeting concerning the feasibility of establishing a regional mechanism are the low level of ratification of human rights treaties, the non-observance of treaty-obligations after ratification, the cultural relativist argument as opposed to universality of human rights by the leadership in the region.

In 1995 the NGO Forum on Asia Pacific Economic Cooperation (APEC) was held in Tokyo, Japan and more than 100 NGOs took part. The statement issued by the Forum urges members of APEC to ratify and implement all major human rights instruments and to engage in regional cooperation to promote socially and ecologically sustainable development, among others.

In 1996 the Asia-Pacific Human Rights NGOs Congress was held in Delhi, India. Approximately 117 delegates from 28 countries attended the Congress. The Congress stressed no-derogation from existing international human rights norms and standards and respect for the universality, indivisibility and non-selectivity of human rights. One of the recommendations of the meeting was establishment of a regional human rights mechanism.

The LAWASIA Human Rights Committee[92] has been working on establishing a Human Rights Commission for the Asia and Pacific region. The Committee considered three steps; first, the dissemination of information concerning human rights and the promotion of awareness of human rights throughout the region, for example, translation of major international human rights treaties into local languages such as Thai, Filipino, Hindi, Malay, and Burmese. Second, the establishment of a coalition of NGOs concerned with human rights issues in the region. LAWASIA's effort resulted in a formation of an Asian Coalition of Human Rights Organizations (ACHRO). Third, efforts have been made to establish sub-regional human rights commissions in ASEAN and the South Pacific regions.

ATTEMPTS TO SET UP REGIONAL HUMAN RIGHTS MECHANISMS IN THE ASSOCIATION OF SOUTHEAST ASIAN NATIONS (ASEAN) REGION

The ASEAN was established in 1967 and is composed of Brunei Darussalam, Indonesia, Malaysia, Philippines, Singapore, Thailand and Myanmar. The main objectives of the ASEAN is to accelerate economic growth, social progress and cultural development in the region; promote regional peace and stability through abiding respect for justice and the rule of law.

In 1983 the Regional Council on Human Rights in Asia, a NGO based in Hong Kong, drafted a "Declaration of the Basic Duties of ASEAN Peoples and Governments," which was presented to ASEAN.[93] Furthermore, the Asian Human Rights Commission and the Christian Conference of Asia, NGOs in Hong Kong, have initiated the process of drafting a Charter of Asia Pacific Understanding on Human Rights.

In 1993, the 26th ASEAN Ministerial Meeting was held in Singapore and the Joint Communique was issued, which declared that the ASEAN Foreign Ministers, in support of the Vienna Declaration and Program of Action of June 1993, agreed, "ASEAN governments should consider the establishment of an appropriate regional mechanism on human rights." The Meeting adopted the Singapore Declaration, which stated, "we should begin the setting up of an appropriate regional human rights mechanism."

Similarly, in 1977 the ASEAN Inter-Parliamentary Organization (AIPO) was formed and adopted the "Kuala Lumpur AIPO Declaration on Human Rights" at its 14th AIPO General Assembly in 1993.[94] Article 21 of the Declaration states that "it is the task and responsibility of Member States to establish an appropriate regional mechanism on human rights."

In 1994 the Colloquium on Human Rights was held in Manila. The Colloquium emphasized the important contribution that independent national institutions can make and the role NGOs can play. The Colloquium was to facilitate the process of developing a sub-regional human rights body for promotion and protection of human rights in South-East Asian nations.

In 1995 representatives of governments, regional organizations and NGOs from the ASEAN regions met in Manila to consider the feasibility of establishing a appropriate human rights arrangement in the region. In 1997 the Workshop was held in Kuala Lumpur. Its focus was on the legal, institutional and political implications of an ASEAN human rights mechanism. The Conclusions and Recommendations of the Workshop include:

1. to pursue ASEAN's commitment to establish a regional human rights mechanism through the Steering Committee and the establishment of national working groups;
2. to work for a draft ASEAN Convention on Human Rights.

National Working Groups have been formed in Indonesia, Malaysia, Philippines and Thailand. The proposed ASEAN Human Rights Mechanism is an inter-governmental mechanism which will not only enable ASEAN states to consult each other on human rights matters but also encourage states to undertake concrete steps to promote and protect human rights. In 1998, the Working Group for an ASEAN Human Rights Mechanism, comprised of prominent political and human rights figures from ASEAN countries, was formally recognized by ASEAN governments as an important vehicle for discussion about the possibility of establishing an ASEAN human rights mechanism.

ATTEMPTS TO SET UP REGIONAL HUMAN RIGHTS MECHANISMS IN SOUTH ASIAN ASSOCIATION FOR REGIONAL COOPERATION (SAARC) REGION

SAARC was established by adopting the Charter of the South Asian Association for Regional Co-operation (SAARC) in 1985. SAARC is based on the principles of sovereign equality, territorial integrity, national independence, non-use of force and non-interference in the internal affairs of other states and peaceful settlement of disputes (Preamble of the Charter and Art II [1]). SAARC is currently made up of India, Pakistan, Bhutan, Bangladesh, Nepal, Sri Lanka, and the Maldives. SAARC's main goal is to strengthen regional cooperation and to accelerate economic and social development in member states through joint action.

The Integrated Program of Action (IPA) identifies eleven areas of cooperation:

1. Agriculture
2. Communications
3. Education, culture and sports
4. Environment and meteorology
5. Health and population activities
6. Prevention of drug trafficking and drug abuse
7. Rural development
8. Science and technology
9. Tourism
10. Transport
11. Women in development

In 1986 SAARC adopted the Bangalore Declaration, which provides that "the needs of all children is the principal means of human resources development. Children should, therefore, be given the highest priority in national development planning. The Declaration recognizes peace, security, and respect for international law are essential for growth and stability."

In 1990 Male Declaration was issued by the SAARC, which states, "there has been integration of national economies into the world economy. There is the trend of increasing integration of the pattern of global production, consumption, trade, and integration of markets. SAARC is convinced that their mutual cooperation can be a critical factor in enabling them to face new challenges."

At the Sixth SAARC Summit in Colombo in 1991, SAARC leaders issued the Colombo Declaration, which recognized the interdependence and equal importance of civil, political, economic and social rights. The Declaration reaffirms their commitment to democracy, human rights and rule of law. The Declaration accords the highest priority to the alleviation of poverty in all South Asian countries. In 1997 the Declaration of the Ninth Summit of SAARC countries was adopted and it recognizes the importance of gender equality and empowerment of women, raising education and literacy rates, and the reduction of population rates, among others. The Declaration expressed concern at the trafficking of women and children within and between countries. They decided upon the feasibility of establishing a Regional Convention on Combating the Crime of Trafficking in Women and Children for Prostitution and Convention on Regional Arrangement on the Promotion of Child Welfare in South Asia.

In 1993 the Declaration of the Seventh SAARC Summit was adopted. The Declaration states that governments commit unequivocally to eradication of poverty in South Asia, the provision of universal primary education, primary health care, shelter for the poor and protection of children.

In 1995 the Delhi Declaration was adopted, which reaffirms the realization of the rights of all, in particular those of the poor, to food, work, shelter, health, and education. Considering that the exploitation of the Girl Child is a direct reflection of the status of women in society, the Leaders reaffirmed their resolve to take necessary measures to eliminate all forms of discrimination against women and female-children.

SAARC also has adopted the Convention on Terrorism and the Regional Convention against Drug Abuse and Drug-Trafficking. SAARC decided to observe the years 1991–2000 as the "SAARC Decade of the Girl Child" and the years 2001–2010 as the "SAARC Decade of the Rights of the Child." The problem with SAARC is India's hegemonic role in the region. India is considered gross violator of human rights and SAARC cannot achieve anything without the blessing of India.[95]

Dias observes, "SAARC countries agreed to take an issue-oriented approach, for example, to focus on child labor, migrant workers, refugees, poverty problems and the education of the girl-child. This is a beginning. From there they can move forward. They are moving forward in the direction of establishing a human rights institution."[96]

ATTEMPTS TO SET UP REGIONAL HUMAN RIGHTS MECHANISMS IN SOUTH PACIFIC REGION

LAWASIA initiated human rights efforts in the South Pacific in 1970s. In 1985 the conference on "Prospects for the Establishment of an Inter-Governmental Human Rights Commission in the South Pacific" was held in Fiji organized by LAWASIA Human Rights Standing Committee. The Drafting Committee was formed at the conference and it drafted a Pacific Charter of Human Rights.[97] The Charter now awaits consideration and adoption by states within the South Pacific.

The Pacific Charter is patterned mainly after the African Charter on Human and Peoples' Rights. It includes civil, political and economic, social and cultural rights,[98] the right to development, the rights of peoples, and the duties of individuals and governments.[99] It also proposes the creation of a Pacific Human Rights Commission with promotional functions and with power to consider complaints from state parties and individuals. The South Pacific has been considered an appropriate region to set up a sub-regional mechanism because of cultural affinity, a good degree of political understanding, a certain historical involvement, trade relationships and movements of people.

Dias observes that the problem in the Pacific region is that Australia and New Zealand have money and they tend to dominate in the whole process. According to Dias, Pacific islands are not happy about it; secondly, the needs of Pacific islands are completely different from Australia and New Zealand.[100]

ASSESSMENT OF HUMAN RIGHTS NGOs IN EAST ASIA

NGOs have historically played little known but critically important roles in the development of intergovernmental human rights organizations. They have been a source of support for the formation of regional human rights institutions, whether in the Americas, Europe or Africa.

The aim of this investigation is to identify the roles of NGOs indigenous to Japan, South Korea, Taiwan, Hong Kong and Mongolia as well as international NGOs that focus on those countries, and to analyze their support for, indifference to, or opposition to regional integration in terms of the formation of East Asian human rights institutions. The presentation of their diverse views tells us much about the range of their views and the substance of their concerns and remaining challenges to be confronted. There is no such existing presentation of participant-observers in existing literature on East Asia. As a first exploratory step to fill this scholarly gap, I must emphasize that this study does not represent a cross-section of NGOs but should be viewed as an exploratory first step. This study should supply a foundation for further future research.

For this study I have sent out questionnaires to 128 human rights NGOs which were selected from the Human Rights Internet Reporter: A Listing of Organizations Concerned with Human Rights and Social Justice Worldwide (Ottawa: Human Rights Internet, 1994) and 45 individuals in South Korea, Japan, Taiwan, Hong Kong, Mongolia, The Philippines and Indonesia, who were selected from Human Rights Connections (American Society of International Law Human Rights Interest Group, 1998–1999). The survey instruments are found in the appendix of this work.[101] The NGOs who have responded to the questionnaires are as follows:

Hong Kong [5]

    Asian Center for the Progress of Peoples
    Asian Human Rights Commission
    The Information Center for Human Rights and Democratic Movement
    Asia Monitor Resource Center
    Christian Conference of Asia

Taiwan [1]

    Taiwan Association for Human Rights

Japan [8]

    Jesuit Social Center
    The Investigation Team on the Truth about forced Korean Labors in Japan
    The Association for Solidarity with Foreign Migrant Workers
    Women's Democratic Club
    Japan Federation of Bar Association
    All Japan Federation of Buraku Liberation Movement
    Asia-Pacific Human Rights Information Center
    The Japanese Committee of World Conference on Religion and Peace

South Korea [4]

    People's Solidarity for Participatory Democracy
    Human Rights Committee of the Korea Youth Progress Party
    The Lawyers for a Democratic Society
    The International Human Rights of Korea

Philippines [1]

    Working Group for an ASEAN Human Rights Mechanism

Mongolia [2]

    The Mongolian Human Rights Committee
    Mongolia Committee

The US [3]

    Human Rights in China
    Human Rights Watch/Asia
    Amnesty International/USA

The NGOs that responded numbered 24 accounting for an 18.8 percent mail return. They identified themselves according to the following categories:

International organization (INGO)	6
Regional organization (RO)	7
National organization (NO)	10

Local community organization (LC)   1
Total: 24

The individuals who have responded to the questionnaires are as follows:

1. Chi Young Pak, Professor, Hanyang University, South Korea
2. Nana N. Soeyono Ma, Lecturer, University of Indonesia
3. V. Chen, International Lawyer, Taiwan
4. John J. Tobin, Law Professor, Japan
5. Sayoko Kodena, Professor, Osaka International University, Japan
6. Shin Hae Bong, Associate Professor, Aoyama Gakuin University, Japan
7. Pae Keun Park, Professor, Kyushu University, Japan

In addition, I have conducted interviews of the following individuals in order to collect experts' opinions:

1. Clarence Dias, President, International Center for Law in Development, New York;
2. Mike Jendrzejczyk, Washington Director, Human Rights Watch/Asia;
3. Xiaorong Li, Vice Chair, Human Rights in China;
4. Christina Cerna, Executive Director,the Inter-American Commission on Human Rights, Washington, D.C.;
5. Hungda Chiu, Director of East Asian Legal Studies Program, University of Maryland Law School and President of the International Law Association.
6. T. Kumar, Advocacy Director, Asia & Pacific, Amnesty International USA

My findings will first be narratively presented in relation to the survey queries. According to the NGO surveys and the interviews of experts, the followings are the findings:

1. Are the "Asian Values" arguments valid, and do Asians need their own concept of human rights?

According to Dias, President of International Center for Law in Development in New York, the Asian values argument is a totally spurious argument. It is advocated by a couple of heads of states who want to justi-fy particular types of policies to pursue economic growth.[102] For example, the argument of Prime Minister Mahathir Mohamad of Malaysia and former Prime Minister Lee Kuan Yew of Singapore is that in developing countries, it is necessary to sacrifice civil and political rights in order to achieve economic development.[103] Singaporean "Shared Values" states, in part, that:

> Nations before community and society above self; Family as the basic unit of society.[104]

The trade-off argument is a question of choice between providing bread and freedom. Dias criticizes such trade-off arguments saying that:

> "if the state gives you lots of bread but you do not have freedom, then the state may stop giving you bread at any moment. What happens then? In the same way, if one has only freedom without bread, one starves to death."

The situation of North Korea is a good example. Dias cited his Indian countryman, Amartya Sen, who wrote, "no substantial famine has ever occurred in any country with a democratic form of government and a relatively free press."[105] Dias stresses that democratic society can check administrative mismanagement and not allow conditions of famine to take place or to go unremedied.

On a related matter, Dias contends that the indivisibility of human rights is a crucial concept, which provides a counterargument to the Asian values thesis. Indivisibility means that if people are deprived of food, it causally affects their right to work and their right to education (and vice versa). In order to fight for his/her job, they have to organize for collective bargaining. Collective bargaining involves civil and political rights of assembly and association. Without them we cannot get economic rights. Similarly, if one does not enjoy basic nutrition, one is not in a position to exercise civil and political rights, a proposition which brings us back to Amartya Sen's ideas.

Interdependence and interrelatedness among rights are very crucial. Dias puts emphasis on the assertion that Asian values need to be redefined in many ways. This does not mean that Asian values are inconsistent with human rights, human rights are not inconsistent with some Asian values, nor that we all have the same basic needs. Rather, because human rights are universal claims to enable us to remain or become human.

In extension of this view, Dias stresses that there is no such thing as Asian human rights because Asians are no different from other human beings. We are all human beings. He explains that vocal critics of the Asian values thesis include a large number of Asian scholars who have documented human rights notions in Asian traditions. Jendrzejczyk of Human

Rights Watch/Asia, Sen and Li agree that the Asian values argument is largely discredited.

2. Is the regional inter-governmental organization (RIGO) useful as compared to the global human rights mechanism available at the UN?

Cerna of the Inter-American Commission points out that most RIGOs have courts, and courts have authority to issue legally binding decisions. For example, the regional court in Strasbourg is a real court with full decision power. The court can decide cases authoritatively. The UN does not have a comparable court mechanism covering the full range of human rights. This is why an attempt has been made to establish the International Criminal Court, which primarily deals with genocide, crimes against humanity, war crimes, and the crime of aggression.[106] Prof. Chiu of University of Maryland Law School agrees that the UN Conventions lack enforcement mechanisms and procedures. Dias concurs that although the UN has established international human rights standards, the protection mechanisms are very weak. He states that:

> "the UN can monitor, make reports, make criticism, and make recommendations. But if governments ignore it, there is nothing the UN can do."

On the other hand, at the national level there are strong enforcement mechanisms. For example, Dias explains that:

> "India has ratified CEDAW and incorporated it into its national laws. Nevertheless, a widow may be burnt after her husband dies. If a bride is unable to bring a dowry, she is killed by her in-laws. The UN publicizes this; the UN can call upon the Indian government to do something about it. However, it depends upon the Indian government. Human rights are universal. Yet most enforcement is made at the national level."[107]

Dias stresses that we need complementary mechanisms at these different levels. It is, therefore, a positive step to have a regional mechanism where one can appeal. Echoing notions from a functional and regional integration theory, Dias emphasizes that RIGO has an advantage because countries in the region share the same language, culture, have trade relations and enjoy proximity to each other, etc. Consequently, the problems in Asia tend to have regional characteristics (e.g. trafficking of women and children, etc).

Dias also argues that even if the US sends an envoy to Mahathir, the Malaysian Prime Minister, will not listen to him. By contrast, the problems can be solved within Asia. With a RIGO, we will be able to deal with regional problems effectively. Dias stresses that human rights are universal but should be applied given the conditions of the region (e.g. level of economic development). Dias points out that the global level human rights protection mechanisms are generally based on the Western standard of living. A RIGO is able to adjust to the regional reality.

Another strength of RIGO is its accessibility. Dias asks:

> "Are you going to expect bondage laborers to have resources to be able to fight cases in Geneva and New York? It is easier for NGOs to do their work in Bangkok than Geneva and New York psychologically and financially."

Dias cautions, however, what RIGO should not do is to function at lower standards of "internationally recognized human rights principles." RIGO should not bypass international law. Therefore, Dias insists that if a country does not ratify an international treaty, the country should not be allowed into the system.

Kumar states that Amnesty International is a worldwide human rights organization and it is always helpful to have a regional mechanism like the European Commission and the African Commission. He argues that regional and sub-regional systems will strengthen the UN system. Jendrzejczyk agrees that RIGO could be, ideally, very useful and can supplant and not compete with the UN mechanisms and procedures.

Cerna of the Inter-American Commission points out, however, the limitations of regional mechanisms involving a smaller number of states, which can be dominated by the superpower in the region. Moreover, regional systems tend to have funding problems.

3. Why has East Asia not had a RIGO so far?

Many states in Asia still consider human rights issues as internal affairs. Chiu points out that human rights implicates questions of sovereignty, and some governments argue that human rights should not be a means to interfere in the internal affairs of another country. For example, China—like Yugoslavia and Chile—has insisted that human rights belong to the domestic jurisdiction of an independent sovereign state. Li, a philosopher and Vice Chair of Human Rights in China argues that:

> "RIGO could do great things but also could do nothing. A regional mechanism may not do anything to a country like China. I am not sure if China will join an Asian mechanism. China has been a member of the UN and has made a commitment by signing a number of documents, which provide NGOs and the international community with weapons to tell the government that they are obliged to respect human

rights. However, the human rights situation in China has hardly improved."[108]

According to Jendrzejczyk, the problem for China "is sensitivity about nationalist integrity being somehow violated as soon as such a mechanism is set up." He argues that in Asia there has been a gentleman's agreement and understanding that human rights problems are very sensitive in many cases. As a result, countries would rather deal with human rights problems internally.

In this context, states are reluctant to accept any RIGO that would likely expose a state to complaints filed by other states, individuals, and NGOs for human rights violations, since it is perceived as a serious threat to their dominance and national sovereignty.

Jendrzejczyk explains that RIGO involves rather a complicated and complex set of relationships among different countries. Europe has had a history of close cooperation. They have had a common set of standards, cultural background, history, and existing political and economic frameworks. In Europe certain human rights standards and principles have been agreed upon because in Europe and the Americas the notion of human rights is a part of history (e.g. Magna Carta, the English Bill of Rights, the French Declaration of Man and of the Citizens, etc) in spite of its tumultuous history. In addition, all European countries are parties to UN human rights conventions.

On the contrary, East Asian countries have not had such close relationships. East Asia has not had any pre-existing framework (e.g. European Union). Cerna states that a political organization is prerequisite for the development of human rights institutions because those countries have to express their political intention to work together in many areas including human rights. Jendrzejczyk asserts that many Asian countries still resist the idea of "international standards." He points out that the difficulty in East Asia is that there are no human rights standards and principles the countries in the region can agree upon. For example, Chiu explains that China's position is that the right to subsistence is more important than other rights.

China also puts emphasis on the right to self-determination and collective rights. In addition, many Asian countries have not ratified UN human rights Conventions. Some Asian leaders argue, "if we pay too much attention to human rights, the society will become chaotic; what we need are order and stability."[109]

Jendrzejczyk indicates that Japan's refusal to make adequate compensation to war victims (e.g. comfort women and forced conscripts) and attend to the Nanking Massacre[110] has failed to remove the legacy of World War II and has prevented countries in the region from building any cooperative framework. Chiu points out that the reason why the regional arrangement has not materialized is due to the indifference of governments in the region and consequently that there is no initiator and little regional leadership.

4. What have been the chief obstacles for setting up a RIGO in East Asia?

Jendrzejczyk points out that many countries in East Asia have not ratified UN human rights treaties. He argues that since so many governments in the region have yet to ratify the most important treaties the question must be raised about their willingness to adhere to international standards. In this situation, it would be difficult to reach agreements or consensus on human rights standards upon which all governments can jointly agree. He asks: "if countries have not ratified human rights treaties and have a regional human rights mechanism, what would be the standards all governments can commit to and abide by. Would it be the Universal Declaration of Human Rights entirely or only certain provisions such as the right to free expression, free association, the freedom of religion, political participation and the right to adequate housing?" Yet if we deal with a specific issue, we will run into problems because the PRC, for example, has a sharply different concept as to how individuals participate in political processes.

According to Dias, the main obstacles for setting up regional mechanisms are the attitudes of some governments, which continue to claim that Asian values are not consistent with human rights norms. And those governments argue that where human rights are valid, they are a matter of national sovereignty and are not open to any international scrutiny. Jendrzejczyk asserts that although international norms have been universally endorsed, when it comes to enforcement and implementation, we encounter a number of problems.

Dias points out another factor. Asian human rights NGOs have not played much of a role on this issue because, in part, NGOs have been disillusioned when they see the African Commission, the European Commission, and the Inter-American Commission in operation. These mechanisms have done some good work but at the same time they have been having many problems. Therefore, people who work for NGOs think that the Asian machinery may not be effective.

In addition, NGOs are worried, for example, that ASEAN can create a ASEAN human rights mechanism and in doing so, lower international standards because many governments have not signed international human rights treaties. In this situation, RIGO may become a device whereby governments can evade higher international standards.

NGOs who have responded to the questionnaire state that the obstacles for establishing RIGO are:

1. political issues such as human rights are the internal affairs of sovereign states, lack of governments' commitment, Taiwan's ambiguous legal status, lack of governments willing to take initiatives, governments' policy in Asia based on Asian Values, lack of governments' cooperation among themselves, the Japanese government's indifference to human rights, governments' aversion to external accountability, prospect that RIGO will scrutinizes human rights records of governments, intervention by the international community, lack of political will, and the application of a Western concept of human rights;
2. cultural issues such as language, ethnic consciousness and ASEAN countries attitudes;
3. legal issues such as the fact that very few governments have signed and ratified international human rights conventions, governments are not willing to be subjected to a higher authority like a regional human rights court and sovereignty is interpreted in a traditional sense; and
4. economic issues such as economic disparity in East Asia.

5. Do human rights NGOs need to cooperate or collaborate with counterparts in other countries to achieve their organizational goals?

Jendrzejczyk explains that, with partners, Human Rights Watch (HRW) determines its priorities (e.g. trafficking of women, extra-judicial killings) and then sets its agenda, e.g., in Burma, Thailand, Philippines, and Japan. HRW does research and advocacy and other projects jointly with partners. HRW shares and combines its resources with partners. HRW engages in the cross-fertilization of ideas because Jendrzejczyk explains that:

> From our point of view, our effectiveness and our ability to be successful depends upon our ability to work closely with NGOs as colleagues. NGOs have limited resources, play different roles and complimentary roles. This is an ad hoc division of labor in many cases. NGOs have different tactics and priorities. Generally there is a recognition among the NGO communities that we have to work together. Voices are limited in terms of how much influence we can have. Working together we can have a better chance of being effective."

As for Amnesty International, Kumar explains that AI sections work independently and cooperatively. It depends on the issue. If there are needs to cooperate, they will. Dias argues that NGOs have been cooperating not only in Asia but also globally over the last 15 years because of globalization. NGOs need to cooperate increasingly on a global scale because many problems require actions in many different places. He stresses that NGOs need to be able to re-mobilize human rights communities, people in Geneva, New York, Brazil and Nigeria, for example.

In the NGO survey, 6 INGOs, 9 NOs, and 7 ROs stated that they cooperate and collaborate with counterparts in other countries. Only 2 NGOs have not done any cooperative work because one NGO works only for foreign residents in Japan and another NGO has just begun their operation. Six out of seven individuals answered that NGOS need to cooperate or collaborate with each other in order to achieve their organizational goals.

NGOs surveyed indicate that their cooperative work includes: personnel exchanges, dissemination of reports, providing information; holding meetings, seminars, educational training sessions and workshops; implementing projects, supporting groups in other countries, doing research projects jointly, providing financial support and technical assistance, distributing publications, organizing regional networking, engaging in regular consultation, and participating in drafting of an NGO Asian Charter.

6. If a RIGO existed in East Asia, would it serve human rights NGOs' organizational goals?

Dias argues that in order to achieve organizational goals, NGOs must participate in the process of establishing a regional human rights mechanism because if NGOs are a part of the process of bringing into creation new machinery, already working relationships between governments and NGOs will have been established when the arrangements begin to operate. NGOs must enhance their working relationships, otherwise, NGOs' ability to contribute to RIGO will be limited.

Dias stresses that NGOs are crucial to any human rights mechanism, whether it is national, regional or global. Without NGOs' participation the mechanism will never work. NGOs provide the impetus for regional mechanisms to work. For instance, Cerna points out that the "African system existed only on a piece of paper until NGOs began working."

Cerna states that NGOs' goals will certainly be served by RIGO because in the Inter-American human rights protection system many NGOs have actively been involved by preparing complaints and presenting cases to the Commission because they know how the system works. States often avoid openness and want to hide everything. Because of NGOs' reports, the facts are revealed. NGOs help victims and the victims' family. They organize conferences and give lectures. They provide information, lobby, advocate certain positions and intervene in litigation (e.g by filing briefs and serving as amicus curiae).   The NGOs survey indicates that 5 ROs out of 7, all 9 NOs, 6 out of 7 ROs stated that RIGO would serve their organizational goals. The reasons RIGO would help their organizational goals are that:

1. the mechanism can put pressure on China's human rights policy;
2. A RIGO would help their organizational goals as long as RIGO adheres to universal principles of human rights and do not present a watered-downed regional version of such rights;
3. A RIGO would have the power to alter the Japanese government's development policy;
4. RIGO provides a forum to exchange information between governments and NGOs and a chance for collaboration between NGOs and government institutions.

Two ROs stated that RIGO would not serve their organizational goals because:

1. RIGO tends to support government policy;
2. RIGO should include the whole Asia instead of limiting it to East Asia; and
3. the human rights concept is Western.

Six out of seven individuals who have responded to the questionnaires state that RIGO would constructively serve NGOs' goals. One individual pointed out that it would depend upon the Charter on which RIGO would be based.

7. Would human rights NGOs' purposes be affected for better or worse by establishing a regional inter-governmental human rights mechanism in East Asia?

Dias argues that NGOs' purposes would be affected for better or worse depending on how such mechanism would develop, operate and be funded. All factors must be taken into consideration. He argues that NGOs' purposes would be more effective if NGOs were involved directly in the process of establishment and have some formal roles to play in the arrangement because one of the goals of the mechanism would be to protect human rights monitors and promote a civil society. NGOs and the would-be mechanism would thus share a division of labor.

Kumar points out that AI's organizational role is to protect and promote the human rights of individuals, and AI's role would be enhanced because the regional mechanism would be an additional instrument that could improve human rights conditions. Dias asserts that NGOs' purposes would be affected for the better as long as the mechanism is genuine and responsive to human rights problems. If the regional mechanism is disingenuous, government representatives will dominate it. Then NGOs will expose it. That is why the mechanism can be a positive force, serving for the better.

The NGOs survey indicates that 9 NOs out of 10, 5 ROs and 6 INGOs stated that RIGO would affect their work for the better:

1. As long as RIGO holds governments accountable.
2. As long as RIGO supports universality of human rights.
3. As long as RIGO includes other sub-regions; e.g., Asian countries.
4. As long as NGOs participate in RIGO's building process.

While five out of seven individuals who have responded to the questionnaires say that RIGO would benefit the work of NGOs., nevertheless, one individual points out that if RIGO is controlled by states and based on, for example, "Asian values" and wrong kind of contextual sensitivity, it would not serve NGOs for the better.

8. Do NGOs support or oppose the development of a RIGO in East Asia?

According to Dias, at the moment most NGOs in the region do not know enough to take a stand one way or another on the establishment of RIGO. Many human rights meetings have been taking place but the issue has not been central to the agenda of regional meetings. There are many urgent issues to deal with. As a result, only a few NGOs have been following regional mechanism issues (e.g HURIGHTS Osaka).

Jendrzejczyk explains the HRW's position that "we do not take a position for or against as to the establishment of RIGO. It is for Asian governments and NGOs to decide. However, HRW is interested in seeing the process continue." If the NGO survey is any indication, that process will continue because 3 ROs, 5 INGOs, 7 NOs and 1 LC stated that they will support establishment of RIGO. Also five out of seven individuals state that NGOs will support RIGO.

9. If it would be difficult to establish an inter-governmental human rights mechanism encompassing the whole of Asia, what sub-regional setting

would be the most realistic and beneficial to promote and protect human rights (e.g. South Asia, East Asia, ASEAN region, etc)?

Dias argues that the contention that Asia is too large for a RIGO has some validity to it. He asserts that there is no such thing as Asia but there are different sub-regions. Each sub-region shares certain attributes (e.g. philosophical traditions, culture, level of economic development, etc). Hence, sub-regions are more meaningful. Dias states that once we have created sub-regional areas, we then can build an institution from sub-regional to regional. The interviewees generally agree that sub-regional mechanisms would be a good starting point and that sub-regional arrangements can satisfy cultural, political, legal and the economic needs of each respective sub-region. Kumar points out, however, that the shortcoming of a sub-regional approach is that if there is a strong country in the sub-region (e.g. PRC, India), it tends to use its power to get its way.

As I have documented in the previous chapter, ASEAN, SAARC and South Pacific regions have already begun their human rights initiatives in their respective region. As for East Asia, Geddes, Secretary General of LAWASIA and Dias agree that it is an appropriate sub-region in which to set up a RIGO. East Asia is a complicated region because of such countries as North Korea and China. However, without China and North Korea, there is no meaning to the human rights mechanism in East Asia. The challenge is, as Jendrzejczyk contends, how to convince the Chinese and North Korean governments that it serves the unique welfare of the people in a large context. I must note Chiu's view that the US could be included, as an observer at first, because its relations with East Asia have been improving.

East Asian countries except Mongolia have been under the strong influence of Confucianism. Li argues that whether Confucianism is anti-human rights is debatable.[111] Chiu contends that Confucius' idea is not necessarily anti-democratic because the basic tenet of Confucianism is benevolence. In fact, Confucianism was once denounced but later restored in China. The Confucius heritage has some positive elements consistent with human rights such as hard working ethics, emphasis on education, respect for the elderly and so on.

Chiu says that when we consider constructing a RIGO in East Asia the issue somehow must be addressed and the Confucius heritage is not insurmountable.[112] It is important to note that, first, Confucianism is not the determining factor. The determining factors are interdependent political, economic and social relations.

Second, as for the level of economic development relative to establishing a RIGO, Jendrzejczyk argues that Cambodia is in a low level of economic development. Yet many Cambodians actively support the promotion of human rights. Therefore, standard of living is not necessarily relevant.

Third, a positive factor for setting up a RIGO in East Asia is a growing civil society in the region; for example, Jendrzejczyk points out that when the Japanese government presented its report to the UN Human Rights Commission, hundreds of Japanese NGOs came to listen at Geneva. Another excellent example is drafting of the Asian Human Rights Charter by East Asian NGOs in 1995.

Fourth, the generational shift has been taking place all the countries in East Asia, which will obliterate the World War II legacy. Those in the younger generation are more educated and share a stronger sense of democracy and human rights.

Fifth, as we saw in chapter I and II, human rights has become a global issue, often referred to as the "internationalization of human rights." In East Asia, China's official position had been that there are no human rights issues in China. However, China began publishing its White Paper on Human Rights, hosted the Beijing Women's Human Rights Conference. China accepted a visit of the UN Commissioner for Human Rights. China opened contacts with Amnesty International. These instances indicate that the universality of human rights is being accepted. That is, a concern for human rights is that there sometimes should be interference in the domestic affairs of a sovereign state. Human rights have become a legitimate concern of the international community.

Sixth, democratization has been advancing in East Asia, especially as regards the introduction of a market economy in PRC. Chiu points out that if the economy reaches a certain stage, people will begin demanding their political rights. Thus, "economic development undermines authoritarianism and serves to validate and legitimate democratic government."[113] Many dissidents and students abroad certainly influence the political process. In China, communist ideology and practice has been losing ground because the leadership does not talk about communism any more. Chiu stresses that on the contrary, the leadership talks about stability and economic development.

Seventh, Chiu points out that legal traditions in the region are similar. For example, Taiwan was ruled by Japan for 50 years and has been influenced by the Japanese legal system. The Korean legal system has been strongly influenced by China.[114]

CONCLUSIONS

The difficulty in establishing a RIGO in East Asia is that the region has quite divergent political and economic conditions, which have contributed to the inability of the various nations to come together in a common human rights regime. At present, both the People's Republic of China and the government in North Korea are led by conservative communist leaders who feel threatened and are quite opposed to any organization that might overtly champion human rights.

In this sense, there is some similarity between East Asia at present and Western Europe during the period when the European human rights regime was initiated. As indicated earlier, the European regime was brought into being as a response to the excesses of the totalitarian Nazi government and the groundbreaking work of NGOs in bringing the regime into being "piece by piece" in the latter half of the 20th century. In a similar manner, the major impetus for developing a regional human rights regime in East Asia comes from those who have become indignant over human rights excesses in China, including especially the leaders and members of regional NGOs. In this context, it is not inconceivable to imagine the birth of a rudimentary regional organization in East Asia at some point in the early 21st century, especially in view of the emerging consensus embodied in the 1998 Asian Charter of Human Rights.

If one compares East Asia to the three areas where regimes have already been established, it is clear that there is not that great a distance at present between the concerns of many East Asian leaders and those of leaders of the three regimes. East Asian perceptions of legitimate human rights organization is perhaps closer to the perceptions of African leaders, with both regional leaderships insisting on strict adherence to sovereignty and state independence in all organizational activities. The African practice of dealing only with clusters of cases, rather than with individual human rights violations in isolation, is one that would appeal to governments throughout East Asia, communist and non-communist alike.

But the experience of the three regional human rights regimes has thus far not been such that it would necessarily scare off all leaders of East Asian nations from the prospect of creating a common association for promoting human rights. A major reason why this is so is the evidence thus far that the existing regional organizations in the three regions have all had serious limitations, and all have been consistently state-centric, respecting national sovereignty, territorial integrity, and noninterference in the internal affairs of other states (again, the African system is most pronounced in this regard" but the other regimes are only different in this respect in degree, not in kind).

Since there would be benefits to be gained by East Asian nations if they could bring into being a regional human rights regime, and since existing regimes have demonstrated an inability to approach anything resembling strict enforcement of human rights, it is conceivable that future East Asian leaderships might view the benefits of such a regime outweighing the liabilities. Potential benefits include especially the movement of East Asian nations toward the community of nations that would occur, at least in a minimal way, were a regional organization to be created that would adhere to widely-accepted international standards for the protection of human rights. This would have the advantage for such nations as China and North Korea of diminishing the efforts by many nations of the world to boycott or condemn the Chinese and North Koreans for their human rights failures, often linking these to trade and security matters and even to relatively mundane aspects of international relations like sporting events and international educational exchange.

For the present, however, the nations of East Asia, and especially the People's Republic of China and North Korea, are unwilling to risk any of their jurisdictional rights to a regional organization. Their observation has been that, under regional organizations, there seem to be an increasing possibility of becoming subject to international human rights norms. The major stumbling block to the creation of regional organization in East Asia, therefore, stems from fear that the raison d'etre of regional human rights mechanisms will be some form of international supervision of human rights. If one looks at the significant attempts to make governments accountable within the three existing human rights regimes and that this is a fear that may, from the perspective of China and North Korea especially, be justified.

A second major stumbling block for governments of East Asia is the emergence of the individual as a procedural actor under international law and the ways in which existing human rights organizations have promoted this trend. There have been growing demands among ordinary people worldwide for direct access to international justice, a phenomenon that has been resisted by sovereign states everywhere, including most intensely recently in East Asia. To the extent that East Asian governments view regional human rights organization as giving people greater access to independent, transnational courts empowered to make binding judgments in individual cases, such regional organization will be resisted.

Even though the three existing regional systems are in no way contradictory to the global human rights system of the United Nations, the states of East Asia are less wary of the UN because they see it as lacking the powers of implementation and enforcement. Regional approaches for the promotion and protection of human rights have thus far been somewhat more successful in this regard, in part because they have been mutually supportive of one another and complementary to other human rights organizations, both within the region and outside. For this reason too, the states of East Asia have been unwilling to establish a regional human rights organization.

In the meantime, however, NGOs in East Asia are beginning to have a major impact on human rights issues, in a manner that is not unlike the impact of NGOs in the three geographic areas where there are existing human rights RIGO. To a considerable extent, there are already human

Chapter V

Conclusions

T HE PURPOSE OF THIS STUDY HAS BEEN TO INVESTIGATE THE POSSIBILITY OF establishing a regional inter-governmental human rights protection mechanism in East Asia with a focus on the contributions of NGOs to such a development. Chapter II investigated such concepts and issues as functionalism, regional integration, interdependence, the global civil society and NGOs as a theoretical tool to explore this research problem. These issues and concepts have indeed proven to be pertinent. Indeed, the Asian Charter of Human Rights (1996) was drafted as an embodiment of these issues and concepts and as a prospective step toward establishing a regional human rights arrangement in East Asia.

Chapter III examined the impacts of globalization on human rights by first presenting the expanding worldwide acceptance of the universality of human rights. That chapter illustrated the relative significance of international human rights treaties and UN human rights mechanisms and procedures. In addition, it demonstrated how the U.S. and other major countries have contributed to the internationalization of human rights by their human rights diplomacy and developmental aid policies.

Chapter IV examined existing regional human rights mechanisms in Europe, the Americas and Africa in order to determine whether their past experience might be relevant for prospective institutions in East Asia. It also investigated current human rights situations in East Asian countries in order to demonstrate why regional human rights promotion and protection arrangements are necessary and useful in the region and to assess whether they meet specific conditions associated with the establishment of a RIGO.

Later sections of chapter IV examined past initiatives taken to set up regional human rights arrangement in other sub-regions of Asia such as ASEAN, SAARC and in the South Pacific. The concluding section of chapter IV investigated the attitudes, activities and outlooks of NGOs indigenous to East Asia and reported on interviews with knowledgeable experts with extensive experience in Asia.

The findings of this exploratory research on the feasibility of establishing a regional inter-governmental human rights mechanism in East Asia are as follows:

First, interviews with experts as well as the responses of NGO leaders indicate that regional human rights protection mechanisms hold a promise of success in protecting human rights and are useful because they can supplement global mechanisms located in New York and Geneva. In this sense, regional mechanisms are not in contradiction with global arrangements although there may be structural and procedural differences. Regional mechanisms provide easier access for most people in the region. Moreover, they have been set up to meet regional needs, priorities, and conditions because they are usually set up by a group of like-minded countries who enjoy geographical proximity and cultural and historical affinity and heritage.

Regional mechanisms themselves can be mutually reinforcing; in fact, judges, lawyers, and administrators working for regional mechanisms have been holding regular meetings, workshops, and seminars with their counterparts to exchange their legal expertise and experiences (e.g. utilizing precedents) so as to improve and expedite their functions and procedures.

Second, literature on civil society as well as views expressed by NGO leaders and experts insist that NGOs appear to be indispensable for both regional and global human rights protection mechanisms to function successfully. As indicated in this study, NGOs have been major contributors to the existing regional and global mechanisms because they gather and evaluate information, provide vital and impartial information, assist victims to file petitions and propagate cases (e.g. Amnesty International' s prisoner of conscience campaign).

Third, we have seen explosive growth of NGOs in such East Asian countries as ROK, Japan, Taiwan, and Mongolia. These NGOs have been forming international networks, strategic alliances and communications because NGOs, whether they are international, regional or national, tend to cooperate and are interested in collaboration with each other in order to achieve their organizational goals. In East Asia, NGOs have been organizing regional meetings, seminars, workshops, conferences, etc. (e.g. the 1999 Northeast Asia training workshop on human rights education attended by delegations of Mongolia, PRC, Japan and ROK). These activities could persuade governments and lead to a condition that might likely facilitate regional integration.

Fourth, NGOs propagate human rights notions of universality and skillfully mediate between regional culture and "internationally recognized standards and principles" of human rights, as illustrated by the Asian

Human Rights Charter. In Asia NGOs have been vocal critics of Asian values as the 1993 NGO Bangkok Declaration indicates. The argument that there are "Asian values" has been, in fact, advocated by authoritarian and despotic rulers in the region to justify their oppressive rule. However, because of progress in democratization and consolidation of democracy in the region, their argument has been losing ground, especially among the young, more educated middle class.

Fifth, according to survey responses of NGOs as well as in interviews with experts, regional human rights protection mechanisms appear to serve NGOs' organizational goals because regional human rights protection mechanisms support NGOs to achieve their goals and thus enhance NGO efficacy and capacity building. As a result, NGOs are likely to support the establishment of regional human rights protection mechanisms. If regional arrangements were to be based on a state-centric outlook — i.e. lacking accountability, transparency and effectiveness while hampering participation of individuals and NGOs—NGOs would expose these institutional deficiencies.

Sixth, in the opinion of several interviewees, East Asia is an appropriate venue for establishing a regional inter-governmental human rights mechanism because other sub-regions of Asia share strong ties among the countries concerned and, as indicated in an earlier chapter, have begun their own human rights initiatives (e.g. ASEAN, SAARC, the South Pacific). Moreover, in East Asia, in addition to geographical proximity, a shared historical and cultural heritage, combined with increasing economic ties has been intensifying the interdependence of the countries in the region.

Seventh, as shown by the chronology of meetings, declarations and UN workshops—including those attended by East Asian governments—increasing East Asian participation shows that an ongoing process is prospectively leading to an East Asian RIGO.

In spite of these positive findings, there are several major impediments existing in the region with regard to setting up a regional inter-governmental human rights implementation mechanism. These include i) indifference of governments concerned; ii) lack of regional political organization; iii) different political and economic systems existing in the region, including strong market economies vs. command economies; iv) diverse stages of economic development in the countries in the region; v) antagonistic histories and national rivalries; and vi) the "Asian Values" argument advocated and supported by governments in the region.

Governments in the region have not historically shown much interest in protecting the human rights of their citizens because of authoritarian/patriarchal Confucian traditions. It has been argued by many leaders that human rights is a Western concept and thus inapplicable to

East Asian people. In East Asia, "law and order" has been considered more important than individual rights. This culture has been reflected in governments' indifference to any human rights initiatives and a low rate of ratification of international human rights instruments.

Moreover, governments in the region have insisted that human rights are "essentially within the domestic jurisdiction of a sovereign state." How states treat their own nationals in their own territory has been considered a prerogative of national sovereignty and thus the business of no one else. Thus, international supervision of a human rights mechanism is viewed as a threat to national sovereignty. To be comprehensive, it should be pointed out that some human rights advocates have viewed the policy of non-interference in the affairs of other countries as having reached its limits. In this view, the time of absolute and exclusive sovereignty has passed. For example, the 1993 NGO Bangkok Declaration stressed that advocacy of human rights cannot be considered an encroachment on national sovereignty.

Because of the globalization of human rights and heightened awareness of human rights instigated by active civil society in countries like Japan, South Korea, Taiwan, and Mongolia, governments in the region have become more sensitive to the human rights of citizens in these countries in recent years. As a result, as indicated earlier in this study, East Asian governments have shown a willingness to participate in UN-initiated regional workshops, with a view to establishing a regional human rights protection mechanism.

Second, it is essential prerequisite to have a regional political organization (e.g. the Council of Europe, OAS, OAU) prior to establishing a RIGO, in order to enforce human rights effectively. As a result of East Asian turbulent history, there are two Koreas and two Chinese entities, which have not had any regional political, economic and culturally cooperative inter-governmental organization. However, because of the advancement of economic interdependence and developments in communications and transportation, people in the region have increasingly come in contact with each other for the last decade. Bilateral trade, cultural exchange, communications, and tourism between the countries in the region have been expanding rapidly.

According to functionalist theory, collaboration in a field may spill over into collaboration in other fields. A recent development is what functionalists call "confidence-building" which may lead to "institution-building." In fact, Kim Dae-jung, president of the ROK, is now advocating that it is time for East Asia to have a regional cooperative institutional framework.

Third, in the region there are countries with a market economy (e.g. Japan, ROK, ROC, and Mongolia), a mixed economy and a command economy (e.g. DPRK and PRC). There are one party states, autocratic governments and parliamentary democracies. As a result, it has been difficult to have a consensus on human rights. Countries in the region claim different priorities and approaches to human rights. For example, the PRC and DPRK consider collective (e.g. state, society, community) rights as being more important than individual rights. This has resulted in suppressing the right to freedom of assembly, association and expression in these countries. Democratic institutions and concepts of civil society are viewed threat to the existing power structure and have been suppressed. Under these circumstances it is difficult to see the growth of NGOs.

Fourth, the countries in the region are at diverse stages of economic development. Japan, Taiwan and ROK have been enjoying a high standard of living while the PRC, DPRK, and Mongolia have been struggling to develop their economies. This has affected their governments' approach to human rights. For example, the PRC argues that the right to subsistence (e.g. the right to food and adequate housing) is more important than promoting and protecting "bourgeois" civil and political rights.

Fifth, countries in the region bitterly fought each other during World War II and some countries colonized others (i.e. Japan colonized Korea from 1910 to 1945 and Taiwan from 1895 to 1945). Since the Korean War (1950–53), DPRK and ROK have been completely cut off from each other. As a result, after half a century, the ill feeling is still lingering among the people of the region. As contrasted with Germany, which has spent 80 billion dollars in war reparations, Japan has refused to make adequate war reparations thus far. Critics argue that after WWII, unlike Germany, because of US occupation policies, the Japanese power structure was not completely dismantled and therefore was not thoroughly "democratized" (e.g. the Emperor system was kept intact).

In addition, the Japanese government has refused to face the "hard facts", in part because of the Japanese prejudiced outlook toward other Asians and the subordinate role women have played in Japanese society. No society is immune from prejudice and bigotry such as racism and sexism. Japan is no exception. The Japanese tend to look up to Westerners and down on fellow Asians. This attitude stems from the Meiji Restoration in 1868 when Japan launched its modernization by westernizing in the country "to catch up to the West." "Datsua Nyuo" (Leave Asia and Join the West) became a national slogan for Japan at that time. As a result of the modernization process, Japanese began looking down upon countries in Asia and their people. These situations have resulted in Japan' s intransigent refusal to make any adequate war reparation.

Sixth, the Asian values argument that has justified authoritarian rule has been strongly supported by governments such as the PRC. The PRC has contended that Asia should have a different standard of human rights. According to Asian values, performing one' s duties is more important than the assertion of individual rights. In Confucian tradition, conformity and submission to social norms and political authority have been stressed at the expense of individual expression. Confucianism emphasizes the proper place for each individual within the hierarchy and discourages individualism. In this context, the argument has been made that East Asia needs to foster a human rights concept that is more in tune with East Asia' s culture and level of economic development. However, in recent years East Asian countries, including the PRC, began acknowledging the universality of human rights by acceding gradually to international human rights instruments.

Thus there are several impediments existing in the region in terms of establishing a regional human rights protection mechanism. Nevertheless, each impediment is not insurmountable and in many cases their significance has been, in fact, eroding. The question is then what human rights protection model would be suitable in view of the East Asian environment? As for the proposed regional protection mechanism, there are three types of regional mechanisms - the European, the Inter-American and the African. As indicated earlier, the respective mechanisms have slightly different institutional and functional characteristics in order to meet regional needs, conditions and priorities.

First, there must be an inter-state convention on human rights, with the collaboration of regional NGOs. The 1998 Asian Human Rights Charter could be an excellent model. The Charter states that the convention must reflect the realities of East Asia (for example, its level of economic development), and an emphasis on group rights and performance of one' s duties in the society. It might reflect Confucian tradition by stressing, for example, group rights and a respect for the elderly. The convention must be comprehensive, including the first, second, and third generations of human rights. At any rate, it must be fully consistent with international human rights norms and standards.

Second, it might be a good idea to focus, at first, to promote human rights (e.g. human rights education) instead of protection and enforcement of human rights in its institutional and functional objectives so that governments in the region can participate without fear of sacrificing their sovereign rights. However, the arrangement ultimately should have the power to receive complaints of the violation of rights, to hear evidence, and to provide redress for violations, including punishment for violators because the judiciary (i.e. the complaint procedure and international court) is a major means for the effective protection of rights.

RECOMMENDATIONS

As a result of research, interviews, surveys and readings, and taking into account many sources including NGOs and experts, this study can conclude with several recommendations. In my research I have heard many opinions about how integration could be conceived, facilitated, implemented and furthered. Some of those ideas I would now like to present as recommendations. These recommendations are put forward with the objective of achieving a supranational human rights body in East Asia with an independent investigation, adjudication, and enforcement power.

First, it is necessary for both human rights-promoting governments in their diplomatic initiatives and NGOs in their political activities to persuade governments in the region to ratify existing international human rights treaties so that they can have common standards and principles of agreement. This is to affirm the universality of human rights and to confirm the globalization of human rights. The universality of human rights represents inter-civilizational "consensus-building" in our multilateral, conflicted world.

Second, it is crucial for regional integration to establish amicable relations among the countries in the region so as to foster regional integration. Consistent with the need for amicable relations is the requirement to address historical sources of friction. There is a growing consensus in international law that (a) the state is obligated to provide compensation to victims of egregious human rights abuses perpetrated by the government, and (b) if the regime that committed the acts in question does not provide compensation, the obligation carries over to the successor government.

In this context, I urge the Japanese government to make war reparations because it is deserved, and in order to eradicate the lingering ill feelings of people in neighboring countries toward Japan and the Japanese people. The abuses of internationally recognized human rights such as war crimes, crimes against humanity and genocide, which have been committed by a government must be dealt with in defense of "transitional justice." For moral accountability, the Japanese government must reckon with an evil past and "hard facts" instead of resorting to "let bygones be bygones" or whitewash and social amnesia. Compensation, restitution or reparation must be made to victims (e.g. comfort women) to restore the status quo ante.

It is, in fact, appalling if Japan is compared to Germany who since World War II has awarded $80 billion to Jews who survived concentration camps. It is the moral responsibility of the Japanese government do the equivalent. One of the strong raisons d' etre of the proposed regional human rights judicial institution is that it might help reckon with past human rights violations such as the war time atrocities committed by Japan. Moreover, the arrangement not only would help defend international security but also individual security.

In this context, Japanese development assistance should not only declare support of human rights but be implemented in a pro-active way supportive of human rights. This is to affirm that human rights are the legitimate concern of the international community in our interdependent global society. Appropriate development assistance and adequate compensation for violations is fundamental to implementing human rights, connecting remedies to rights, and bringing these standards into the everyday lives of the common people. Japan is expected to play a more responsible role in the international community in proportion to its economic power. However, meaningful reconciliation among countries in East Asia cannot be achieved if resentment and bitterness linger in the minds of citizens due to Japan' s inaction.

Third, NGOs facilitate democratization by demanding accountability and transparency. Many NGOs are not tied to the territoriality of the state and participate in regional and global governance. They are the impetus for regional integration. NGOs are agents for strengthening global civil society and for building a human rights culture. Consistent with the need for countries not only to sign treaties, but to abide by these treaties, I urge the Chinese and North Korean governments to guarantee constitutional rights of freedom of expression, association, and assembly so that independent NGOs can function in both countries. Since China and North Korea are members of the UN, they are obliged to observe the Universal Declaration of Human Rights, which guarantees these fundamental rights. This is consistent with the "Framework for Regional Technical Cooperation in the Asia-Pacific" adopted by the Teheran workshop in 1998,[1] (in which China and North Korea participated) which urged governments to develop "national plans of actions and the strengthening of national capacities."

Fourth, I call upon the governments in the region to complete the process now initiated by such countries as the Philippines and Indonesia to establish national human rights commissions with advisory, educative, investigative as well as promotion and protection functions.[2] This is consistent with the "Framework for Regional Technical Cooperation in the Asia-Pacific" adopted by the Teheran workshop in 1998, which urged governments to develop "national institutions for the promotion and protection of human rights." It is also consistent with the efforts of the Canadian Human Rights Foundation to underwrite and facilitate collaborative regional meetings of existing national human rights commissions in Asia.[3]

Fifth, I call upon governments in the region to strengthen human rights education at all levels of their education system to create national, regional and global human rights cultures. This is consistent with the "Framework for Regional Technical Cooperation in the Asia-Pacific," which urged governments "to develop human rights education." It is also consistent with the program of support now undertaken by the Asia Foundation[4] to promote such education among Asian countries, including those in East Asia, and the plans of the Asia Development Bank to foster "legal literacy training" among loan recipient countries.

It should be noted that the link between human rights education and RIGO is that such "grass roots popular education" has the twofold effect of (1) influencing indigenous cultural acceptance of human rights standards, and (2) creating and raising expectations that human rights complaints can be heard and remedied, if not at the local level and national level, then at the regional level, especially as some of the complaints are regional in nature, such as the rights of migrant workers.

DATA-BASED THEORY CONSTRUCTION

As for future research designed to answer the question of whether the condition prevails in which it becomes reasonable to expect the development of a regional inter-governmental human rights institution, I would like to recommend using measurement techniques to construct and test a development model for an East Asian RIGO. The analytical components of such a model and the conceptual framework from which appropriate hypotheses may be devised is inherent in the United Nations "Framework for Regional Technical Cooperation in the Asia-Pacific." The exploration of the literature on theory, on the review of history and interviews in addition to survey lead me to identify measurable variables which could be linked to the model and related hypotheses addressed to the subject of rigorous future scientific work.

The independent variables are of four kinds;[5] Economic variables include global trade, market economy, regional trade, regional labor interdependence; Social variables include education and literacy, human rights-respecting culture, prevalence of the middle class, civil society, status of minorities and women; Political variables include prevalence and status of NGOs, human rights education, human rights-respecting regime, free domestic and international communication; Legal variables include national human rights governmental organizations, human rights in national constitution and law, government participation in intergovernmental organizations, and the ratification of human rights treaties.

In closing, I must say that quantification is useful, but impossible until the historical and conceptual underbrush has been cleared. This requires mapping the field of action of the actors, their intentions, and the normative aspirations, of those forces affecting them, and their involvement with human rights NGOs.

The purpose of this book was to investigate the possibility of establishing a regional inter-governmental human rights mechanism in East Asia. The seed of the topic was sewn when I was in London, England in 1976–80 where I became acutely aware of brutal oppression and human rights abuses in Latin America. I joined Amnesty International, and have been an active member in London, Tokyo, Columbia, SC, and Los Angeles,

CA. Through those years, a question I have had in my mind is, why has an RIGO not been established in Asia as elsewhere, and what are the obstacles? This study is an attempt to offer an answer to the question. As I indicated earlier, the Asian Human Rights Charter was drafted by regional NGOs in East Asia. Now we need a response from the East Asian governments to the Charter and their participation in establishing a human rights enforcement arrangement.

Appendix A

A Cover Letter

Dear Friends and Colleagues:

I am a researcher working at the University of Maryland, College Park. As you may well know, regional inter-governmental human rights organizations have been in operation for sometime in Europe, the Americas and Africa (e.g. the European Commission and Court of Human Rights).

My current research is an investigation into the prospects of establishing a regional intergovernmental human rights mechanism in East Asia, with a focus on nongovernmental organizations' (NGOs) contributions to the development of such a regional human rights institution.

The questionnaire enclosed is directly related to the above topic and is being sent to a small but representative sample of human rights NGOs such as yours in Japan, South Korea, Taiwan, and Hong Kong. Therefore, your participation is extremely important. My research has been supported by such prominent scholars and professors as Drs. Marcus Franda, Richard Pierre Claude, and Edy Kaufman.

Your questionnaire will certainly be treated confidentially. If interested in the research results, please so indicate in order that they may be made available to you. Please find enclosed international return coupon for your convenience. Thank you very much for your assistance with this important study.

Yours sincerely,
Henry A. Hashimoto

Appendix B

A Questionnaire Sent to Nongovernmental Organizations

PROSPECTS FOR ESTABLISHING A REGIONAL INTER-GOVERNMENTAL HUMAN RIGHTS MECHANISM IN EAST ASIA QUESTIONNAIRE

Date:

1. Name of the Organization:
2. Person who fills out this questionnaire:
3. His/her position in the organization:
4. Network Address (E-mail):
5. Please check the one category that best describes your organization:

    [ ] International (i.e. global) organization
    [ ] Regional office of an international organization
    [ ] Regional organization
    [ ] National organization
    [ ] Local or community organization
    [ ] Other

6. Serial publications of your organization (include journals, newsletters, bulletins). Please indicate title and frequency of the publication.
7. Objectives: Please state the purpose or objectives of your organization in the field of human rights.
8. Has your organization cooperated or collaborated with organizations in other countries, especially in East Asia, to achieve your organizational goals? If yes, please explain what kind of works your organization has done with those others (e.g. exchange information, hold regular meetings, etc). Please indicate whether your organiza-

tion intends to cooperate with counterparts in other countries in the future.

9.   If a regional inter-governmental human rights mechanism (e.g. the European Commission and Court of Human Rights, the Inter-American Commission and Court of Human Rights) existed in East Asia, would it serve your organizational goals?

10.   Would your organizational purposes be affected for better or worse by establishing a regional inter-governmental human rights mechanism in East Asia? Please explain whether your organization supports or opposes the development of a regional inter- governmental human rights organization in East Asia.

11.   What are the chief obstacles to setting up an inter-governmental human rights mechanism in which your country could participate?

12.   [Optional] If it would be difficult to establish an inter-governmental human rights mechanism encompassing the whole of Asia, what sub-regional setting would be the most realistic and beneficial to promote and protect human rights (e.g. South Asia, East Asia, ASEAN region, etc)? Please state the reasons.

Appendix C
A Questionnaire Sent to Individuals

PROSPECTS FOR ESTABLISHING A REGIONAL INTER-GOVERNMENTAL HUMAN RIGHTS MECHANISM IN EAST ASIA QUESTIONNAIRE

Date:

1. Name:
2. Occupation:
3. Network Address (E-mail):
4. If a regional inter-governmental human rights mechanism (e.g. the European Commission and Court of Human Rights, the Inter-American Commission and Court of Human Rights) existed in East Asia, would it serve constructively human rights organizations' goals?
5. Do you think that non-governmental human rights organizations need to cooperate or collaborate with counterparts in other countries, especially in East Asia, to achieve their organizational goals?
6. Would human rights NGOs' purposes be affected for better or worse by establishing a regional inter-governmental human rights mechanism in East Asia?
7. Do you think that non-governmental human rights organizations support or oppose the development of a regional inter-governmental human rights organization in East Asia?
8. What are the chief obstacles to setting up an inter-governmental human rights mechanism in which your country could participate?
9. If it would be difficult to establish an inter-governmental human rights mechanism encompassing the whole of Asia, what sub-regional setting would be the most realistic and beneficial to promote and

protect human rights (e.g. South Asia, East Asia, ASEAN region, etc)? Please state the reasons.

10. Would your government benefit by participating in such a mechanism?

11. Can you refer me to any scholarly literature on this project published in your country?

Notes

NOTES TO CHAPTER II

[1] Frederick L. Schuman. The Commonwealth of Man (New York: Knoph, 1952), p. 314.

[2] Philippe C. Schmitter "A Revised Theory of Regional Integration" in Leon N. Lindberg and Stuart A. Scheingold, ed. Regional Integration: Theory and Research. (London: Oxford University Press, 1971), p. 242.

[3] Leon Lindberg, for example, has adopted a behavioral approach, applying David Easton's system analysis to the study of European integration.

[4] On federalism, see, for example, Peter Hay. Federalism and Supranational Organizations: Pattern for New Legal Structures (Urbana, IL: University of Illinois Press, 1966).

[5] See Ernst B. Haas. The Obsolescence of Regional Integration Theory. (Berkeley, CA: Institute of International Studies, University of California, 1975).

[6] Sir Oliver Franks, quoted in Francis O. Wilcox, "Regionalism and the United Nations," International Organization, XIX (Summer 1965), p. 811.

[7] See Philip E. Jacob and Henry Tenue "The Integrative Process: Guidelines for Analysis of the Bases of Political Community" in Philip E. Jacob and James V. Toscano, ed. The Integration of Political Communities. (Philadelphia: J.B. Lippincott, 1964),
p. 1–45.

[8] See Ernst B. Haas, "The Study of Regional Integration: Reflections on the Joy and Angst of Pretheorizing" in Leon Lindberg and Scheingold, Stuart, ed. Regional Integration: Theory and Research. (Cambridge: Harvard University Press, 1971), p. 6.

[9] Karl W. Deutsch and Sidney A. Burrel, et al. "Political Community and the North Atlantic Area," in International Political Communities, An Anthology, p. 2

[10] See Karl Deutsch et al. Political Community and the North Atlantic Area: International Organization in the Light of Historical Experience (Princeton, N.J.: Princeton University Press, 1957), p. 5–8.

[11] Donald J. Puchara. "Of Blind Men, Elephants, and International Organization," *Journal of Common Market Studies* (1972), p. 277

[12] See Donald J. Puchara "International Transactions and Regional Integration" in Leon N. Lindberg and Stuart A. Scheingold, ed. Regional Integration: Theory and Research (Cambridge, MA: Harvard University Press, 1971), p. 158.

[13] James A. Caporaso. Functionalism and Regional Integration: A Logical and Empirical Assessment. (Biverly Hills, CA: Sage Pub., 1972).

[14] Ernst B. Haas, The Uniting of Europe: Political, Social and Economic Forces, 1950–1957 (Stanford, CA: Stanford University Press, 1957), p. 16 and p. 382.

[15] Bela Balassa, The Theory of Economic Integration (Homewood, Ill: Richard D. Irwin, 1961), p. 1.

[16] Ibid. p. 1–7. Balassa indicates that the example of customs union is the European Coal and Steel Community and common market are the European Economic Community and the European Free Trade Association respectively. See Robert O. Keohane and Joseph S. Nye, Jr. "International Interdependence and Integration" in Fred Greenstein and Nelson W. Polsby. Handbook of Political Science vol. 8 (Menlo Park, CA: Addison-Wesley Pub., 1975), p. 369, Table I.

[17] Joseph S. Nye "Comparing Common Markets: Concept and Measurement" *International Organization* (1968), p. 861.

[18] Hayward Alker, Jr., and Donald Puchara, "Trends in Economic Partnership: The North Atlantic Area, 19281963," in David Singer, ed., Quantitative International Politics (New York: Free Press, 1968), p. 288.

[19] Ernst B. Haas and Philippe C. Schmitter. "Economics and Differential Patterns of Political Integration: Projections About Unity in Latin America" *International Organization* 18 (Autumn 1964), p. 705.

[20] See Leon N. Lindgerg. "Political Integration as a Multidimensional Phenomenon Requiring Multivariate Measurement" in Leon N. Lindberg and Stuart A. Scheingold, ed. Regional Integration: Theory and Research (Cambridge, MA: Harvard University Press, 1971), p. 45.

[21] Hayward defines adaptation as the response of individuals to directives to them made in the name of the political structure and orientation as actors' identification with and evaluation of the political structure.

[22] The communications approach suggests that an intensive pattern of communication between national units will result in a closer community among the units. A community, by definition, is a group of people who share certain attributes and members of a community share values, preferences, and life-styles. Political community must have three kinds of inte-

gration: 1) control over force; 2) control over allocation of resources; and 3) provision of a chief focus of identification (Etzioni, 1965). Communications are measured by trade, mail, and tourist flow. See Karl Deutsche et al. France, Germany and the Western Alliance: A Study of Elite Attitudes on European Integration and World Politics (New York: Charles Scribner's Sons, 1967), p. 218.

[23] Jaap de Wilde "Norman Angell: Ancestor of Interdependence Theory" in James Rosenau and Hylke Tromp, ed. Interdependence and Conflict in World Politics. (Aldershot: Avebury, 1989), p. 26.

[24] Marina v. N. Witman, Reflections of Interdependence: Issues for Economic Theory and U.S. Policy (Pittsburgh: University of Pittsburgh Press, 1979), p. 265

[25] For example, the vulnerability would be: (1) high export product concentration; (2) a high ratio of exports to GNP; (3) geographic concentration of exports; and (4) geographic concentration in sources of supply (Holsti, 1978, p. 516).

[26] David M. Rowe, "The Trade and Security Paradox in International Politics," (Unpublished manuscript, Ohio State University, 15 Sept, 1994), p. 16.

[27] Dale C. Copeland, "Economic Interdependence and War: A Theory of Trade Expectations" International Security 20 (Spring 1996), p. 25.

[28] See Lester R. Brown "Redefining National Security" in Charles W. Kegley, Jr. and Eugene R. Wittkoph. The Global Agenda. (New York: Random House, 1984).

[29] See Barbara Ward. Spaceship Earth. (New York: Columbia University Press, 1966).

[30] Philip A. Reynolds and Roberts D. Mckinley "The Concept of Interdependence: Its Uses and Misuses" in Kjell Goldmann and Gunnar Sjostedt. Power, Capabilities, Interdependence: Problems in the Study of International Influence. (Beverly Hills, CA: Sage Pub., 1979), p.141–166.

[31] United Nations Statistical Yearbook, 1997.

[32] See Andre Gunter Frank, Latin America: Underdevelopment or Revolution (New York: Monthly Review Press, 1969) and Johan Galtung, "A Structural Theory of Imperialism," Journal of Peace Research No. 2 (1971): 81–117.

[33] Howard V. Perlmutter, "The Tortuous Evolution of the Multinational Corporation," Columbia Journal of World Business, 4 (January-February 1969): 9–18.

[34] See Francis Fukuyama "The End of History?" The National Interest (Summer 1989): 3–18.

[35] See Samuel P. Huntington. The Third Wave: Democratization in the Late Twentieth Century. (Norman: University of Oklahoma Press, 1991).

[36] Kim Dae Jung "Is Culture Destiny? The Myth of Asia's Anti-Democratic Values" *Foreign Affairs* (November/December 1994): 189–194.

[37] The Treaty of Westphalia in 1648 ended an era of religious warfare and inaugurated the modern European state system. The characteristics of Westphalian system includes: the consent of states determines the content of international law; the liberty of states is protected by the principles of nonintervention in domestic jurisdictions; sovereign equality and the balance of power are recognized by voting rules of the UN.

[38] Luis Kunter. World Habeas Corpus (New York: Oceana Pub., 1962), p. 168

[39] See Richard Pierre Claude and David R. Davis. "The Global Society Perspective on International Human Rights" in Kenneth W. Hunter and Timothy C. Mack. International Rights and Responsibilities for the Future. (Westport, CT: Praeger, 1996), p. 83–90

[40] See Gordon A. Christenson. "World Civil Society and the International Rule of Law" *Human Rights Quarterly* 19 (1997), p. 731.

[41] J. Martin Rochester, Waiting for the Millennium: The United Nations and the Future of World Order (Columbia, S.C.: University of South Carolina Press, 1993), p. 36.

[42] Alberto Melucci, Nomads of the Present: Social Movements and Individual Needs in Contemporary Society, in J. Keane and Paul Mier, eds. (London: Hutchinson Radius, 1989), p.74 and 86.

[43] The "Year of Truth" was the term used by Garton Ash to characterize the Wonder Year, 1989. See Chapter 6 of Timothy Ash Garton. The Magic Lantern: The Revolution of '89 Witnessed in Warsaw, Budapest, Berlin and Prague. (New York: Random House, 1990).

[44] See Gordon A. Christenson. "World Civil Society and the International Rule of Law" *Human Rights Quarterly* 19 (1997), p. 731.

[45] Leon Gordenker and Thomas G. Weiss define global governance in their article "Pluralizing Global Governance: Analytical Approaches and Dimensions," in NGOs, the UN, and Global Governance, (Boulder, CO: Lynne Rienner Pub., 1997) that efforts to bring more orderly and reliable responses to social and political issues that go beyond capacities of states to address individually.

[46] See Ruben Cesar Fernandes "Threads of Planetary Citizenship" in World Assembly, ed. Citizens: Strengthening Global Civil Society (Washington, D.C.: World Alliance for Citizen Participation, 1994), p. 319–346.

[47] See World Assembly, ed. Citizens: Strengthening Global Civil Society (Washington, D.C.: World Alliance for Citizen Participation, 1994).

[48] Miguel Darcy de Oliveira and Rajesh Tandon, "An Emerging Global Civil Society" in World Assembly, ed. Citizens: Strengthening Global Civil Society (Washington, D.C.: World Alliance for Citizen Participation, 1994), p. 16.

[49] See John Baylis and Steve Smith, ed. The Globalization of World Politics: An Introduction to International Relations. (New York: Oxford University Press, 1997), p. 288

[50] See Charles W. Kegley, Jr. and Eugene R. Wittkoph. "The Multinational Cooperation in World Politics" in Charles W. Kegley, Jr., and Eugene R. Wittkoph. The Global Agenda. (New York: Random House, 1984), p. 262.

[51] See John Baylis and Steve Smith, ed. *op.cit* p. 288.

[52] Ibid. p.288

According to Adam Dieng, Secretary-General of the International Commission of Jurists, a NGO is a non-profit entity whose members are citizens or associations of citizens of one or more countries and whose activities are determined by the collective will of its members in response to the needs of the members or of one or more communities with which the NGO cooperates. Philippe Schmitter argues that NGOs are intermediary organizations and arrangements that lie between the primary units of society - individuals, families, clans, ethnic groups of various kinds, village units - and the ruling collective institutions and agencies of the society. See Michael Clough, Free at Last? U.S. Policy Toward Africa and the End of the Cold War (New York: Council on Foreign Relations, 1992), p. 55. According to Yearbook of International Associations (1993/94), the actual figure of NGOs is 16,142 and it is constantly increasing. The figure has doubled since 1991. For example, over 1,100 NGOs participated in the UN World Conference on Human Rights held in Vienna in 1993.

[53] The term "NGO revolution" was used by Claude E. Welch, Jr. "Civil Society and Human Rights NGOs: Themes for the 1990s in Africa" in Claude E. Welch, Jr. Protecting Human Rights in Africa: Roles and Strategies of Non-Governmental Organizations. (Philadelphia: University of Pennsylvania Press, 1995), p. 45

[54] Gordon A. Christenson. "World Civil Society and the International Rule of Law" *Human Rights Quarterly* 19 (1997). See also Jessica T. Matthews. "Power Shift" *Foreign Affairs* (January/February 1997): 50–66.

[55] Laurie S. Wiseberg. "Protecting Human Rights Activists and NGOs: What More Can Be Done?" *Human Rights Quarterly* 13 (1991), p. 529. For a discussion on what constitutes a human rights NGO, see Henry J. Steiner, Diverse Partners: Non-Governmental Organizations in the Human Rights Movement, the Report of a Retreat of Human Rights Activists (Cambridge, MA: Harvard Law School Human Rights Program and Human Rights Internet, 1990), 5–15. It is important to note that what distinguishes a human rights NGO from other political actors is that the political powers seek to protect the rights of their members or constituents; a human rights group seeks to secure the rights for all members of the society. According to Blaser, human rights NGOs are based on progressive incentives, unions on material incentives, and fraternal organizations on

solidarity incentives. See Arthur W. Blaser, "Human Rights in the Third World and Development of International Nongovernmental Organizations" in George Shepherd, Jr. and Ved P. Nanda., ed. Human Rights and Third World Development. (Westport, CT: Greenwood Press, 1985), p. 281.

[56] See Egon Larsen. A Flame in Barbed Wire: The Story of Amnesty International. (New York: W.W. Norton & Co., 1979), Scoble & Wiseberg. Amnesty International: Evaluating Effectiveness in the Human Rights Arena. *Intellect*, (Sept./Oct.1976), at 79, and Scoble and Wiseberg, Human Rights & Amnesty International, 413 *Annals Am. Acad. Pol. & Soc. Sci* 11 (1974).

[57] See Laurie S. Wiseberg and Harry M. Scoble. "The International League for Human Rights: The Strategy of a Human Rights NGO" *Georgia Journal of International and comparative Law* 7 (1977): 289–313 and Roger Clark. "The International League for Human Rights and South West Africa, 1947–1957: The Human Rights NGO as Catalyst in the International Legal Process" *Human Rights Quarterly* 3 (Fall 1981): 101–136.

[58] Niall MacDermont "The Work of the International Commission of Jurists" *Index on Censorship* 1 (1972): 15; Howard B Tolley, Jr. The International Commission of Jurists: Global Advocates for Human Rights (Philadelphia: University of Pennsylvania, 1994).

[59] See "Human Rights and Private Transactional Action: The International Committee of the Red Cross" in David P. Forsythe. The Internationalization of Human Rights. (Lexington, MA: Lexington Books, 1991), p. 143–170; David P. Forsythe. Humanitarian Politics: The International Committee of the Red Cross (Baltimore: The Johns Hopkins University Press, 1977); J.Bissell. "The International Committee of the Red Cross and Protection of Human Rights" *Human Rights Journal* 1 (1968); John F. Hutchinson Champions of Charity: War and the Rise of the Red Cross (Boulder: Westview, 1996); George Willemin and Roger Heacok. The International Committee of the Red Cross (The Hague: Martinus Nijhoff, 1984).

[60] Bracre Waly Ndiaye, UN Special Rapporteur on Summary or Arbitrary Executions said, when he visited Australia in 1993, he relied on Amnesty International for over 65 percent of the information he used. 11(10) Amnesty International Australian Newsletter 10 (1993).

[61] Irwin Cotler, "The Role of Non-Governmental Organizations in the Promotion and Protection of Human Rights in a Revolutionary Age: The Helsinki Process as a Case Study," in Irwin Cotler and F. Pearl Eliadis. International Human Rights: Theory and Practice. (Montreal: The Canadian Human Rights Foundation, 1992), p.463.

Mr. Cees Flinterman, Head of the Delegation of the Kingdom of the Netherlands, stated at the 50th session of the United Nations Commission on Human Rights:

> I believe that the Commission on Human Rights would not be able to function the way it does without the indefatigable and courageous individual and NGOs who are, as it were, the eyes and ears of the Commission and who provide essential information to enable it to fulfill its task of upholding the universal application of human rights.

[62] Category I - those in general consultative status. These are organizations concerned with most of the activities of the Council, which are deemed to be able to make significant contribution to the work of the U.N., are closely involved with the social and economic life of the people of the areas they represent, and whose membership is broadly representative of major segments of population in a large number of countries.

Category II - those in special consultative status. There are organizations which are concerned specifically with only a few of the field of activity covered by the Council and which are known internationally within those fields. Organizations accorded this status because of their interest in human rights should have a general international concern in this field. This status may also be granted to major organizations one of whose primary purposes is to promote the objectives of the U.N.

The Roster - this includes other NGOs which the Council, or the Secretary-General in consultation with the Council, considers able to make occasional and useful contributions to the Council or its subsidiary bodies or other U.N. bodies. [Rules of Procedure of the Functional Commissions of ECOSOC, U.N. Doc. E/4767, rule 75, at 16 (1970)].

By 1993 over 1,000 NGOs had been granted formal consultative status with ECOSOC. It should be noted, however, that ECOSOC Resolution 1296 effectively precluded local human rights NGOs from receiving consultative status and limited the capacity of local NGOs to participate in key UN meetings on human rights because it restricted the granting of consultative status to NGOs with an international focus. The exclusion of national organizations from ECOSOC accreditation operates to specifically disadvantage Third World NGOs.

[63] The Article 71 of the United Nations Charter provides: The Economic and Social Council may make suitable arrangements for consultation with non-governmental organizations that are concerned with matters within its competence.

[64] See Nicolas Valticos. "The International Labor Organization (ILO)" in Karel Vasak, ed. The International Dimensions of Human Rights (Paris:

UNESCO, 1982), p. 363–400; Ernst B. Haas Human Rights and International Action. (Stanford, CA: Stanford University Press, 1970).
⁶⁵ See Hanna Saba "UNESCO and Human Rights" in Karel Vasak, ed. The International Dimensions of Human Rights (Paris: UNESCO, 1982), p. 401– 426.
⁶⁶ According to Marek Antoni Norwicki, "NGOs before the European Commission and the Court of Human Rights." *Netherlands Quarterly of Human Rights*. 14 (September 1996), p. 292, at present over 350 NGOs have been granted the consultative status by the Council of Europe.
⁶⁷ Standards on Cooperative Relations Between the Organization of American States and the United Nations, its Specialized Agencies, and Other National and International Organizations, O.A.S. Doc. AG/Res. 57(1971).
⁶⁸ See O.A.U. Doc. CM/Res.330 (XXII) (1974).
⁶⁹ Laurie Wiseberg "Human Rights Nongovernmental Organizations" in Richard Pierre Claude and Burns H. Weston. Human Rights in the World Community 2nd. ed. (Philadelphia: University of Pennsylvania Press, 1992), p. 373.
⁷⁰ In 1968, U.N. Secretary-General U Thant addressed NGO Conference convened to commemorate the twentieth anniversary of the Universal Declaration of Human Rights and stated [U.N. Doc. SG/SM/999, at 2 (1968)]:

> During 1947 and 1948, non-governmental organizations participated at every stage in the strenuous process of preparing the Universal Declaration of Human Rights.

See John Humphrey, "The U.N. Charter and the Universal Declaration of Human Rights," in E. Laurd, ed. The International Protection of Human Rights (New York: Frederick A. Praeger, 1967), p. 39–58.
⁷¹ See Virginia Leary, "A New Role for Non-governmental Organizations in Human Rights: A Case Study of Non-governmental Participation in the Development of International Norms on Torture" in Antonio Cassese, ed. UN Law/Fundamental Rights: Two Topics in International Law. (Alphen aan den Rijn: Sijihoff & Noordhoff, 1979). p. 197–210. Amnesty International was actively involved with drafting the 1975 Declaration on the Protection of All Persons from Being Subjected to Torture or Other Cruel, Inhuman or Degrading Treatment or Punishment and the 1984 Convention against Torture and Other Cruel, Inhuman or Degrading treatment or Punishment. Subsequently, the Committee against Torture was established in 1987 in accordance with Article 17 of the Convention. Moreover, the Special Rapporteur on Torture was created in 1985 pursuant to the commission on Human Rights Resolution 1985/33. Amnesty

International, "Torture" in Richard Pierre Claude and Burns H. Weston. Human Rights in the World Community 2nd ed. (Philadelphia: University of Pennsylvania Press, 1982), pp. 79–80.

[72] See Cynthia Price Cohen, The Role of Nongovernmental Organizations in the Drafting of the Convention of the Child, 12 *Human Rights Quarterly* 137 (1990). Laurence J. LeBlanc. The Convention on the Rights of the Child (Lincoln: University of Nebraska Press, 1995).

[73] The Article 25 of the European Convention on Human Rights states:

> "Any person or group of persons, or any non-governmental entity legally recognized in one or more Member States of the organization, may lodge petitions with the Commission containing denunciations or complaints of violation of this Convention by a State Party."

Article 44 of American Convention of Human Rights states: Any person or group of persons, or any non-governmental entity legally recognized in one or more Member States of the organization may lodge petitions with the Commission containing denunciations or complaints of violation of this Convention by a State Party. This is also true of various complaints that have reached the European Court of Human Rights and the Inter-American Court of Human Rights. The Courts have permitted NGO's to file amicus curiae briefs in advisory proceedings. See Dinah Shelton. "The Participation of Nongovernmental Organizations in International Judicial Proceedings" *American Journal of International Law* 88 (Oct. 1994), p. 630–640.

[74] For example, in 1979, the Lawyers Committee for International Human Rights submitted a communication to the Sub-Commission on the widespread violations of human rights in Argentina. In 1979, Amnesty International submitted communications on Afghanistan, Argentina, the Central African Empire, Ethiopia, Indonesia, Paraguay, and Uruguay.

[75] Sub-Commission on Prevention of Discrimination and Protection of Minorities Res. 1 (XXIV), para. (2)(a), U.N. doc.E/CN.4/1070, E/CN.4/Sub.2/323, at 50–51 (1971).

[76] Today NGOs deliver more official development assistance than the entire U.N. system, excluding the World Bank and the International Monetary Fund. See Jessica T. Matthews. "Power Shift" *Foreign Affairs* 76 (January/February 1997), p. 51.

[77] Francis M. Deng. "Sovereignty and Humanitarian Responsibilities: A Challenge for NGOs in Africa and the Sudan," in Vigilance and Vengeance: NGOs and Preventing Ethnic Conflict in Divided Societies, ed. Robert I. Rotberg (Cambridge, MA: World Peace Foundation, 1996), p. 188.

[78] Discussion, *The Center Magazine* (May/June 1984), p. 58.

[79] See Hans Thoolen and Berth Verstappen. Human Rights Missions: A Study of the Fact-Finding Practice of Non-governmental Organizations. (Dordrecht: Martinus Nijhoff Pub., 1986) and David Weissbrodt and James McCarthy "Fact-Finding by International Nongovernmental Human Rights Organizations" *Virginia Journal of International Law* 22 (1981): 1–89. The prominent NGOs that send regularly fact-finding mission are Amnesty International, the Anti-Slavery Society, the International Association of Democratic Lawyers (IADL), the International Commission of Jurists (ICJ), the International Committee of Red Cross, the International Federation of Human Rights, the International League for Human Rights, the Minority Rights Group, Survival International, and the World Peace Council. For example, Iran received representatives of IADL in 1972, the ICJ, and the International Federation of Human Rights; Chile received missions from AI and the ICJ in 1973 and 1974; South Korea received AI in 1974; Greece received the ICJ in 1972. Spain and Yugoslavia received the International League for Human Rights in 1973 and 1975 respectively.

[80] See Claude E Welch Jr. Protecting Human Rights in Africa: Roles and Strategies of Non-Governmental Organizations. (Philadelphia: University of Pennsylvania Press, 1995), p. 61. Amnesty International reported in 1972 on allegations of torture in Brazil contained a listing of more than one thousand torture victims and demonstrated a consistent pattern of gross violations of human rights in Brazil. The ICJ has issued reports on violations of human rights in such countries as Uganda, Uruguay, and Chile. The International League for Human Rights and the Lawyers Committee for International Human Rights have produced reports on Argentina, Burundi, Greece, the USSR, Northern Island, and Yugoslavia.

[81] See lists of Urgent Action Network established by NGOs in Appendix in Laurie S. Wiseberg. "Protecting Human Rights Activists and NGOs: What More Can Be Done?" *Human Rights Quarterly* 13 (1991), p. 543–544.

[82] Amnesty International and the People's Decade of Human Rights Education (PDHRE - New York-based) are prominent NGOs in the field of HRE. On HRE for law enforcement, see Edy Kaufman, "Human Rights Education for Law Enforcement" in George Andreopolos and Richard Pierre Claude. The Human Rights Education for the Twenty-First Century. (Philadelphia, PA: University of Pennsylvania, 1997), pp. 278–295.

[83] See Richard Pierre Claude "Global Human Rights Education: The Challenges for Nongovernmental Organizations" in Andreopolos, G. and Richard Pierre Claude. The Human Rights Education for the Twenty-First Century. (Philadelphia, PA: University of Pennsylvania, 1997), pp. 394–415. Richard Pierre Claude. "Human Rights Education: The Case of the Philippines" *Human Rights Quarterly* 13 (1991), p. 524. On formal, informal and nonformal education, see, Richard Pierre Claude "Inventing

New Educational Ideas" in David P. Forsythe, ed. Human Rights in the New Europe. (Lincoln: University of Nebraska Press, 1994), pp. 230–232. Shulamith Koenig, Executive Director, Organizing Committee of the People's Decade of Human Rights Education, USA, argues that "mass education in human rights is, in the long term, the most effective means of preventive abuse; promoting participation, accountability, reciprocity, and good governance; sustaining democracy and civil society; and establishing a climate in which societies and economies can prosper and human needs can be met with dignity."

[84] This is called lobbying; it means the informed communication from private individuals and groups to public decision-makers in support of or in opposition to some pending policy decision. Lobbying is considered the essence of the democratic process - the process through which interests are articulated and aggregated.

[85] See David P. Forsythe. Human Rights and U.S. Foreign Policy: Congress Reconsidered. (Gainesville: University of Florida Press, 1988).

[86] Governments hesitate to criticize one another because most governments are concerned with keeping their diplomatic relations on a friendly basis. See David Weissbrodt, "The Contribution of International Nongovernmental Organizations to the Protection of Human Rights" in Theodore, Meron ed. Human Rights in International Law: Legal and Policy Issues (Oxford: Clarendon Press, 1984), p. 412.

[87] Although NGO share a commitment to "human rights," their understanding about goals, priorities and strategies are not identical. "First World" NGOs usually committed to traditional Western values - civil and political rights, and concentrate on individual rights rather than group rights (e.g. Amnesty International, the Lawyers Committee for Human Rights, Human Rights Watch). On the contrary, "Third World" NGOs emphasize the importance of social and economic rights.

[88] Menno Kamminga and Nigel Rodley,"Direct Intervention at the UN: NGO Participation in the Commission on Human Rights and Its Sub-Commission" in Hurst Hunnum, ed. Guide to International Human Rights Practice (Philadelphia: University of Pennsylvania, 1984), p. 198.

[89] Morten Kjaerum, "The Contributions of Voluntary Organizations to the Development of Democratic Governance," in Ann McKinstry Micou and Birgit Lindsnaes, eds., The Role of Voluntary Organizations in Emerging Democracies: Experience and Strategies in Eastern and Central Europe and in South Africa (New York and Copenhagen: Institute of International Education and Danish Center for Human Rights, 1993), p. 15–16.

[90] See Laurie Wiseberg. "Protecting Human Rights Activists and NGOs: What More Can Be Done?" *Human Rights Quarterly* 13 (1991), p. 542–543. Suggestion have been made to alleviate financial difficulties of

NGOs. For example, in Germany traffic violators can pay their fine either to the government or to Amnesty International.

[91] See Nigel S. Rodley "Monitoring Human Rights Violations in the 1980s" in Jorge I. Dominguez, et al. Enhancing Global Human Rights. (New York: McGraw-Hill Book Co., 1979), p. 148.

Nigel S. Rodley proposes an ideal model of NGOs, whose principal desiderata include:

1. It should be completely independent of governments;
2. It should be completely independent of all power elites, particularly economic ones;
3. It should be free of all ideological or politically partisan prejudice. It should not be committed to, or otherwise permeated by, any single socio-cultural norm;
4. It should be staffed by and responsible to people who, individually or collectively, can ensure compliance with the above;
5. it should be financially secure;
6. It should be legally secure;
7. Its investigations should seek to approximate scientific accuracy;
8. The information it disseminates should be detailed and accurate;
9. It must have access to and seek to work effectively with such international media of communication as are willing to give it attention;
10. It should be based in a country that is stable enough to protect the human rights of its own citizens and to accept without retaliation such criticism as the institution may be called upon to level against it.

[92] For example, the Egyptian Organization for Human Rights (EOHR) has not been granted official permission to operate, although they applied for registration in July 1987. According to Michael H. Posner and Candy Whittome, "The Status of Human Rights NGOs" *Columbia Human Rights Law Review* 25 (1994), p. 274, state-sponsored physical attacks on and persecution of human rights advocates are well-documented and widespread. For example, in 1993 the Lawyers Committee for Human Rights documented over 250 cases of attacks on lawyers and judges, involving some 450 people in fifty countries. When activists are arrested, NGOs have been able to provide them with direct or indirect legal assistance and extend financial assistance to members of activists' families who might also be at risk. For instance, Amnesty International has a fund that can be used to provide humanitarian assistance to political prisoners and their families.

[93] Governmental restrictions on NGOs in Singapore, Egypt, Mexico, Sri Lanka and Tunisia are documented in Michael H. Posner, Michael H. and Candy Whittome. "The Status of Human Rights NGOs" *Columbia Human Rights Law Review* 25 (1994), p. 277–281.

[94] Article 20 of the Universal Declaration of Human Rights provides:

"[E]veryone has the right to freedom of peaceful assembly and association."

Similar provisions are found in Article 22 of the International Covenant on Civil and Political Rights (ICCPR), Article 11 of the European Convention for the Protection of Human Rights and Fundamental Freedoms, Article 16 of the American Convention on Human Rights, and Article 10 of the African Charter on Human and Peoples' Rights. ICCPR, a binding treaty that has been ratified by over 120 nations, elaborates on the right of association and provides that:

> No restrictions may be placed on the exercise of this right other than those that are prescribed by law and that are   necessary in a democratic society in the interests of national security or public safety, public order (order public), the protection of public health or morals or the protection of the rights and freedoms of others.

It must be noted that Article 10 of the African Charter of Human and Peoples' Rights is problematic because it gives virtual carte blanche to states to decide what restrictions they choose to impose: Article 10 (1) states that "every individual shall have the right to free association provided that he abides by the law," June 27, 1981, O.A.U. doc. CAB/LEG/67/3 rev.5.

[95] See Clarence J. Dias "Relationships between Human Rights NGOs in the Third World" in Saksena, K.P. ed. Human Rights Perspective & Challenges (In 1990 and Beyond). (New Delhi: World Congress on Human Rights, 1994), p. 105–128.

[96] See Michael Posner "The Establishment of the Right of Nongovernmental Human Rights Groups to Operate" in Louis Henkin and John Lawrence Hargrove, ed. Human Rights: An Agenda for the Next Century. (Washington, D.C.: The American Society of International Law, 1994) p. 415. Posner explains that at one session in the 1993 Commission, more than 120 NGOs signed up to speak. The Commission was obliged to hold sessions late into the night to accommodate them. As a result, most of the NGO representatives addressed an empty room.

[97] Posner argues that the Working Group on Enforced or Involuntary Disappearances, which holds its sessions in Geneva and New York, and to which local NGOs and victims are invited to participate, could serve as a model in this respect.

[98] Arthur W. Blaser, "Human Rights in the Third World and Development of International Nongovernmental Organizations" in George Shepherd, Jr. and Ved P. Nanda., ed. Human Rights and Third World Development. (Westport, CT: Greenwood Press, 1985), p. 276.

[99] NGOs in the Third World must be assisted in having access to the modern means of communications, faxes, telexes, electronic mail, tape recorder and video cameras. It is necessary to set up a special fund to encourage greater participation by Third World NGOs. See Richard Pierre Claude, Educating for Human Rights: The Philippines and Beyond (Manila: University of Philippines Press, 1996). Claude explains about "Diplomacy Training for NGOs", which was organized in recognition of the worldwide maldistribution of NGOs that put such groups in "the South" at a disadvantage. The training sessions promote NGO familiarity and competence in using the United Nations human rights system without undertaking expensive travel to Geneva or other Western fora.

[100] Jack Donnelly. "International Human Rights: A Regime Analysis," *International Organization* 40 (1986), p. 604–5.

[101] Irwin Cotler, "The Role of Non-Governmental Organizations in the Promotion and Protection of Human Rights in a Revolutionary Age: The Helsinki Process as a Case Study" in Irwin Cotler and F. Pearl Eliadis. International Human Rights: Theory and Practice. (Montreal: The Canadian Human Rights Foundation, 1992), p. 468.

[102] Dianne Otto. "Nongovernmental Organizations in the United Nations System: the Emerging Role of International Civil Society" *Human Rights Quarterly* 18(1996), p. 141.; John W. Harbeson et al., ed. Civil Society and the State in Africa. (Boulder, CO: Lynne Rienner Pub., 1994).

[103] B.G. Ramcharan. "Strategies for the International Protection of Human Rights in the 1990s" *Human Rights Quarterly* 13 (1991), p. 163; Bertram Gross "Towards a Human Rights Century" *Human Rights Quarterly* 13 (1991): 387–395.

[104] Richard Doner "Japanese Foreign Investment and the Creation of a Pacific Asian Region" in Frankel and Kahler, eds. Regionalism and Rivalry, p. 196.

[105] Address by President Kim Dae-jung of the Republic of Korea at Bijing University on November 12, 1998. Visit website: www.kocis.go.kr/Statevisit/china/address/4–1.html

[106] The workshop is part of the technical cooperation programme of the Office of the High Commissioner for Human Rights, which benefits 40 countries worldwide, and springs from the Framework for Regional Technical Cooperation in the Asia-Pacific Region. For more information, visit website: www.uhhchr.ch/html/menu2/techcoop.htm

[107] The full text of the Asian Human Rights Charter is obtainable at Asian Human Rights Commission/Asian Legal Resource Center: Unit 4, 7th Floor, Mongkok Commercial Center 16 Argyle Street, Kowloon, Hong Kong, SAR China. E-mail: ahrchk@ahrchk.org
Internet: http://www.hk.super.net/~ahrchk

[108] The Asian Human Rights Commission (AHRC) is an independent non-governmental body, which seeks to promote greater awareness and realization of human rights in the Asian region. AHRC mobilizes Asian and international public opinion to obtain relief and redress for the victims of human rights violations. Their address is: Unit 4, 7th Floor, Mongkok, Commercial Center, 16 Argyle Street, Kowloon, Hong Kong, SAR China.

[109] Stephen S. Lee, Taiwan Association for Human Rights. An Open Letter of Support and Appreciation on Asian Charter on Human Rights. Visit website: http:/www.ahrchk.net/east.htm

[110] Yasushi Higashizawa, Japan Civil Liberties Union. The Guiding Principles of the Draft Asian Human Rights Charter: The Constitution of Japan and Human Rights. Visit website: http:/www.ahrchk.net/east.htm

[111] On "internationalization" of human rights, see W. Paul Gormiley. Human Rights and Environment: The Need for International Cooperation (Leyden: A.W. Sijihoff, 1976); Section IV (c) The Right to Environment in Kathleen E. Mahoney and Paul Mahoney. Human Rights in the Twenty-first Century: A Global Challenge. (Dordrecht: Marinus Nijhoff Pub., 1993); Dinah Shelton. "The Right to Environment" in Asbjorn Eide and Jan Helgesen, eds. The Future of Human Rights Protection in a Changing World. (Oslo: Norwegian University Press, 1991), p.197–212; David P. Forsythe. The Internationalization of Human Rights. (Lexington, MA: D.C. Heath and Co., 1991); Stanley Hoffmann. Duties Beyond Borders. (New York: Syracuse University Press, 1981); Edith Brown Weiss. "Planetary Rights" and Philip Alston "Peace as a Human Rights" in Richard Pierre Claude and Burns H. Weston. Human Rights in the World Community: Issues and Action, 2nd ed. (Philadelphia: University of Pennsylvania, 1992), p.187–198 and p.198–211.

NOTES TO CHAPTER III

[1] Samuel P. Huntington "The Clash of Civilization?" *Foreign Affairs* 72 (1993), p. 25. See also Samuel P. Huntington, The Clash of Civilizations and the Remaking of World Order. (New York: Simon & Schuster, 1996). As a native of Japan, I would like to point out that although Huntington recognizes Japan as a distinctive culture among eight major civilizations, I argue that historically Japan has been in Confucian civilization. It is estimated that some 1.5 billion people share Confucian culture, followed by Islam with 1.1 billion.

[2] The First World designates the developed Western countries of Europe and North America, plus Japan and Australia. The Second World refers to the non-Asian communist countries. The salient characteristic of the Third World is a lower level of economic development. The Third World shares little in values or ideology except for a desire for economic development.

Since the end of the cold war, this crude trichotomy has blurred. See James Nickel. Making Sense of Human Rights: Philosophical Reflections on the Universal Declaration of Human Rights. (Berkeley: University of California Press, 1987), p. 62–68; Alice Ehr-Soon Tay, "Marxism, Socialism and Human Rights," in Eugene Kamenka and Ehr-Soon Tay, eds., Human Rights (London: Edward Arnold, 1978), p. 112; Adamantia Pollis," Human Rights in Liberal, Socialist, and Third World Perspective" in Richard Pierre Claude and Burns H. Weston. Human Rights in the World Community: Issues and Action, 2nd ed. (Philadelphia: University of Pennsylvania, 1992), p. 146–158. On North-South framework and human rights, see "Human Rights in North-South Relations" in R.J. Vincent. Human Rights and International Relations. (Cambridge: Cambridge University Press, 1986), p. 76–91. Louis Henkin "Constitutions and Human Rights in the Third World" in Louis Henkin. The Rights of Man Today. (Boulder. CO: Westview Press, 1978), p. 78–88; "Third World" in Peter Baehr. The Role of Human Rights in Foreign Policy. (New York: St. Martin's Press, 1994). Graciela Chichilnisky and H.S.D. Cole "Human Rights and Basic Needs in a North-South Context" in Paula R. Newberg. The Politics of Human Rights. (New York: New York University Press, 1980), p.113–142; Richard Falk "Comparative Protection of Human Rights in Capitalist and Socialist Third World Countries" in Richard A. Falk Human Rights and State Sovereignty. (New York: Holms and Meier, 1981), p.125–152.

[3] See Bramsted, E.K. and K.J. Melhuish. Western Liberalism: A History in Documents from Locke to Croce. (London: Longman, 1978); Burns H. Weston,"Human Rights" in Richard Pierre Claude and Burns H. Weston. Human Rights in the World Community: Issues and Action, 2nd ed. (Philadelphia: University of Pennsylvania, 1992). Jack Donnelly "Human Rights and Western Liberalism" in Abdullahi Ahmed An-Naim and Francis M. Deng. Human Rights in Africa: Cross-Cultural Perspectives. (Washington, D.C.: The Brookings Institution, 1990), p. 31–55. The idea of human rights can be traced to the philosophical traditions of Greek, Roman and Judaeo-Christian, which include the English Magna Carta (1215), the United States Declaration of Independence (1776), and the French Declaration of the Rights of Man and of the Citizens (1789) and such thinkers as natural law theorist Locke as well as Hobbes, Mill, Montesquieu, Voltaire, and Jean-Jacques Rousseau, among others. The characteristic of liberal tradition is its emphasis on individualism and the protection of private property.

[4] Macpherson, "Natural Rights in Hobbes and Locke," in D.D. Raphael ed., Political Theory and the Rights of Man (London: Macmillan, 1976), p. 1–2. John Locke (1632–1704), English philosopher, wrote that certain rights self-evidently pertain to individuals as human beings in "the state of

nature" prior to humankind entered civil society, that among them are the right to life, liberty (freedom from arbitrary rule) and property.

5 Abdullahi Ahmed An-Naim and Francis M. Deng. Human Rights in Africa: Cross-Cultural Perspectives. (Washington, D.C.: The Brookings Institution, 1990), p. xi,

6 Joan Bauer "International Human Rights and Asian Commitment" in *Human Rights Dialogue* 3 (December 1995), p. 2.

7 See Hedley Bull and Adam Watson, ed. The Expansion of International Society. (Oxford: The Clarendon Press, 1984).

8 On "The Asian Values Debate" speech by Prime Minister of Malaysia Dr. Mahathir bin Mohamad at the 29th International General Meeting of the Pacific Basin Economic Council at Washington, D.C. on 21 May 1996.

9 See Abdullahi Ahmed An-Naim and Francis M. Deng. Human Rights in Africa: Cross-Cultural Perspectives. (Washington, D.C.: The Brookings Institution, 1990); Rhoda Howard, Human Rights in Commonwealth Africa (Totawa, N.J.: Rowman and Littlefield, 1986);

Rhoda Howard."Evaluating Human Rights in Africa: Some Problems of Implicit Comparison" *Human Rights Quarterly* 6 (May 1984): 160–179.

10 See James T. H. Tang, ed. Human Rights and International Relations in the Asia-Pacific Region. (London: Pinter, 1995). James Hsiung, ed. Human Rights in East Asia: A Cultural Perspective. (New York: Paragon House Pub., 1985); Michael Davis, et al, ed. Human Rights and Chinese Values: Legal, Philosophical, and Political Perspectives. (Oxford: Oxford University Press, 1995).

11 See Ann Elizabeth Mayer, Islam and Human Rights: Tradition and Politics (Boulder, CO: Westview Press, 1991); Bassam Tibi, "Universality of Human Rights and Authenticity of non-Western Cultures, Islam, and the Western Concept of Human Rights" *Harvard Human Rights Journal* 5 (Spring 1992): 221–226; Tore Lindholm and Kari Vogt, ed. Islamic Law Reform and Human Rights (Oslo: Nordic Human Rights Pub., 1993); Mohammed Allal Sinaceur "Islamic tradition and human rights" in Paul Ricoeur. Philosophical Foundations of Human Rights. (Paris: UNESCO, 1986), p.193–225; Fouad Zakaria, "Human Rights in the Arab world: the Islamic Context" in Paul Ricoeur. Philosophical Foundations of Human Rights. (Paris: UNESCO, 1986), pp. 227–241; Snna E. Arzt, The Application of International Human Rights Law in Islamic States" *Human Rights Quarterly* 12 (1990): 202–230; Abdullahi Ahmed an-Na'im "Islam, Islamic Law and the Dilemma of Cultural Legitimacy for Universal Human Rights" in Claude E. Welch Jr and Virginia A. Leary. Asian Perspectives on Human Rights. (Boulder, CO: Westview Press, 1990), p.31–54; Ali Abedl Wahid Wafi, "Human Rights in Islam" *Islamic Quarterly* 27 (1967); Ismai'il al-Farugi "Islam and Human Rights" *Islamic Quarterly* 27 (1983);

Raffat Hassan's "On Human Rights and the Qur'anic Perspectives" *Journal of Ecumenical Studies* 19 (1982).

[12] The African Charter was adopted in Nairobi in June 1981. Its preamble refers to the "value of their historical tradition and the values of African civilization, which should inspire and characterize their reflection on the concept of human rights and peoples' rights." See Richard Gittleman, "The Banjul Charter on Human and Peoples' Rights: A Legal Analysis," in Claude E. Welch, Jr. and Ronald I. Meltzer, eds., Human Rights and Development in Africa (Albany: State University of New York Press, 1984), p.156–176; On collective rights, see Douglas Sanders. "Collective Rights" *Human Rights Quarterly* 13 (1991): 368–386; William F. Felice, Taking Suffering Seriously: The Importance of Collective Human Rights. (New York: State University of New York Press, 1996).
Collective rights include the right of peoples to self-determination, rights of minorities, development rights and environment rights.

[13] Rhoda Howard, "Is There an African Concept of Human Rights?" in R.J. Vincent, ed. Foreign Policy and Human Rights Issues and Responses. (Cambridge: Cambridge University Press, 1986), p. 13

[14] John S. Mbiti, African Religions and Philosophy (New York: Doubleday, 1970) sums up a philosophy of existence in Africa as: "I am because we are, and because we are, therefore I am." Shue argues that there are three types of correlative duties all of which must be performed if the basic right is to be fully honored. These duties are: (1) the duty to avoid depriving others; (2) the duty to protect from deprivation; (3) the duty to aid the deprived. See Henry Shue Basic Rights: Subsistence, Affluence, and U.S. Foreign Policy. (Princeton, N.J.: Princeton University Press, 1980).

[15] Tom W. Bennett, "Human Rights and the African Cultural Tradition," Wolfgang Schmale, ed. Human Rights and Cultural Diversity: Europe-Arabic-Islamic World Africa-China. (Goldbach, Germany: Keip Publishing, 1993), p. 273. In many parts of Africa, a woman was not allowed to sue for divorce or for the guardianship of her children; she would not be entitled to hold or dispose property; she could not approach a court unassisted; she might not have any say in the government.

[16] See Roberta Cohen. Book Review of Abdullahi Ahmed An-Naih, Human Rights in Africa: Cross-Cultural Perspectives (Washington, D.C.: The Brookings Institution, 1990) in *Human Rights Quarterly* (May 1993), p. 459–461.

[17] See Keba M'Baye. "Human Rights in Africa" in Karel Vasak, ed. The International Dimensions of Human Rights. (Westport, CT: Greenwood Press, 1982), p. 583–601.

[18] According to Confucius, the individual exists solely in the framework of group such as family, society, and state and the well being of community takes priority over that of individual. The individual is not an independent

or self-sufficient entity, but is always thought of as a member of a group and as dependent on the harmony and strength of the group. Therefore, it is considered that individualism is an alien concept to the Confucian society - the concept of individual rights is an import from the West.

[19] John Stuart Mill. On Liberty (New York: Penguin Books, 1979), p. 19.

[20] Lee Manwoo "North Korea and the Western Notion of Human Rights" in James C. Hsiung, ed. Human Rights in East Asia: A Cultural Perspective. (New York: Paragon House Pub., 1985), p. 129–151.

[21] See Lawrence W. Beer "Freedom of Expression in Japan" in Richard P. Claude, ed. Comparative Human Rights (Baltimore: The Johns Hopkins University Press, 1976). Beer notes that seniority and hierarchy may stifle the free expression of individual thought.

[22] See Fareed Zakaria. "Culture is Destiny: A Conversation with Lee Kuan Yew" *Foreign Affairs* 73 (March/April 1994): 109–125.

[23] Professors Andrew Nathan and Randle Edwards have characterized China's human rights tradition - rights are not inherent in humanhood as under natural doctrine but are created by the State. See Randle Edwards, Louis Henkin and Andrew J. Nathan. Human Rights in Contemporary China. (New York: Columbia University Press, 1986).

[24] See James Hsiung ed. Human Rights in East Asia: A Cultural Perspective. (New York: Paragon House Pub., 1985).

[25] Hiroko Yamane observes that "Asia is a conglomeration of countries with radically different social structures, and diverse religious, philosophical, and cultural traditions; their political ideologies, legal systems, and degrees of economic development vary greatly; and above all, there is no shared historical past even from the times of colonialism." See Hiroko Yamane, "Asia and Human Rights," in Karel Vasak, ed. International Dimensions of Human Rights, vol.2 (Westport CT: Greenwood Press, 1982), p.651–670.
On "Asian Values," see Xiaorong Li. "Asian Values and the Universality of Human Rights" *Philosophy & Public Policy.* 16 (Spring 1996): 18–23.

[26] Nathan Gardels, Interview with Lee Kuan Yew, New Perspectives Q. (1992).

[27] Christopher Tremewan. "Human Rights in Asia" *The Pacific Review* 6 (1993), p. 17. According to Asia Watch, alleged violations in Singapore include the use of preventive detention, imprisonment without trial, restrictions on freedom of movement, association, and speech, physical and psychological mistreatment of detainees, limits placed on judicial review, intimidation and harassment of opposition, restriction on media, and intervention in the judiciary. See Silencing All Critics: Human Rights Violations in Singapore (Washington, D.C. and New York: Asia Watch, 1989).

[28] Amartya Sen, "Human Rights and Economic Achievements" in Joanne R. Bauer and Daniel A. Bell, ed. The East Asian Challenge for Human

Rights. (Cambridge: Cambridge University Press, 1999), p. 92. Jack
Donnelly argues that regimes that sacrifice either civil and political rights
or economic, social and cultural rights to development do not represent an
inherently desirable form of government because authoritarian rule often
entails bureaucratic incompetence, unbridled nepotism and corruption. See
Jack Donnelly, "Human Rights and Asian Values: A Defense of 'Western'
Universalism" in Joanne R. Bauer and Daniel A. Bell, ed. The East Asian
Challenge for Human Rights. (Cambridge: Cambridge University Press,
1999), p. 72; Sidney Jones of Human Rights Watch in "The Impact of
Asian Economic Growth on Human Rights" Asia Project Working Paper,
Council on Foreign Relations, January, 1995.

[29] The White Paper "Human Rights in China" (1991) published by the
State Council of Chinese Government stated, "despite its international
aspect, the issue of human rights falls by and large within the sovereignty
of each state." However, China's sovereignty argument was rejected by the
Vienna Declaration and Programme of Action adopted at the World
Human Rights Conference in June 1993. The United Nations' subsequent
establishment of the UN High Commissioner for Human Rights further
rejected Chinese resistance to international human rights.

[30] See Yi Ding. "Opposing Interference in Other Countries' Internal Affairs
Through Human Rights" *Beijing Review* 32 (1989): 10–12.

[31] See Abdullahi Ahmed El Naiem "A Modern Approach to Human Rights
in Islam: Foundations and Implications for Africa" in Welch Jr.Claude E.,
and Ronald I. Meltzer, ed. Human Rights and Development in Africa.
(Albany, NY: State University of New York, 1984), p. 75–89.

[32] According to An-Na'im, the Shari'a is not divine because it is the product of human interpretation of Koran. It is misleading to think of Shari'a
as merely law in the strict modern sense of the term. Shari'a is the Islamic
view of the whole duty of humankind, and includes moral and pastoral the-
ology and ethics, high spiritual aspirations and detailed ritualistic and formal observance as well as legal rules in the formal sense. See Abdullahi
Ahmed An-Na'im, Toward an Islamic Reformation: Civil Liberties, Human
Rights and International Law (Syracuse, NY: Syracuse University Press,
1990), p.185. On Islamic law, see Joseph Schacht, An Introduction to
Islamic Law (Oxford: Clarendon Press, 1964), Ann Elizabeth Mayer, "The
Sharia'h: A Methodology or a Body of Substantive Rules?" in Islamic Law
and Jurisprudence, ed Nicholas Heer (Seattle: University of Washington
Press, 1990), 177–198. Islamic Law Reform and Human Rights (Oslo:
Nordic Human Rights Publications, 1993). Abdul Aziz Said, "Precept and
Practice of Human Rights in Islam," *Universal Human Rights,* vol. I
(1979), no. 1, p. 64–5; S.G. Vesey-Fitzgerald, "The Nature and Sources of
the Shari'a" in M. Khadduri and H.J. Liebersny, eds., Law in the Middle
East (Washington: The Middle East Institute, 1955), p. 85ff; Majid

Khadduri, "Nature and Sources of Islamic Law" *George Washington Law Review* 22 (1953), p.6–10; Majid Khadduri, "Human Rights in Islam" *The Annals of the American Academy of Political Social Science* 243 (1946).

33 Abdul Aziz Said. "Precept and Practice of Human Rights in Islam" *Universal Human Rights.* I (April 1979), p. 63, 73–74.

34 Individual is conceived of as a limb of an organically defined religious-cultural collectivity. Ahmad Farrag, "Human Rights and Liberties in Islam," in Jan Bertin, et al, ed. Human Rights in a Pluralist World: Individuals and Collectivities. (London: Meckler, 1990), p. 133.

35 Jack Donnelly. Universal Human Rights in Theory and Practice. (Ithaca, N.Y.: Cornell University Press, 1989), p. 111.

36 Khalid M. Ishaque, Human Rights in Islamic Law, *Review of the International Commission of Jurists*, 12 (1974): 30–39.

37 In Islamic societies, the man is permitted to marry up to four women; The husband can repudiate his wife unilaterally; Saudi women are not permitted to drive cars and Kuwaiti women do not have a right to vote. See Jack Donnelly, Universal Human Rights in Theory and Practice. (Ithaca, N.Y.: Cornell University Press, 1989), p. 52. Many Islamic states have made reservations to the 1979 Convention on the Elimination of All Forms of Discrimination against Women [adopted 18 Dec. 1979, G.A. Res. 34/180, 34 U.N. GAOR supp. No.46 at 193, U.N. Doc. A/34/36. (1980)] See Riffat Hassan, "On Human Rights and the Qur'anic Perspective," in Human Rights in Religious Traditions 64 (Ardene Swindler ed, 1982). The Pakistani feminist Riffat Hassan points out that "Many Muslims, when they speak of human rights, either do not speak of women's rights at all or are mainly concerned with the question of how a women's chastity may be protected." On general situations of women in Muslim world, see Part Eight, "The Arab-Muslim World" in Eschel M. Rhoodie, Discrimination Against Women. (Jefferson, NC: McFarland & Co., 1989), p. 345–381.

38 The conversion of Muslims to other faith is considered to be an act of betrayal warranting the death penalty. See Donna E. Arzt, "The Application of International Human Rights Law in Islamic States," *Human Rights Quarterly* 12 (1990): 202–230. It should be noted that the restriction of interreligious marriages practiced in some Muslim states are in contrary to Article 16 of the Universal Declaration of Human Rights, which recognizes the right to marry "without any limitation due to race, nationality or religion."

39 See Abdullahi Ahmed An-Na'im. "Islam, Islamic law and the Dilemma of Cultural Legitimacy for Universal Human Rights" in Claude E. Welch Jr. and Virginia A. Leary. Asian Perspectives on Human Rights. (Boulder, CO: Westview Press, 1990), p. 38.

40 Sami Aldeeb Abu-Salhieh points out Article 20 of the Universal Declaration of Human Rights, which provides, in part:

"The will of the people shall be the basis of the authority of government; this shall be expressed in periodic elections which shall be by universal and equal suffrage"

and argues that "in almost all the Arab and Islamic countries, power is in
the hands of persons without any popular legitimacy." See Sami A. Aldeeb
Abu-Sahlieh "Muslims and Human Rights: Challenges and Perspectives"
in Wolfgang Schmale, ed. Human Rights and Cultural Diversity: Europe-
Arabic-Islamic World Africa-China. (Goldbach, Germany: Keip Publishing,
1993), p. 239–268.

[41]James Nickel. Making Sense of Human Rights: Philosophical Reflections
on the Universal Declaration of Human Rights. (Berkeley: University of
California Press, 1987).

[42] See David Crocker "Moral Relativism and International Affairs"
Colorado State University, 1979.

[43] See Jack Donnelly. Universal Human Rights in Theory and Practice.
(Ithaca, N.Y.: Cornell University Press, 1989), p. 109

[44] See Fernando R. Teson "International Human Rights and Cultural
Relativism" in Richard Pierre Claude and Burns H. Weston. Human Rights
in the World Community: Issues and Action, 2nd ed. (Philadelphia:
University of Pennsylvania, 1992), p.42–54.

[45] Raimundo Panikkar. "Is the Notion of Human Rights A Western
Concept?" *Diogenes* (Winter/1982), p. 75.

[46] Abdullahi Ahmed An-Naim and Francis M. Deng. Human Rights in
Africa: Cross-Cultural Perspectives. (Washington, D.C.: The Brookings
Institution, 1990), p. xii.

[47] Kishore Mahbubani "Live and let live; Allow Asians to choose their own
course," *Far Easter Economic Review,* (17 June 1993), p. 26.

[48] Douglas Lee Donoho. "Relativism Versus Universalism in Human
Rights: The Search for Meaningful Standards," *Stanford Journal of
International Law* (Spring 1991), p. 351.

[49] Jack Donnelly, "Cultural Relativism and Universal Human Rights,"
Human Rights Quarterly, vol.6 (1984), no. 4.

[50] The principle of self-determination was affirmed in Article 1 of the
International Covenants on Civil and Political Rights and Economic, Social
and Cultural Rights, that is, "All people have the right of self-determination. By virtue of that right they freely determine their political status and
freely pursue their economic, social and cultural development."

[51] R.J. Vincent. Human Rights and International Relations. (New York:
Cambridge University Press, 1991), p 52.

[52] Ethnocentricity is the belief that one's own value system is superior to all
others.

[53] See Virginia A. Leary. "The Effect of Western Perspectives on International Human Rights" in Abdullahi Ahmed An-Naim and Francis M. Deng. Human Rights in Africa: Cross-Cultural Perspectives. (Washington, D.C.: The Brookings Institution, 1990), p.15–55 and
Admantia Pollis & Peter Schwab, Human Rights: A Western Construct with Limited Applicability, in Human Rights: Cultural and Ideological Perspectives (Admantia Pollis & Peter Schwab, eds., 1979), p. 1–18.

[54] See Admantia Pollis, "Human Rights in Liberal, Socialist, and Third World Perspective" in Richard Pierre Claude and Burns H. Weston. Human Rights in the World Community: Issues and Action, 2nd ed. (Philadelphia: University of Pennsylvania, 1992), p. 146–158. Y. Khushalani, Human Rights in Asia and Africa, in Third World Attitudes Toward International Law 331–34 (F. Snyder & S. Sathirathai eds. 1987).

[55] R.J. Vincent. *op.cit.* p 52.

[56] It must be noted that most of present Asian and African member states of the United Nations were still colonies in 1948 and thus did not participate in drafting of the "common standard of achievement for all peoples and nations." The lack of influence of major non-Western cultures in the early drafting of international human rights standards has been cited as a serious deficiency in the development of a universally acceptable concept of human rights. See Pollis & Schwab. Human Rights: Cultural and Ideological Perspectives (1979), p. 14.

[57] See Xiaorong Li. "Asian Values and the Universality of Human Rights" *Philosophy & Public Policy.* 16 (Spring 1996): 18–23.

[58] Maurice Cranston. What are Human Rights? (New York: Basic Books, 1973), p. 36

[59] Henry Shue. Basic Rights: Subsistence, Affluence, and U.S. Foreign Policy. (Princeton, N.J.: Princeton University Press, 1980), p. 13.

[60] Jack Donnelly. Universal Human Rights in Theory and Practice. (Ithaca, N.Y.: Cornell University Press, 1989), p. 116.

[61] Onuma Yasuaki "Toward an Intercivilizational Approach to Human Rights" in Joanne R. Bauer and Daniel A. Bell, ed. The East Asian Challenge for Human Rights. (Cambridge: Cambridge University Press, 1999), p. 103–123.

[62] Henry Shue, *op.cit.*

[63] Morton E. Winston The Philosophy of Human Rights. (Belmont, CA: Wadsworth Pub., 1989), p. 27.

[64] He made this statement at the 1993 World Conference on Human Rights. *Human Rights Dialogue* 1 (May 1994), p. 10.

[65] Sidney Jones "The organic growth: Asian NGOs have come into their own" *Far Eastern Economic Review*, 17 June 1993, p. 23. Amartya Sen, for example, points out the existence of concepts such as freedom, tolerance and equality in Asian traditions. See Amartya Sen "Human Rights

and Asian Values" in Joel H. Rosenthal, ed. Ethics and International Affairs A Reader, 2nd ed. (Washington, D.C.: Georgetown University Press, 1999).

[66] A Conference Report. Human Rights in the Post-Cold War Era: The Cases of North Korea, China and Burma. *Human Rights Dialogue* 1 (May 1994), p. 7.

[67] This is a phrase of U.N General Secretary U Thant. See, John P. Humphrey."The Magna Carta of Mankind" in Peter Davies., ed. Human Rights. (London: Routledge, 1988), p. 31–39.

[68] The Universal Declaration of Human Rights, adopted 10 Dec. 1948, G.A. res. 217A (III), 3 U.N. GAOR (Resolution, part 1) at 71, U.N. Doc. A/810 (1948). The Charter of the Organization of African Unity was adopted by thirty heads of African States and Governments assembled in May 1963 in Addis Ababa, Ethiopia. In the Preamble the heads of States and Governments declare "that the United Nations Charter and the Universal Declaration of Human Rights provide a solid foundation for peaceful and productive cooperation among States" and add that they reaffirm their adherence to the principles of the UN Charter and of the Declaration.

[69] The representatives of 172 states adopted by consensus the Vienna Declaration and Programme of Action at the Second World Conference on Human Rights, 14–25 June 1993. U.N. GAOR, 48th Sess., 22nd plen. mtg., U.N. Doc. A/CONF. 157/24 (Part I) at 20 (1993).

[70] Press Release, SG/SM/6359, 15 October 1997.

[71] Jack Donnelly. Universal Human Rights in Theory and Practice. (Ithaca, N.Y.: Cornell University Press, 1989), p. 122.

[72] See Richard B. Bilder "Possibilities for Development of New International Judicial Mechanisms" in Louis Henkin and John Lawrence Hargrove, ed. Human Rights: An Agenda for the Next Century. (Washington, D.C.: The American Society of International Law, 1994), p. 317–346.

[73] Abdullahi Ahmed An-Naim and Francis M. Deng. Human Rights in Africa: Cross-Cultural Perspectives. (Washington, D.C.: The Brookings Institution, 1990), p. xiii.

[74] Heiner Bielefeldt. "Muslim Voices in the Human Rights Debate." *Human Rights Quarterly* 17 (1995), p. 616.

[75] See John Rawls, "The Idea of an Overlapping Consensus" in Political Liberalism. (New York: Columbia University Press, 1993), p. 133–172.

[76] See Robert O. Keohane and Joseph S. Nye Power and Interdependence: World Politics in Transition (Boston: little, Brown and Co., 1977); Stanley Hoffmann, Duties Beyond Borders (Syracuse, N.Y.: Syracuse University Press, 1981); Lester R. Brown World Without Borders (New York: Vintage

Books, 1973); and David Jacobson. Rights Across Borders (Baltimore: The Johns Hopkins University Press, 1997).

[77] Sami A. Aldeeb Abu-Sahlieh. "Muslims and Human Rights: Challenges and Perspectives," in Wolfgang Schmale, ed. Human Rights and Cultural Diversity: Europe-Arabic-Islamic World Africa-China. (Goldbach, Germany: Keip Publishing, 1993), p. 239–268.

[78] Yash Ghai "Rights, Social Justice, and Globalization in East Asia" in Joanne R. Bauer and Daniel A. Bell, ed. The East Asian Challenge for Human Rights. (Cambridge: Cambridge University Press, 1999), p. 250.

[79] Abdullahi Ahmed An-Naim and Francis M. Deng. Human Rights in Africa: Cross-Cultural Perspectives. (Washington, D.C.: The Brookings Institution, 1990), p. xiii.

[80] A Conference Report Cultural Sources of Human Rights in East Asia: Consensus Building Towards a Rights Regime. *Human Rights Dialogue 5* (June 1996), p. 4.

[81] Annette Marfording. "Cultural Relativism and the Construction of Culture: An Examination of Japan." *Human Rights Quarterly* 19 (1997), p. 432.

[82] Wm. Theodore de Bary, "Human Rites - An Essay on Confucianism and Human Rights" in Irene Eber, ed. Confucianism: The Dynamics of Tradition. (New York: Macmillan Pub., 1986), p. 115.

[83] Francis Fukuyama "The Illusion of Exceptionalism" *Journal of Democracy* 8.3 (1997): 146–149.

[84] As of February 1998, 140 states ratified the International Covenant on Civil and Political Rights and 137 states, the International Covenant on Economic, Social and Cultural Rights, 150 states ratified the International Convention on the Elimination of All Forms of Racial Discrimination, 161 states, the Convention on the Elimination of All Forms of Discrimination against Women, 191 states, the Convention on the Rights of the Child.

[85] Diana Ayton-Shenker, "The Challenge of Human Rights and Cultural Diversity" United Nations Background Note, http://www.un.org/dpi1627e.htm

[86] Won Kan Seng, "The real world of human rights," speech by the Singapore Foreign Minister, Second World Conference on Human Rights, Vienna, 1993, p. 2.

[87] Douglas Lee Donoho. "Relativism Versus Universalism in Human Rights: The Search for Meaningful Standards." *Stanford Journal of International Law* (1991), p. 378.

[88] Abdullahi Ahmed An-Naim elaborates cross-cultural approach to human rights in his work. See Human Rights in Cross-Cultural Perspectives: A Quest for Consensus. (Philadelphia: University of Pennsylvania, 1992).

[89] Richard Schwartz, "Human Rights in an Evolving World Culture" in Abdullahi Ahmed An-Naim and Francis M. Deng. Human Rights in Africa:

Cross-Cultural Perspectives. (Washington, D.C.: The Brookings Institution, 1990), p. 382.

[90] Ibid. p. 368.

[91] See David P, Forsythe. The Internationalization of Human Rights. (Lexington, MA: Lexington Books, 1991) and Kenneth W. Hunter and Timothy C. Mack, ed. International Rights and Responsibilities for the Future. (Westport, CT: Praeger, 1996).

[92] Onuma Yasuaki "Toward an Intercivilizational Approach to Human Rights" in Joanne R. Bauer and Daniel A. Bell, ed. The East Asian Challenge for Human Rights. (Cambridge: Cambridge University Press, 1999). p. 103–123.

[93] Modernity has two dimensions: it is a cultural concept. On the other hand, it has a structural-institutional dimension. See Juergen Habermas, The Philosophical Discourse of Modernity (Cambridge, MA: MIT Press, 1989), Anthony Giddens, The Consequences of Modernity (Stanford, CA: Stanford University Press, 1990).

[94] See Samuel P. Huntington The Third Wave: Democratization in the Late Twentieth Century (Norman: Oxford University Press, 1991); Larry Diamond and Marc F. Plattner, ed. The Global Resurgence of Democracy (Baltimore: The Johns Hopkins University Press, 1993);

Thomas M. Franck "The Emerging Right to Democratic Governance" *American Journal of International Law* 92 (1992): 46–91.

[95] See the United Nations Human Rights Website: http://www.unhchr.ch, maintained by the Office of the High Commissioner for Human Rights, Geneva, Switzerland.

[96] U.N. G.A. Res. 217A (III), 3(1)U.N. GAOR Res. 71, U.N. Doc. A/810 (1948).

[97] U.N. G.A. Res. 2200 (XXI), 21 U.N. GAOR, Supp. (No.16) 49, U.N. Doc.A/6316 (1967).

[98] U.N.G.A.2200 (XXI), 21 U.N. GAOR Supp. (No.16) 52 U.N. Doc. A/6316 (1967).

[99] The Optional Protocol was adopted by the UN in December 1966 and entered into force in March 1976. The Optional Protocol provides for consideration by the UN Human Rights Committee of communications from individuals or groups of individuals who claim to be victims of violations of any rights set forth in the Covenant on Civil and Political Rights. The Second Optional Protocol adopted in December 1989. The Second Optional Protocol aims at abolishing the death penalty.

[100] Jack Donnelly, Universal Human Rights in Theory and Practice (Ithaca: Cornell University Press, 1987), p. 3.

[101] On the third generation of human rights, see, for example, Kemal Baslar. The Concept of the Common Heritage of Mankind in International Law. (The Hague: Martinus Nijhoff Pub., 1998),

pp. 318–334.

[102] See Hans Danelius "The United Nations Fund for Torture Victims: The First Years of Activity" *Human Rights Quarterly* (May 1986): 294–305.

[103] The Declaration was adopted by the General Assembly without a global consensus. The developed countries (the major aid donors) did not support it and remain opposed to it.

[104] The global and regional human rights treaties have much in common. Their common features are:

1. They specify the particular obligations of all their state parties in respect of certain human rights and fundamental freedoms of all the persons within their territories and subject to their jurisdictions;
2. They contain general provisions applying to the protection of realization of all those rights;
3. They define and circumscribe the rights and freedoms concerned;
4. They establish institutions and protections for the international supervision, interpretation, and application of their substantive provisions.

[105] Within Europe, the European Union and the Organization for Security and Co-operation in Europe (OSCE) also provide human rights protection mechanisms.

[106] The Committee is composed of a number of members equal to that of the State parties. It is composed of independent experts in the fields of law, prison administration, medicine, psychiatry, sociology, etc. See for details, Antonio Cassese. "A New Approach to Human Rights: The European Convention for the Prevention of Torture" *American Journal of International Law* 83 (1989): 128–153; Malcolm Evans and Rod Morgan. "The European Convention for the Prevention of Torture: Operational Practice" *International and Comparative Law Quarterly* 4 (July 1992): 590–614.

[107] The Inter-American Convention to Prevent and Punish Torture was signed at Cartagena de Indias, Colombia, on December 9, 1985 and went into force on February 28, 1987. The Inter-American Convention on the Forced Disappearance of Persons was adopted at Belem do Para on March 29, 1991 and went into force on June 9, 1994. The Inter-American Convention on the Prevention, Punishment and Eradication of Violence Against Women was adopted at Belem do Para, Brasil on June 9, 1994.

[108] Imre Szabo "Historical Foundations of Human Rights and Subsequent Development" in Karel Vasak, ed. The International Dimensions of Human Rights. (Westport, CT: Greenwood Press, 1982), p. 23.

[109] Theo van Boven, "Strengthening Un Human Rights Capacity," Working Paper I, Seminar on Human Rights in the United Nations, Geneva, 8–10 Sept 1986.

[110] See Daniel P. Moynihan "The politics of human rights" *Commentary*, 64:2 (August 1977): 19–26.

[111] Laurie S. Wiseberg. "Access to United Nations Human Rights Documentation" *Human Rights Quarterly* (1997), p. 351.

[112] The reporting procedure is laid down in Article 40 CCPR, Article 17 CESCR, Article 9 CERD, Article 18 CEDAW, Article 19 CAT, and in Article 44 CRC. The reporting procedure requires state parties to the human rights treaties to submit periodic reports on the implementation of the obligation laid down in the treaty and the problems they encounter. The reporting procedure was meant to serve a forum in which a "constructive dialogue" could take place between governments and independent experts on the implementation of the standards. The reporting procedure offers state parties the opportunity to identify problems and to search for solutions. The treaty bodies provide "general comments" or "general recommendations" in response to state reports. See United Nation. Manual on Human Rights Reporting. (Geneva: the UN Human Rights Center, 1991).

[113] Katarina Tomasevski. Development Aid and Human Rights Revisited. (New York: Pinter Pub., 1993). In 1985 there were 384 overdue reports, in 1986, 460. Reporting obligations of States parties to United Nations conventions on human rights, Reports of the Secretary-General, U.N. Doc. A/41/510, 11 August 1986.

[114] Ann Bayefsky, "Making the Human Rights Treaties Work," in Louis Henkin and John Lawrence Hargrove, ed. Human Rights: An Agenda for the Next Century. (Washington, D.C.: The American Society of International Law, 1994), p. 239.

[115] Whereas the International Covenant on Civil and Political Rights (ICCPR) and the American Convention make the inter-state complaint procedures optional for state parties, the European Convention and the African Charter make it compulsory.

[116] See, for example, Denmark, the Netherlands, Norway and Sweden vs. Greece in 1967 in European human rights system in A.H. Robertson and J.G. Merrills. Human Rights in the World: An Introduction to the Study of the International Protection of Human Rights, 4th ed. (Manchester: Manchester University Press, 1996), p. 136–138.

[117] The individual petition is subject to the state complained of having made a declaration recognizing the competence of the treaty body to receive and consider such communications. If such a declaration has not been notified by a state, the treaty body has no authority to hear a petition against the state.

[118] 22 Trial of Major War Criminals, p. 579 (1948).

119 G.A. Res. 217B (III), U.N. doc. A/810, at 77 (1948).

120 Presently membership of the Commission is allocated 15 for Africa, 12 for Asia, 11 for Latin America and Caribbean, 5 for East Europe, and 10 for the West and they serve as state representatives.

121 ECOSOC Res. 1235 (XLII), 42 U.N. ESCOR Supp. No. 1, at 17, U.N. Doc. E/4393 (1967).

122 ECOSOC Res. 1503 (XLVIII), 48 U.N. ESCOR Supp. No. 1A, at 8, U.N. Doc. E/4832.Add.1 (1970). For in-depth analysis of the 1503 Procedure, see M.E. Tardu, "United Nations Response to Gross Violations of Human Rights: The 1503 Procedure" *Santa Clara Law Review* 20 (Summer 1980): 559–601.

123 Henry Steiner and Philip Alston. International Human Rights in Context: Law, Politics, Morals. (Oxford: Clarendon Press, 1996), p. 387.

124 Philip Alston. "The Commission on Human Rights" in Philip Alston, ed. The United Nations and Human Rights: A Critical Appraisal. (Oxford: Clarendon Press, 1992), p. 146.

125 Manfred Nowak. "Proposals for Improving the UN Human Rights Programme" *Netherlands Quarterly of Human Rights* (1993), p. 156.

126 From 1992 to 1996, the Special Rapporteur on Summary and Arbitrary Executions, for example, made 818 urgent appeals on behalf of more than 6,500 person to 91 different countries and received nearly half of the instances.

127 M.T. Kamminga. "The Thematic Procedures of the UN Commission on Human Rights" *Netherlands International Law Review* (1987), p.322.

128 See Peter Haver "The United Nations Sub-Commission on the Prevention of Discrimination and the Protection of Minorities" *Columbia Journal of Transnational Law* 21 (1982): 103–134; Theo van Boven "The United Nations Sub-Commission on Prevention of Discrimination and Protection of Minorities" *Netherlands Quarterly of Human Rights* (1989): 464–471; Inis L. Claude, Jr. "The Nature and Status of the Sub-Commission on Prevention of Discrimination and Protection of Minorities" *International Organization* (May 1951): 300–312.

129 Laura Reanda "The Commission on the Status of Women" in Philip Alston, ed. The United Nations and Human Rights: A Critical Appraisal. (Oxford: Clarendon Press, 1992), p. 301.

130 See Felice Gaer. Non-Governmental Organizations and the UN High Commissioner for Human Rights, April 1997.

131 The Division of Human Rights was renamed the Center for Human Rights in 1982. The Center was consolidated into a single Office of the United Nations High Commissioner for Human Rights (OHCHR) in September 1997. The Office has staff of some 200 and a limited annual budget of about $200 million, about 1.7 percent of the United Nations regular budget. As of 1999, the top seven contributors to the UN general

budget are the US (25%), Japan (19.98%), Germany (9.08%), France (6.54%), Italy (5.43%), the UK (5.09%), and Canada (2.75%). Collectively they account for more than 73.87% of the regular UN budget.

132 Torkel Opsahl. "The Human Rights Committee" in Philip Alston, ed. The United Nations and Human Rights: A Critical Appraisal. (Oxford: Clarendon Press, 1992), p. 369.

133 The inter-state procedure became available in 1979, when ten states had made the necessary declarations. A number of states have made it clear that they will never accept this optional procedure, as they are opposed to the basic principle on which it rests. It has been argued that it is hard to believe that many governments, other than those of democracies with genuine guarantees of freedom of expression and association, free elections, protection against arbitrary arrest and due process of law, will be willing to expose themselves to the possibility of complaints by other states that they are violating civil and political rights. Therefore, the prospects of inter-state procedures being used in practice are not substantial.

134 Both the complainant and object state must have made declarations to recognize the competence of the Committee. The Committee seeks to resolve the issue and, if it is not successful, it may appoint, with the consent of states, an ad hoc Conciliation Commission. Admissibility requirements of the individual communication include:

1. the communication is not anonymous;
2. the individual claims to be a victim of a violation by that state party of any of the rights set forth in the Covenant;
3. the communication is not an abuse of the right to submit a communications under the Protocol;
4. the same matter is not being examined under another procedure of international investigation or settlement.

135 See Roberta Jacobson "The Committee on the Elimination of Discrimination against Women" in Philip Alston, ed. The United Nations and Human Rights: A Critical Appraisal. (Oxford: Clarendon Press, 1992), p. 452.

136 See American Bar Association (ABA), Washington, D.C. Draft recommendation adopted by the House of Delegates August 3–4, 1998. Recommendations towards consolidating into two committees the existing six UN committees currently monitoring UN human rights treaties. *Human Rights Law Journal* 20 (1999): 272–275.

137 Nicholas Valticos. "The International Labor Organization (ILO)" in Philip Alston, ed. The United Nations and Human Rights: A Critical Appraisal. (Oxford: Clarendon Press, 1992), p. 393.

[138] Virginia A. Leary "Lessons from the Experience of the International Labor Organization" in Philip Alston, ed. The United Nations and Human Rights: A Critical Appraisal. (Oxford: Clarendon Press, 1992), p. 619.

[139] List of Ratifications by Convention and by Country ILO, Geneva 87th Session 1999 ILO Conference Report III (Part II); Nicolas Valticos "The International Labour Organization (ILO) in Karel Vasak, ed The International Dimensions of Human Rights. Westport, CT: Greenwood Press, 1982), p. 367.

[140] See David Weissbrodt and Rose Farley. "The UNESCO Human Rights Procedure: An Evaluation" *Human Rights Quarterly* (1994), p. 397.

[141] Stephen P. Marks "The Complaint Procedure of the United Nations Educational, Scientific and Cultural Organization" in Hurst Hannum. Guide to International Human Rights Practice. 2nd ed. (Philadelphia: University of Pennsylvania Press, 1992), p. 86–98.

[142] A principle (interdependence) applicable to all human rights that whatever "generation" of human rights - first, second, or third - is involved, each generation is dependent upon every other generation. A principle (indivisibility) provides that all human rights together form a whole that cannot be divided into subsets. For example, the state cannot accept economic and social rights and not respect civil and political rights. A principle (interrelatedness) provides that all human rights are closely related to each other (e.g. the right to food, expression, movement, association, and the right to vote).

[143] In addition to the UN Charter provisions, in 1965 the Declaration on Inadmissibility of Intervention in Domestic Affairs of States and Protection of their Independence and Sovereignty and in 1970 the Declaration on Principles of International Law Concerning Friendly Relations and Co-operation Among States in Accordance with the Charter of the United Nations were adopted at the UN. The 1970 Declaration makes clear that no state or group of states has the right to intervene, directly or indirectly, for any reason whatever, in the internal or external affairs of any other state.

[144] See L. Oppenheim, International Law: A Treatise, vol. I: Peace, 8th ed. by H. Lauterpacht, (London, Longmans Green & Co, 1955), p. 305. Oppenheim-Lauterpacht define intervention as "dictatorial interference by a state in the affairs of another state for the purpose of maintaining or altering the actual condition of things."

[145] H. Lauterpacht, ed. International Law, A Treaties by L. Oppenheim, vol. I, Peace, 8th ed. (London: Longmans Green & Co., 1955), p. 312.

[146] Sean D. Murphy. Humanitarian Intervention: The United Nations in an Evolving World Order. (Philadelphia: University of Pennsylvania, 1996), p. 296–297.

[147] Kurt Mills "Reconstructing Sovereignty: A Human Rights Perspective" *Netherlands Quarterly of Human Rights* (September 1997): 267–290.

[148] See Sei Fujii v. California, 217P. 2d 481 (1950), rehearing denied, 218 P. 2d 595 (Cal. App. 1950), 38 Cal. 2d 718, 242 P. 2d 617 (1952). Quincy Wright "National Courts and Human Rights - the Fujii Case" 45 *AJIL* 62 (1951).

[149] The Bricker Amendment states:

> Section 1:
> A provision of a treaty which conflicts with this constitution shall not be any force or effect.
> Section 2:
> A treaty shall become effective as international law in the United States only through legislation, which would be valid in the absence of a treaty.
> Section 3:
> Congress shall have power to regulate all executive and other agreements with any foreign power or international organization. All such agreements shall be subject to the limitations imposed on treaties by this article.
> Section 4:
> Congress shall have power to enforce this article by appropriate legislation.

See Natalie Hevener Kaufman. Human Rights Treaties and the Senate: A History of Opposition. (Chapel Hill, N.C.: The University of North Carolina Press, 1990), p. 94–116; Natalie Hevener Kaufman and David Whiteman. "Opposition to human rights treaties in the United States: The Legacy of the Bricker Amendment" *Human Rights Quarterly* (August 1988): 309–338.

[150] "Human Rights in the World Community: A Call for U.S. Leadership," Reports of the Subcommittee on International Organizations and Movements, Committee on Foreign Affairs, 93rd Cong., 2d Sess, (1974).

[151] The concept of "gross violation of internationally recognized human rights" is defined as "... torture or cruel, inhuman, or degrading treatment or punishment, prolonged detention without charges and trial, causing the disappearance of persons by the abduction and clandestine detention of those persons, and other flagrant denial of the right to life, liberty, or the security of persons (Sec. 116 (a) and Sec. 502B (d)(1).

[152] International Security Assistance and Arms Export Control Act, Pub. L. No. 94–329, 90 Stat. 729 (1976) (codified at 22 U.S.C. Sec. 2151 n(b) (1982).

[153] See Henry Kissinger "Continuity and Change in American Foreign Policy" in Abdul Aziz Said, ed. Human Rights and World Order. (New York: Praeger Pub., 1978).

[154] Transcript of President Carter's Address at the United Nations, New York Times, March 18, 1977, p. A10.

[155] "Report to Congress on Arms Transfer Policy," June 30, 1977, Senate Foreign Relations Committee, Arms Transfer Policy, July 1977.

[156] Cyrus R. Vance "Law Day Address on Human Rights Policy," delivered at the University of Georgia's Law School, Athens, Georgia, April 30, 1977.

[157] The first State Department's annual Country Reports on Human Rights Practices was submitted to Congress by the Reagan administration in 1982. Department of State, Country Reports on Human Rights Practices for 1981, 97th Cong., 2nd Sess. 2 (1982). See Judith Innes de Neufville "Human Rights Reporting as a Policy Tool: An Examination of the State Department Country Reports" Human Rights Quarterly (Nov. 1986): 681–699. In 1993, the State Department reorganized the Bureau of Human Rights and Humanitarian Affairs and renamed it as the Bureau of Democracy, Human Rights and Labor.

[158] See D. Cingranelli and T. Pasquarello. "Human rights practices and the distribution of U.S. foreign aid to Latin American countries" American Journal of Political Science (1986): 539–563;
D. Carleton and M. Stohl. "The role of human rights in U.S. foreign assistance policy: A critique and reappraisal" American Journal of Political Science (1987): 1002–1018. The punitive approach is defined as that the US has used development aid and human rights to punish foes and opponents discriminately.

[159] President Franklin Delano Roosevelt stated by referring to one of the Latin American dictators as "He may be an SOB, but he's our SOB."

[160] Jean Kirkpatrick. "Dictatorship and Double Standard" Commentary 68 (November 1979).

[161] Daniel P. Moynihan. "The Politics of Human Rights" Commentary (Aug. 1977).

[162] One explicit example of this is the introduction to the Department of State "Reports on Human Rights Practices for 1981," Washington, 1981. This reads: "Internationally recognized human rights can be grouped into broad categories: first, the right to be free from governmental violations of the integrity of the person...second, the right to enjoy civil and political rights." There is no mention of economic, social and cultural rights.

[163] As of May 2002, the U.S. has not ratified the International Covenant on Economic, Social and Cultural Rights, the Convention on the Elimination of All Forms of Discrimination Against Women, the American Convention on Human Rights, and the Convention on the Rights of the Child.

[164] Lawyers Committee for Human Rights. Human Rights and U.S. Foreign Policy: Report and Recommendations, 1992. (New York: Lawyers Committee for Human Rights, 1992).

[165] Ministry of Foreign Affairs, A World of Difference. A New Framework for Development Co-Operation in the 1990s. Public Document, The Hague, March 1991.

[166] Human Rights and Foreign Policy. The Hague: Ministry of Foreign Affairs of the Kingdom of the Netherlands, 1979, p. 105.

[167] See Helge Kjekhus "Development Aid and Human Rights - Some Observations by the Norwegian Ministry of Development Co-Operation" in Lars Adam Rehf & Claus Gulmann, ed. Human Rights in Domestic Law and Development Assistance Policies of the Nordic Countries. (Dordrecht: Martinus Nijhoff Pub., 1989), p. 30.

[168] Canadian International Development Assistance: To Benefit a Better World. Response of the Government of Canada to the Report by the Standing Committee on External Affairs and International Trade, Ottawa, September 1987.

[169] Gaimusho Keizai Kyoryoku Kyoku [Department of Economic Co-operation, Ministry of Foreign Affairs], Wagakuni no Seifu Kaihatsu Enjo [Japan Official Development Assistance], (1991), p. 58.

[170] See Human Rights Watch World Report 1992 (New York: Human Rights Watch, 1992).

[171] Winegard Report: Report of the Standing Committee on External Affairs and International Trade of the Canadian Parliament on Canada's Official Development Assistance Policies and Programmes, Ottawa, 1987.

[172] See, for example, David Arase, Buying Power: The Political Economy of Japan's Foreign Aid (Boulder, CO: Lynne Reinner, 1995); Margee Ensign, Doing Good or Doing Well? Japan's Foreign Aid Program (New York: Columbia University Press, 1992).

[173] Marie Soderberg. The Business of Japanese Foreign Aid: Five case studies from Asia (London: Routledge, 1996), p. vii

[174] While all four organizations are often referred to collectively as the "World Bank Group," it is the IBRD which is generally referred to as the World Bank.

[175] David Gillies. "Human Rights, Democracy, and 'Good Governance' Stretching the World Bank's Policy Frontiers," a paper presented at the International Conference on Human Rights in a New World Order, Prague, Czech Republic, June 9–12, 1992.

[176] According to Far Eastern Economic Review, 11 November 1991, Burma's trade Minister David Abel received a tongue-lashing from Attila Karaosmanoglu, the World Bank official in charge of the Asian region, at the IMF/World Bank conference in Bangkok in mid-October [1991]. Karaosmanoglu castigated the ruling State Law and Order Restoration Council (SLORC) for its human rights record, its excessive military expenditure and its disregard for the environment. Burma has neither sought nor

received any assistance from the World Bank or the IMF since the SLORC took power in 1988.

[177] The principal provision of the IBRD's Article of Agreement is Article IV, Section 10, which provides:

> The Bank and its officers shall not interfere in the political affairs of any member; nor shall they be influenced in their decisions by the political character of the member or members concerned. Only economic considerations shall be relevant to their decisions, and these considerations shall be weighed impartially in order to achieve the purposes stated in Article I.

[178] David Gillies. "Human Rights, Democracy, and 'Good Governance' Stretching the World Bank's Policy Frontiers," a paper presented at the International Conference on Human Rights in a New World Order, Prague, Czech Republic, June 9–12, 1992, p. 4.

[179] Louis Henkin and John Lawrence Hargrove, ed. Human Rights: An Agenda for the Next Century. (Washington, D.C.: The American Society of International Law, 1994), p. 383.

[180] R.J. Vincent. Human Rights and International Relations. (New York: Cambridge University Press, 1986), p. 125.

[181] Figures quoted by Pictet, "Armed conflicts - laws and customs," I.C.J. Review, 1969, p. 30.

NOTES TO CHAPTER IV

[1] International regimes are defined as "principles, norms, rules, and decision-making procedures around which actor expectations converge in a given issue-area." Stephen D. Krasner, "Structural Causes and Regime consequences: Regimes as Intervening variables," *International Organizations* 36 (Spring 1982), p. 185.

[2] Virginia A. Leary "The Asian Region and the International Human Rights Movement" in Claude Welch, Jr. and Virginia A. Leary, ed. Asian Perspectives on Human Rights. (Boulder, CO: Westview Press, 1990), p. 13.

[3] On cultural relativism, see, for example, Douglas Lee Donoho. "Relativism Versus Universalism in Human Rights: The Search for Meaningful Standards." *Stanford Journal of International Law* (1991): 345–391; Fernando R. Teson. "International Human Rights and Cultural Relativism" in Richard Pierre Claude and Burns H. Weston. Human Rights in the World Community: Issues and Action, 2nd ed. (Philadelphia: University of Pennsylvania, 1992), p. 42–54; Jack Donnelly. Universal Human Rights in Theory and Practice. (Ithaca, N.Y.: Cornell University Press, 1989); Alison Dundes Renteln. International Human Rights:

Universalism Versus Relativism. (London: Sage Pub., 1990) and Abdullahi
Ahmed An-Naim. Human Rights in Cross-Cultural Perspectives: A Quest
for Consensus. (Philadelphia: University of Pennsylvania, 1992).

[4] The European Convention on Human Rights was signed on November 4,
1950 and entered into force on September 3, 1953. Some of the studies on
the Convention include A.H. Robertson and J.G. Merrills, Human Rights
in Europe (Dobbs Ferry, NY: Oceana Pub, 1963); P. Van Dijk and G.J.H.
Van Hoof, Theory and Practice of the European Convention on Human
Rights, 2nd ed. Thomas Buergenthal and Louis Sohn. International
Protection of Human Rights. (New York: The Bobbs-Merrill Co., 1973).

[5] The Charter was opened for signature on October 18, 1961 and entered
into force on February 26, 1965. As of March 1995, 20 States were parties
to the Charter. The Charter also established a regional European system
(i.e. the Committee of Experts, the Governmental Committee of the Social
Charter, the Consultative Assembly, and the Committee of Ministers) for
the protection of economic and social rights guaranteed in the Charter.

[6] Civil and Political rights covered by the Convention include protection of
physical well-being (right to life, prohibition of torture, inhuman or
degrading treatment or punishment, prohibition of slavery, servitude,
forced or compulsory labor); protection of freedom (freedom of movement,
right to freedom and security); protection of the right to justice (right to be
granted effective remedy, right to a fair hearing, rights of the accused); protection of privacy (right to marry, right to respect for private and family
life, right to respect for one's home and correspondence);protection of
intellectual activity (freedom of thought, conscience and religion, freedom
of expression, right to education and right of parents over the education
and teaching of their children); protection of political activity (freedom of
assembly and association, free elections) protection of economic activity
(right to enjoy one's possessions); prohibition of discrimination on whatever grounds.

[7] Economic, social and cultural rights the Charter has guaranteed are not
legally binding per se. Those rights are, right to an occupation, right to just
conditions of work, right to safe and healthy working conditions, right to
fair remuneration, right to freedom of association, right to bargain collectively, right of children and young persons to protection, right of employed
women to protection, right to benefit from social security, right to voca-
tional training, right to health protection, right to social security, right to
social and medical assistance, right to benefit from social welfare services,
right of disabled persons to protection, right of the family to social, and
economic protection, right of mothers and children to social and economic protection, right to work in a country other than one's own, right of
migrant workers and their families to protection and assistance.

8 See Hurst Hannum. "Minorities, Indigenous Peoples, and Self-Determination" in Louis Henkin and John Lawrence Hargrove, ed. Human Rights: An Agenda for the Next Century (Washington, D.C: The American Society of International Law, 1994), p. 1–16.

9 Manfred Nowak "Future Strategies for the International Protection and Realization of Human Rights" in Asbjorn Eide and Jan Helgesen, eds. The Future of Human Rights Protection in a Changing World. (Oslo: Norwegian University Press, 1991), p. 63.

10 A.H. Robertson. Human Rights in the World, 2nd ed. (Manchester: Manchester University Press, 1982), p. 81.

11 Henry Steiner and Philip Alston. International Human Rights in Context: Law, Politics, Morals. (Oxford: Clarendon Press, 1996), p. 572.

12 The Council of Europe was established in 1949. By March 1995 the Council of Europe has 34 Member States. After the Cold War, Finland, Hungary, Poland, Bulgaria, Estonia, Lithuania, Slovania, the Czech Republic, Slovakia, Romania, and Latvia joined the Council of Europe. Yet the Convention had 30 parties because four members of the Council of Europe - Andorra, Estonia, Latvia and Lithuania had signed the Convention but not yet ratified. The Council is composed of three organs, a Committee of Foreign Ministers, a Consultative Assembly, and the Secretariat. The aim of the Council is "to achieve a greater unity between its members for the purpose of safeguarding and realizing the ideals and principles which are their common heritage." In Europe there are two other political organizations, that is, the European Union (EU) and the Organization for Security and Co-operation in Europe (OSCE). The EU has such auxiliary institutions as European Parliament and European Court of Justice.

13 See Stefan Trechsel "Towards the Merger of the Supervisory Organs: Seeking a Way Out of the Deadlock." *Human Rights Law Journal* 8 (1987): 11–23.

14 See Hans-Jurgen Bartsch "The supervisory functions of the Committee of Ministers under Article 54– a postscript to Luedicke-Belkacem-Koc" in Gerard J. Wiarda Protecting Human Rights: The European Dimension (Berlin: Carl Heymanns Verlag KG, 1988), p. 47–54.

15 The European Court often hears cases in a chamber of seven judges and the plenary sessions of the Court are convened at least once a year. The European Court sits at Strasbourg. In Europe, national courts within the state parties to the Convention increasingly turn to the case-law of the European Court when deciding on a human rights issue and apply the standards and principles developed by the Commission and Court. In both procedures, in order to accept the jurisdiction of the Court, a state must file the declaration to accept the Court's jurisdiction.

[16] Inter-state complaints are not subject to the admissibility requirements prescribed for private petitions other than the obligation to exhaust domestic remedies. As of March 1995 eighteen inter-state application had been lodged.

[17] It must be noted that this is not always the case. For example, the proceedings, which were instigated against Greece and Turkey by various Scandinavian nations were compelled by humanitarian considerations. See Denmark, Norway, Sweden, Netherlands v. Greece in Sohn, Louis and Thomas Buergenthal. International Protection of Human Rights. (New York: The Bobbs-Merrill Co., 1973), p.1059–1090.

[18] The requirement that the petitioner must be "a victim of a violation" has been interpreted by the European Court to mean that "an individual applicant should claim to have been actually affected by the violation he alleges." See, as an example of individual petition; Lawless v. Ireland in Sohn, Louis and Thomas Buergenthal. International Protection of Human Rights. (New York: The Bobbs-Merrill Co., 1973), p. 1020–1028.

[19] The most frequent reason for the rejection of complaints is that the applicant had no grounds for invoking international remedies, given the state of protection secured for his or her rights under domestic law.

[20] The requirement that a petition not be "manifestly ill-founded" calls for a determination whether the petition states a prima facie case. The Commission rejects petitions as manifestly ill-founded after concluding that the application "does not disclose ... any appearance of a violation" by the respondent state of the right involved by the applicant or petitions are solely motivated by political consideration.

[21] The "abuse of the right of petition" refers to conduct such as knowingly making false or groundless allegations, using abusive and defamatory language about the respondent government, or intentionally breaking the rule of confidentiality applicable to the proceedings.

[22] See David Weissbrodt and James McCarthy. "Fact-Finding by International Nongovernmental Human Rights Organizations" *Virginia Journal of International* Law 22 (1981), p. 31–37.

[23] Ratification of the Eleventh Protocol by state parties to the European Convention for the Protection of Human Rights and Fundamental Freedoms allows individuals and states to take a case directly to the European Court of Human Rights.

[24] See Marek Antoni Nowicki. "NGOs before the European Commission and the Court of Human Rights" *Netherlands Quarterly of Human Rights* 14 (Sept. 1996), p. 292.

[25] Between 1981 and 1993, the European Commission received a tenfold increase in communications. See Steiner and Alston, *op.cit.* p. 590. Tom Zwart argues in his work The Admissibility of Human Rights Petitions: The Case Law of the European Commission of Human Rights and the

Human Rights Committee (Dordrecht: Martinus Nijhoff Pub., 1994) that to enable the court to cope with its workload, the Convention should be amended to introduce a form of discretionary jurisdiction, comparable to the certiorari review. In addition, the members of the court should be authorized to hire personal assistants to assist them in selecting cases for review.

26 The expression "victim of its own success" was used by Andrew Drzemczewski in "The Need for a Racial Overhaul" 143 *New Law Journal* 1266 (1993).

27 According to Tom Zwart. *op.cit*, p. 1, in 1980, 2,225 new petitions were brought. The number skyrocketed to 9,323 in 1993. However, approximately 90 percent of all registered petitions are found inadmissible by the Commission.

28 The Organization of American States (OAS) was established in 1948. The Charter of the OAS signed in Bogota, Columbia in May 1948 states that: "the historic mission of America is to offer to man a land of liberty, and a favorable environment for the development of his personality and the realization of his just aspirations." The OAS is a regional inter-governmental organizations consisting of 35 members. The purposes of the Organization include: strengthen peace and security, to ensure the peaceful settlement of disputes, to provide for common action in the event of aggression, and to promote economic, social and cultural development.

29 The Ninth International Conference of American States adopted the Declaration in May 1948, seven months before the adoption of the Universal Declaration of Human Rights. The American Declaration of the Rights and Duties of Man (1948) was adopted as non-binding resolution, which included civil and political as well as economic, social and cultural rights. The Declaration contains ten articles of duties and twenty-eight articles of rights. The Inter-American Commission held that the Declaration established standards of conduct that were binding on all members of states of the OAS. The Commission also held that the Declaration has become an authoritative interpretation of the human rights provisions of the Charter.

30 The American Convention on Human Rights was adopted in 1969 by the Organization of American States (OAS) and entered into force in July 1978. The American Convention is patterned on the European Convention in terms of institutional framework that is quite similar to its European counterpart. The Convention contains 82 articles. In 1988 the OAS adopted an Additional Protocol to the American Convention on Human Rights in the Area of Economic, Social and Cultural Rights. It has received four ratifications and has not entered into force. The rights recognized in the Protocol are similar to those in the International Economic, Social and Cultural Rights. The Protocol does not recognize the right to adequate

housing or to adequate standard of living, but it does include the right to a healthy environment, the right of the persons with disabilities. Although the system of supervision relies primarily on reporting, the Protocol provides the right to petition when trade union rights or the right to education are violated by action directly attributable to a State Party.

[31] For example, Article 32 of American Convention states:

1. Every person has responsibilities to his family, his community, and mankind.

2. The rights of each person are limited by the rights of others, by the security of all, and by the just demands of the general welfare, in a democratic society.

[32] Cecilia Medina. "The Inter-American Commission on Human Rights and the Inter-American Court of Human Rights: Reflections on a Joint Venture." *Human Rights Quarterly* 12 (November 1990), p. 442

[33] Medina, *op.cit.* p. 448 The Commission has an annual budget (1995 figures) of $1,734,000. Of that about $1,000,000 is spent on salaries and other fixed expenses, leaving only a little over $400,000 to cover meetings of the Commissioners, on-site visits, witness and expert expenses and the preparation of reports. Medina notes that many states keep the Commission starved for funding.

[34] Ibid.

[35] It could hold its sessions in any member country of the OAS, with the prior consent of the state concerned when a majority of the Court considers it desirable.

[36] Advisory opinions are not legally binding. Nevertheless, the Court is a judicial institution whose purpose is the application and interpretation of the American Convention on Human Rights. Therefore, the advisory opinion possesses legal authority from its character as a judicial institution. Any OAS member state, the General Assembly, all OAS organs, the Permanent Council, and the Commission have standing to request advisory opinions.

[37] For details of CEJIL's works, visit website: www.derechos.org.

[38] See Tom Farer. "The Rise of the Inter-American Human Rights Regime: No Longer a Unicorn, Not Yet an Ox" *Human Rights Quarterly* 19 (1977), p. 544–545.

[39] The Charter entered into force in 1986. As of January 1995, the Charter had been ratified by 49 states.

[40] People's rights include the right of peoples to self-determination, the right to development, the right to peace and the right to satisfactory environment. The right to development is formulated in Article 22 (1) as follows: "All peoples shall have the right to their economic, social, and cultural development with due regard to their freedom and identity and in the equal enjoyment of the common heritage of mankind."

[41] The African Charter considers duties as important. Article 27 (2) states that "the rights and freedoms of each individual shall be exercised with due regard to the rights of others, collective security, morality and common interest."

[42] Keba M'Baye. "Les Dimensions Internationales des Droits de l'homme (Paris 1978), p. 602.

[43] Makau wa Mutua. "The African Human Rights System in a Comparative Perspective: the Need for Urgent Reformation" *The Nairobi Law Monthly* 44 (July 1993), p. 28.

[44] The solidarity rights include the right of all peoples to equality without domination of a people by another; the right of all peoples to existence and self-determination; the right of all peoples to freely dispose of their wealth and natural resources; the right of all peoples to their economic, social and cultural development, including equal enjoyment of the common heritage of mankind; the right of all peoples to national and international peace and security and the right of all peoples to a general satisfactory environment favorable to their development. On the right to development, see Danilo Turk "Development and Human Rights" in Louis Henkin and John Lawrence Hargrove, ed. Human Rights: An Agenda for the Next Century (Washington, D.C: The American Society of International Law, 1994), p. 167–182; Hector Gros Espiell "The Right of Development as a Human Right" in   Richard Pierre Claude and Burns H. Weston. Human Rights in the World Community: Issues and Action, 2nd ed. (Philadelphia: University of Pennsylvania, 1992), p. 167–174; John O'Manique. "Human Rights and Development" *Human Rights Quarterly* 14 (1992): 202–230 and Frances Stewart."Basic Needs Strategies, Human Rights and the Right to Development" *Human Rights Quarterly* 11(1989): 347–374.

[45] The substantive provisions of the African Charter contain "clawback" clauses that permit a state to restrict rights to the extent permitted by domestic law. The "claw back" means one that permits, in normal circumstances, breach of an obligation for a specified number of public reasons. It, thus, differs from a derogation clause "which allows suspension or breach of certain obligations in circumstances of war or public emergency.

[46] The members are chosen among African personalities of the highest reputation, known for their high morality, integrity, impartiality and competence in matters of human and peoples' rights.

[47] The function of the African Commission are:

1. to promote human and peoples' rights and in particular:
    a. to collect documents, undertake studies and researches on African problems in the field of human and people's rights, organize seminars, symposia and conferences, disseminate information, encourage national and local institutions concerned with

human and people's rights, and should the case arise, give its
views or make recommendations to Governments.

    b. to formulate and lay down, principles and rules aimed at solving
legal problems relating to human and people's rights and fundamental freedoms upon which African Governments may base
their legislations.

    c. to co-operate with other African and international institutions
concerned with the promotion and protection of human and
people's rights.

2. to ensure the protection of human and people's rights under conditions laid down by the present Charter.

3. to interpret all the provisions of the present charter at the request of
a State Party, an institution of the OAU or an African organization recognized by the OAU.

4. perform any other tasks which may be entrusted to it by the Assembly
of Heads of State and Government.

[48] Guidelines for National Periodic Reports (AFR/COM/HPR.5(VI) (1989)
specify both the form and content of reports.

[49] Communications indicate authors; are not written in a language that is
insulting or disparaging to the state or the OAU; are not incompatible with
the OAU Charter and African Charter; are sent after the petitioner
exhausts local remedies; and do not deal with a matter that has already
been settled by the states concerned.

[50] In 1990 the Commission opened a special account into which voluntary
donation may be made. Support has so far come from the Danish Agency
for International Development, the Swedish International Development
Agency and the Raoul Wallenberg Institute of Human Rights and
Humanitarian Law, Lund.

[51] Steiner and Alston, *op.cit.* p. 689.

[52] The Protocol for the Establishment of an African Court on Human and
Peoples' Rights was adopted in February 1998 by the OAU Assembly and
opened for signature. The Court will come into effect once 15 countries
have signed the Protocol.

[53] The judges are elected by the OAU Assembly of Heads of States and
Governments and are jurists of high moral character and of recognized
practical, judicial or academic competence and experience in the field of
human and peoples' rights. Judges are eligible for re-election once.

[54] See Makau Mutua. "The African Human Rights Court: A Two-Legged
Stool?" *Human Rights Quarterly* 21 (1999), p. 355.

[55] As of April 1996, the Commission granted 183 NGOs observer status.

[56] See complete lists of NGOs in Appendix C in U. Oji Umozurike. The
African Charter on Human and Peoples' Rights. (The Hague: Martinus
Nijhoff Pub., 1997).

⁵⁷ In Europe and Africa, by ratifying the Conventions, a state accepts the jurisdiction of the Commission to receive complaints from other state parties alleging a violation of the treaty. On the contrary, the Inter-American Commission may deal with inter-state complaints, only if both states have recognized the inter-state jurisdiction of the Commission in addition to ratifying the Convention. The African Commission may examine communications from private individuals, non-governmental institutions and groups only if the OAU Assembly of Heads of State and Government so request and only if a majority of the Commission so decides.

⁵⁸ See Hans Christian Kruger and Carl Aage Norgaad "Reflections concerning friendly settlement under the European Convention on Human Rights" in Gerard J. Wiarda Protecting Human Rights: The European Dimension (Berlin: Carl Heymanns Verlag KG, 1988), p. 329–334.

⁵⁹ The European Court consists of thirty-four judges, whereas the Inter-American Court has seven judges. The European Convention does not require that the judges and Commission members be nationals of the Member States of the Council of Europe.

⁶⁰ The Court can render advisory opinions only at the request of the Committee of Ministers.

⁶¹ Other worst rated countries include Afghanistan, Bhutan, Burma, Burundi, Cuba, Equatorial Guinea, Iraq, Libya, Saudi Arabia, Somalia, Sudan, Syria, Turkmenistan and Vietnam. See Roger Kaplan, ed. Freedom in the World: The Annual Survey of Political Rights & Civil Liberties 1997–1998. (London: Transaction Pub., 1998), p. 6.

⁶² See Thomas Franck. "The Emerging Right to Democratic Governance" *American Journal of International Law* 86 (1992): 46–91.

⁶³ Ibid. p. 88.

⁶⁴ See Robert Chambers "North Korean Human Rights: A View from the International Community" in Sung-Chul Choi, ed. International Community and Human Rights in North Korea. (Seoul: The Institute of Unification Policy, 1996).

⁶⁵ See Lawrence Beer "Comparative Perspectives on Human Rights in Korea" in William Shaw, ed. Human Rights in Korea: Historical and Policy Perspectives (Cambridge: Harvard University Press, 1991), p. 265–282.

⁶⁶ Amnesty International Report 1999 (London: Amnesty International Pub., 1998), p. 226.

⁶⁷ Soh Young-A. "Is the Budding Civic Movement for Real or a Bubble?" *Korea Focus* 7 (May/June 1999), p. 94.

⁶⁸ The Korean peninsula was annexed by Japan between 1910 and 1945. During this colonial period, a large number of Koreans were brought to Japan. Today Korean residents represent approximately 0.6 percent of the Japanese population and 80 percent of resident aliens. Although the major-

ity of Koreans are born and brought up in Japan, they are classified as "resident aliens" as citizenship is granted on the basis of Japanese parentage.
Korean residents are subject to various forms of entrenched social discrimination, especially in employment and marriage. Among others, the legal
obligation to carry an alien registration card and to be fingerprinted have
been leading concerns among permanent resident aliens in Japan.
According to the Alien Registration Law of 1988, fingerprinting became a
one time requirement rather than having to be renewed at five-year inter-
vals as had been the case up till then. Communications alleging violations
of the human rights of Koreans in Japan were filed with the United Nations
under the ECOSOC Resolution 1503 procedure in 1979. The 1503 procedure provides a mechanism to deal with "consistent patterns of gross and
attested violations of human rights and fundamental freedoms."
Communications were first filed by a group in Japan in 1979 and later by
the International Human Rights Law Group, in Washington, D.C. Thus,
Japan became one of the few developed countries whose situations was
taken up by the 1503 procedure. Korean residents constitute 82 percent of
resident aliens in Japan.

[69] Burakumin are descendants of feudal-era outcasts and take up approximately 2.5 percent of the population. They live in roughly 6,000 Buraku
hamlets. In 1871 the Meiji government passed the Emancipation Edict,
which officially abolished discrimination against Burakumin. In 1922 an
organized liberation movement called the Suiheisha (Leveler's Association)
was founded and they called for equal rights and equal treatment. After
World War II the Buraku Liberation League was formed. They adopted
Dowa (integration) measures, which aimed at improving living conditions
of Buraku communities.

[70] See "Case Study: Japan" in Eschel M. Rhoodie. Discrimination Against
Women: A Global Survey of the Economic, Educational, Social and
Political Status of Women. (Jefferson, NC: McFarland & Co., 1989),
p.407. Occupational segregation in Japan is evident from the fact that only
6.4 percent of all scientists are women, 2.4 percent engineers, 9.3 percent
lawyers, and 6.2 percent managers. The position of women in Japan continue to reflect deep-seated traditional values in a patriarchal society, which
assign woman a subordinate role - "the structural embeddedness of sex
roles - man the worker, woman the housekeeper and mother." (Lebra,
1984). Condon observes that Japanese women's status is the lowest of all
industrial societies. Rhoodie observes that Japanese women are as much
subordinate to men as in any Muslim state (Rhoodie, 1989, p. 402). The
Equal Employment Opportunity Law was enacted in 1986, which was
aimed at eliminating sex discrimination in employment recruitment.
However, the law merely states that an employer should "endeavor" to
give women equal opportunity with men. There are no provisions and no

penalty for failure to enforce the law. In 1985 Japan ratified the UN Convention on the Elimination of Discrimination Against Women.

[71] International law recognizes several ways in which states confer nationality. Some states confer nationality at birth to individuals born within the territory (jus soli); while others confer it to individuals born of parents who are already nationals (jus sanguinis). Japan's Nationality Law is based on the latter principle. A child born in Japan of foreign parents does not acquire Japanese nationality. As a result, even though more than 80 percent of Koreans were born in Japan, they are considered aliens.

[72] Members of comfort women were not only Koreans but also Filipinos, Chinese, Indonesians, Burmese, Dutch, and Japanese and comfort stations existed in Japan, China, the Philippines, Indonesia, the then Malaya, Thailand, Burma, New Guinea, Hong Kong, Macao, the then French Indo-China and many of the Pacific islands. Enslaved women ranged in age from 13 to the mid 20s. Historians estimate that less than 30 percent of the comfort women survived the war. See George Hicks. The Comfort Women: Japan's Brutal Regime of Enforced Prostitution in the Second World War (New York: W.W. Norton & Co., 1995)

[73] Relief measures for war victims have been paid to Japanese nationals. The measures, however, have not been extended to Koeans and Taiwanese because the Relief Law for the Wounded, Sick, and Bereaved Because of War is interpreted as inapplicable to them. Therefore, Koreans and Taiwanese who fought for Japan as Japanese nationals have not been able to receive relief from any source.

Japanese government claims that the San Francisco Peace Treaty between Japan and the Allied Powers of 1951 and subsequent agreements completely settled all war claims and absolved Japan of any legal obligation.

[74] Asahi Shimbun (November 26, 1999) reported that Nonprofit Organization Act had been enacted in December 1998 and according to the Act, there are 1,005 registered nonprofit organizations in Japan today.

[75] See Hsin-Huang Michael Hsiao. "Emerging Social Movement and the Rise of a Demanding Society in Taiwan" *The Australian Journal of Chinese Affairs* (July 1990): 163–179.

[76] J.F. Cooper, F. Michael, and Y.L. Wu, Human Rights in Post-Mao China (Boulder, CO: Westview Press, 1985), p. 11. The "Four Basic Principles" enshrined in the preamble to the Constitution are: keeping to the socialist road, upholding the people's democratic dictatorship, insisting on the leadership of the CCP, and Marxist-Leninism-Mao Zedong Thought.

[77] According to Marx, the concept of human rights is an ideological expression of class (bourgeois) egoism. Cooper argues that Mao was suspicious of the concept of human rights. The notion of inalienable human liberties contradicts his ideal of totalitarian political control and the socialist man. See John F. Copper "Defining Human Rights in the People's Republic of

China" in Yuan-li Wu, et al. Human Rights in the People's Republic of China. (Boulder, CO: Westview Press, 1988).

[78] See Louis Henkin "The Human Rights Idea in China: A Comparative Perspective" in R. Randle Edwards, Louis Henkin and Andrew J. Nathan. Human Rights in Contemporary China. (New York: Columbia University Press, 1986), p. 7–39. Louis Henkin explains that in traditional China the ideal was not individual liberty but order and harmony, not individual independence or equality but cooperation, not the freedom of individual conscience but conformity to orthodox. There was no distinction, no separation, no confrontation between the individual and society, but essential unity and harmony.

[79] See Aryeh Neier. "Asia's Unacceptable Standard" *Foreign Policy* (Fall 1993): 42–51.

[80] State Council. White Paper on Human Rights in China (Beijing: Information Office of the State Council of China, 1991). Chinese scholars reject the notion that individuals can be subjects of international law with respect to human rights or any other purposes. Therefore, any inquiry into the Chinese rights situation by a foreign government or international organization is regarded as intervention in Chinese domestic affairs and, thus, violation of international law.

[81] Christian Science Monitor (3/20/1998).

[82] Torture and other forms of mistreatment most often occur during interrogation and reportedly include: beatings, assaults with electric batons, use of handcuffs, shackles and chains, suspension by the arms or feet, confinement in tiny and/or dark cells, deprivation of sleep or food, exposure to cold or heat, prolonged solitary confinement, and force feeding of prisoners on hunger strike. See Amnesty International China: No One is Safe Political Repression and Abuse of Power in the 1990s (London: Amnesty International Pub., 1996).

[83] See Hongda Harry Wu. Laogai - The Chinese Gulag. (Boulder, CO: Westview Press, 1992).

[84] Nick Young. "Are there any real NGOs in China?" *Alliance* 4 (March 1999), p. 18.

[85] For full text, see Appendix B in Yuan-li Wu, et al. Human Rights in the People's Republic of China. (Boulder, CO: Westview Press, 1988), p. 316–319.

[86] According to Principles Governing a National Plan of Action for Human Rights Education (UN document A/52/469/Add. 1, October 20, 1997), governments should develop national plan that:

1. Promotes respect for and protection of all human rights through educational activities all members of society;

2. Promotes the interdependence, indivisibility and universality of human rights, including civil, cultural, economic, political and social rights and the right to development;

3. Integrate women's rights as human rights in all aspects of the national plan;

4. Recognize the importance of human rights education for democracy, sustainable development, the rule of law, the environment and peace;

5. Recognize the role of human rights education as a strategy for the prevention of human rights violations;

6. Encourage analysis of chronic and emerging human rights problems which would lead to solutions consistent with human rights standards;

7. Foster knowledge of and skills to use global, regional, national and local human rights instrument and mechanisms for the protection of human rights;

8. Empower communities and individuals to identify their human rights needs and to ensure that they are met;

9. Develop pedagogues that include knowledge, critical analysis and skills for action furthering human rights;

10. Promote research and the development of educational materials to sustain these general principles;

11. Foster learning environments free from want and fear that encourage participation, enjoyment of human rights and the full development of the human personality.

[87] See *Focus,* Newsletter of the Asia-Pacific Human Rights Information Center (HURIGHTS Osaka) 17 (Sept. 1999), p. 7–8.

[88] Mario Gomez "Sri Lanka's New Human Rights Commission" *Human Rights Quarterly* 20 (1998): 281–302; Juliane Kokott "Indonesian National Commission on Human Rights: Two Years of Activities" *Human Rights Law Journal* 16 (1995): 420–421.

[89] These functions were identified by the Seminar on National and Local Institutions for the Promotion and Protection of Human Rights held in Geneva in 1978. These functions were amended by the first International Workshop on National Institutions for the Promotion and Protection of Human Rights held in Paris in 1991. The modified versions of responsibilities of the commission are:

> To submit recommendations, proposals and reports on any matter relating to human rights (including legislative and administrative provision and any situation of violation of human rights) to the Government, parliament and any other competent body;
> To promote conformity of national laws and practices with international human rights standards;

To encourage ratification and implementation of international standards;

To contribute to the reporting procedure under international instruments;

To assist in formulating and executing human rights teaching and research programs and to increase public awareness of human rights through information and education;

To cooperate with the United Nations, regional institutions, and national institutions of other countries.

[90] For full text, see Our Voice: Bangkok NGO Declaration on Human Rights Reports of the Asia Pacific NGO Conference on Human Rights and NGOs' Statements to the Asia Regional Meeting. Asia Cultural Forum on Development (ACFOD), Pub. 1993.

[91] See *Conclusions and Recommendations* adopted at the Experts Meeting on United Nations' Activities in the Field of Human Rights and the Realization of Human Rights in the Asia-Pacific Region organized by the Asia-Pacific Human Rights Information Center (HURIGHTS Osaka), 26–28 July, 1995.

[92] LAWASIA, organized in August 1966, is a professional NGO of lawyers, judges and law teachers. Membership is restricted to Asia and the Pacific. LAWASIA has a consultative status with the United Nations. The objectives of LAWASIA includes:

1. promoting the administration of justice, the protection of human rights and the maintenance of the rule of law;
2. advancing legal education, diffusing knowledge of the laws of member countries;
3. promoting development of the law and uniformity where appropriate;
4. furthering international understanding and goodwill;
5. fostering relations and intercourse among lawyers in the region; and
6. upholding and advancing the status of the legal profession in the region.

[93] The Declaration was adopted by the First General Assembly of the Regional Council on Human Rights in Asia in Jakarta, Indonesia on December 9, 1983 and presented to the ASEAN Secretariat on the same day. The Regional Council is a NGO largely composed of jurists and others interested in human rights. The Declaration deplores the failure of Asian governments to ratify the International Covenants on Human Rights and urges governments and peoples of the region to incorporate the Declaration in their national constitutions and laws, and to implement and

enforce them. For full text, see Asia-Pacific Human Rights Documents and Resources vol. 1 (The Hague: Martinus Nijhoff Pub., 1998).

[94] The Declaration consists of 22 articles. The Preamble of the Declaration reaffirms the observance of the Universal Declaration of Human Rights and the Vienna Declaration and Programme of Action. For full text, see Asia-Pacific Human Rights Documents and Resources vol. 1 (The Hague: Martinus Nijhoff Pub., 1998).

[95] The success of SAARC lies, to a great extent, on the mood of India. See Madhave K. Rimal, India, SAARC and Its Future, *Spotlight* Jan. 7, 1992.

[96] Statement of Clarence Dias, President, International Center for Law in Development, New York, in the interview conducted in New York on July 13, 1999.

[97] LAWASIA held a seminar entitled "Pacific Charter of Human Rights" in Apia, Western Samoa in 1989. The seminar made amendments to the Pacific Charter. For full text of the Charter, see Asia-Pacific Human Rights Documents and Resources vol. 1 (The Hague: Martinus Nijhoff Pub., 1998).

[98] See Jon M. Van Dyke "Economic, Social and Cultural Rights in the Proposed Pacific Charter of Human Rights" in Report of the Lawasia Seminar on Draft Pacific Charter of Human Rights, 1989, p. 59–65; and Nick O'Neill "Civil and Political Rights" in Report of the Lawasia Seminar on Draft Pacific Charter of Human Rights, 1989, p. 66–67.

[99] See Guy Powles "The Articulation of Duties in Human Rights Documents" in Report of the Lawasia Seminar on Draft Pacific Charter of Human Rights, 1989, p. 75–93.

[100] Statement of Clarence Dias, President, International Center for Law in Development, New York, in the interview conducted in New York on July 13, 1999.

[101] The questionnaires were prepared in consultation with Dr. Johnny Blair, Associate Director, Survey Research Center in the Department of Sociology at the University of Maryland, College Park.

[102] Dias also mentioned in his interview that the Asian value argument has been made by Asian scholars writing primarily from religious and philosophical backgrounds because different countries and religions have different value structures. On East Asian economic development model, see Michael C. Davis "The Price of Rights: Constitutionalism and East Asian Economic Development" *Human Rights Quarterly* 20 (1998): 303–337.

[103] This is called the "Lee thesis." Amartya Sen interprets the Lee thesis that it is based on very selective statistics, rather than on general statistical test over the wide-ranging information that is available.

[104] Government of Singapore, Shared Values (Singapore:Cmd. No. 1 of 1991, 2 January 1991)

[105] See Amartya Sen "Human Rights and Economic Achievements" in Joanne R. Bauer and Daniel A. Bell, eds. The East Asian Challenge for Human Rights (Cambridge: Cambridge University Press, 1999), p. 92.

[106] See Mahnoush H. Arsanjan "The Rome Statute of the International Criminal Court" 93 *American Journal of International Law* (January 1999): 22–43; Hans-peter Kaul. "Towards A Permanent International Criminal Court" *Human Rights Law Journal* 18 (Nov. 1998): 169–174.

[107] Statement of Clarence Dias in the interview conducted in New York on July 13, 1999.

[108] Statement of Xioraong Li in the interview conducted at the University of Maryland, College Park on July 27, 1999.

[109] See Bilahari Kausikan "Asia's Different Standard" *Foreign Policy* (Fall 1993): 24–41.

[110] In 1937 roughly 800,000 Japanese soldiers moved into China and full-scale war broke out. The "Rape of Nanking" involved mass rape of the female population, indiscriminate acts of arson, pillage, looting and massacres on an unbelievable scale. Historians estimate that at least 200–300,000 civilians were slaughtered in a week-long orgy of carnage.

[111] Xiaorong Li stated in the interview on July 27, 1999 that in his original text Confucius never employed the ideas of human rights and democracy. Society then was very different. Whether Confucianism is democratic or not hard to tell because it has a long tradition and depends on what periods, for example, classic or neo-Confucianism. Some scholars argue that in the original text there are some democratic elements and argue for democracy and human rights.

[112] Statement made by Prof. Hungda Chiu, Director of East Asian Legal Studies Program, University of Maryland Law School and President of International Law Association on September 29, 1999.

[113] Gerald L. Curtis "For Democratic Development: The East Asian Prospect" *Journal of Democracy* 8.3 (1997): 139–145. Curtis stresses that democratization has a better chance of succeeding where there is not only economic growth but also a conscious effort on the part of the state to achieve a degree of economic equity.

[114] See William Shaw "Traditional Korean Law and Its Relations to China" in Jerome Alan Cohen, Randle Edwards, and Fu-mei Chang Chen, eds. Essays on China's Legal Tradition (Princeton, NJ: Princeton University Press, 1980), p. 302–326.

NOTES TO CHAPTER V

[1] For full text of "Framework of Regional Technical Cooperation Programme in Asia and the Pacific," visit website: http://www.unhchr.ch/html/menu4/chrrep/98chr50.htm

2 See Professional Training Series NO.4 National Human Rights Institution A Handbook on the Establishment and Strengthening of National Institutions for the Promotion and Protection of Human Rights (Geneva: UN Pub., 1995).

3 See Canadian Human Rights Foundation and Philippine Commission on Human Rights. Developing Capacity in Asia National Human Rights Institutions at Work: Regional Training Manual Tagaytay City, Philippines February 8–13, 1998.

4 Since its inception in 1954 the Asia Foundation has supported the rule of law, development of civil society, good governance with accountability and transparency in Asia.

5 These variables were identified when I had a conversation with Dr. Richard Pierre Claude, Professor Emeritus, University of Maryland, College Park in Washington, D.C. on December 1, 1999.

Bibliography

Ake, Claude. A Theory of Political Integration. Homewood, Ill: Dorsey Press, 1967.

Alston, Philip, ed. Human Rights Law. Aldershot: Dartmouth, 1996.

———, ed. The United Nations and Human Rights: A Critical Appraisal. Oxford: Clarendon Press, 1992.

An-Naim, Abdullahi Ahmed and Francis M. Deng. Human Rights in Africa: Cross-Cultural Perspectives. Washington, D.C.: The Brookings Institution, 1990.

An-Naim, Abdullahi Ahmed. Human Rights in Cross-Cultural Perspectives: A Quest for Consensus. Philadelphia: University of Pennsylvania, 1992.

———. Toward and Islamic Reformation: Civil Liberties, Human Rights and International Law. Syracuse, N.Y.: Syracuse University Press, 1990.

Andic, Fuat, Suphan Andic and Douglas Dosser. A Theory of Economic Integration for Developing Countries: Illustrated by Caribbean Countries. London: George Allen and Unwin, Ltd. 1971.

Archer, Clive. International Organizations. London: Geroge Allen & Wnwin, 1983.

Andreopolos, G. and Richard Pierre Claude. The Human Rights Education for the Twenty-First Century. Philadelphia, PA: University of Pennsylvania, 1997.

Arase, David. Buying Power: The Political Economy of Japan's Foreign Aid. Boulder, CO: Lynne Rienner Pub., 1995.

Azar, Edward E. The Management of Protracted Social Conflict: Theory and Cases. Hampshire: Dartmouth, 1990.

Azar, Edward E. and John W. Burton. International Conflict Resolution: Theory and Practice. Boulder, CO: Lynne Rienner Pub., 1986.

The Asian Coalition of Human Rights Organizations Human Rights Activism in Asia: Some Perspectives, Problems and Approaches. New York: Council on International and Public Affairs, 1984.

Baehr, Peter. The Role of Human Rights in Foreign Policy. New York: St. Martin's Press, 1994.

Baehr, Peter, Hilde Hey, Jacqueline Smith and Theresa Swinehart, ed. Human Rights in Developing Countries Yearbook 1994. Boston, MA: Kluwer Law and Taxation Pub., 1994.

Bailey, Peter H. Human Rights: Australia in an International Context. Sydney: Butterworth, 1990.

Baslar, Kemal. The Concept of the Common Heritage of Mankind in International Law. The Hague: Martinus Nijhoff Pub., 1998.

Balassa, Bela. The Theory of Economic Integration. London: George Allen & Unwin Ltd.

Barry Jones, R.J. and Peter Willetts, ed. Interdependence on Trial: Studies in the Theory and Reality of Contemporary Interdependence. New York: St. Martin's Press, 1984.

Baylis, John and Steve Smith, ed. The Globalization of World Politics: An Introduction to International Relations. New York: Oxford University Press, 1997.

Bauer, Joanne R. and Daniel A. Bell, ed. The East Asian Challenge for Human Rights. Cambridge: Cambridge University Press, 1999.

Beer, Lawrence, ed. Constitutional Systems in Late Twentieth Century Asia Seatle, WA: University of Washington Press, 1992.

Bernhandt, Rudolf and John Anthony Jolowicz, ed. International Enforcement of Human Rights. Berlin: Springer-Verlag, 1986.

Bernstein, Richard J. Beyond Objectivism and Relativism. Oxford: Basil Blackwell Pub., 1983.

Berting, Jan, et al, ed. Human Rights in a Pluralist World: Individuals and Collectivities. London: Meckler, 1990.

Bennett, LeRoy A. International Organizations: Principles and Issues, 6th ed. Englewood Cliffs, N.J.: Prentice Hall, 1995.

Beddard, Ralph. Human Rights and Europe. 3rd ed. Cambridge: Grotius Pub., 1993.

Berting, Jan., ed. Human Rights in a Pluralist World: Individuals and Collectivities. London: Meckler, 1990.

Bernhandt, Rudolf and John Anthony Jolowicz, ed. International Enforcement of Human Rights. Berlin: Springer-Verlag, 1986.

Bloed, Arie, et al. Monitoring Human Rights in Europe: Comparing International Procedures and Mechanisms. Dordrecht: Martinus Nijhoff Pub., 1993.

Boven, Theo van. People Matter: Views on International Human Rights Policy. Amsterdam: Meulenhoff, 1982.

Bramsted, E.K. and K.J. Melhuish. Western Liberalism: A History in Documents from Locke to Croce. London: Longman, 1978

Brown, P.G. and D. Maclean. Human Rights and U.S. Foreign Policy: Principles and Applications, Lexington, Lexington Books, 1979.

Buergenthal, Thomas. International Human Rights in a Nutshell. St. Paul, MN: West Pub., 1988.

———. International Human Rights. 2nd ed. St. Paul, MN: West Pub., 1995.

Buergenthal, Thomas, Robert Norris and Dinah Shelton. Protecting Human Rights in the Americas: Selected Problems. Kehl: N.P. Engel, Pub., 1982.

Buergenthal, Thomas and Sohn, Louis. International Protection of Human Rights. New York: The Bobbs-Merrill Co., 1973.

Bull, Hedley and Adam Watson, ed. The Expansion of International Society. Oxford: The Clarendon Press, 1984.

Brook, Tomothy and B. Michael Frolic, ed. Civil Society in China. London: M.E. Sharpe, 1997.

Buhmann, Karin. Civil and Political Rights in Japan. Copenhagen: The Danish Center for Human Rights, 1989.

Brook, Timothy and B. Michael Frolic, ed. Civil Society in China. Armonk, NY: M.E. Sharpe, 1997.

Brown, Lester R. The Interdependence of Nations. Headline Series, No. 212. New York: Foreign Policy Association Pub., 1972.

———. World Without Borders. New York: Random House, 1972.

Camilleri, Joseph A., Anthony P. Jarvis, Albert J. Paolini, ed. The State in Transition: Reimagining Political Space. Boulder, CO: Lynne Rienner Pub., 1995.

Camilleri, Joseph A. and Jim Falk. The End of Sovereignty?: The Politics of a Shrinking and Fragmenting World. Aldershot: Edward Elgar, 1992.

Cantori, Louis and Steven Spiegel. The International Politics of Regions: A Comparative Approach. Englewood Cliffs, N.J. Prentice Hall, 1970.

Carey, John. United Nations Protection of Civil and Political Rights. New York: Syracuse University Press, 1970.

Cassese, Antonio. Human Rights in a Changing World. Cambridge: Polity Press, 1990.

Castberg, Frede. The European Convention on Human Rights. A.W. Sijithoff-Leiden. Oceana Pub., 1974.

Caporaso, James A. Functionalism and Regional Integration: A Logical and Empirical Assessment. Biverly Hills, CA: Sage Pub., 1972.

———. The Structure and Function of European Integration. Pacific Palisades, CA: Goodyear Pub., 1974.

Carroll, Thomas f. Intermediary NGOs: The Supporting Link in Grassroots Development. West Hartford, CT: Kumarian Press, 1992.

Cassese, Antonio, ed. UN Law/Fundamental Rights: Two Topics in International Law. Alphen aan den Rijn: Sijihoff & Noordhoff, 1979.

Chomsky, Noam and Edward S. Herman. The Political Economy of Human Rights. Boston: South End Press, 1979.

Chan, Steve. International Relations in Perspective: The Pursuit of Security, Welfare, and Justice. New York: Macmillan Pub., 1984.

Chiang, Pei-leng. Non-Governmental Organizations at the United Nations: Identity, Role and Functions. New York: Praeger, 1981.

Choi, Sung-Chul, ed. International Community and Human Rights in North Korea. Seoul: The Institute of Unification Policy, 1996.

Chilcote, Ronald H, ed., Dependency and Marxism: Toward a Resolution of the Debate. Boulder, CO: Westview Press, 1982.

Cingranelli, David Louis., ed. Human Rights Theory and Measurement. New York: St. Martin's Press, 1988.

Claude, Richard Pierre. Comparative Human Rights. Baltimore: The Johns Hopkins University Press, 1976.

———. Human Rights Education in the Philippines. Manila, Kalikasan Press, 1991.

————. Educating for Human Rights: The Philippines and Beyond. Quezon City: University of the Philippines, 1996.

Claude, Richard Pierre and Burns H. Weston. Human Rights in the World Community: Issues and Action, 2nd ed. Philadelphia: University of Pennsylvania, 1992.

Claude, Richard P. and Thomas B. Jabine. Human Rights and Statistics: Getting the Record Straight. Philadelphia, PA: University of Pennsylvania Press, 1992.

Claude Jr, Inis L. Swords into Plowshares: The Problems and Progress of International Organization. New York: Random House, 1971.

Cohen, Ronald, et al, ed. Human Rights and Governance in Africa. Gainesville: University Press of Florida, 1993.

Cotler, Irwin and F. Pearl Eliadis. International Human Rights: Theory and Practice. Montreal: The Canadian Human Rights Foundation, 1992.

Cohen, Jean L. and Andrew Arato. Civil Society and Political Theory. Cambridge, MA: The MIT Press, 1992.

Cooper, R.N. The Economics of Interdependence: Economic Policy in the Atlantic Community. New York: McGraw Hill, 1968.

Cooper, J.F., F. Michael, and Y.L. Wu. Human Rights in Post-Mao China. Boulder, CO: Westview Press, 1985.

Cranston, Maurice. What are Human Rights? New York: Basic Books, 1964.

Craven, Matthew C.R. The International Covenant on Economic, Social and Cultural Rights: A Perspective on its Development. Oxford: Clarendon Press, 1995.

Curtis, W Martin. The History and Theory of the Functional Approach to International Organization. Cambridge, MA: Harvard University, unpublished Ph.D dissertation, 1950.

Davies, Peter., ed. Human Rights. London: Routledge, 1988.

Davis, Michael, et al, ed. Human Rights and Chinese Values: Legal, Philosophical, and Political Perspectives. Oxford: Oxford University Press, 1995.

Davidson, Scott. Human Rights. Buckingham: Open University Press, 1993.

————. The Inter-American Human Rights System. Aldershot: Dartmouth, 1997.

————. The Inter-American Court of Human Rights. Aldershot: Dartmouth, 1997.

de Bary, Wm Theodore. Asian Values and Human Rights: A Confucian Communitarian Perspective. Cambridge: Harvard University Press, 1998.

————. The Trouble with Confucianism. Cambridge, MA: Harvard University Press, 1991.

de Bary, Wm Theodore, Tu Weiming, eds. Confucianism and Human Rights. New York: Columbia University Press, 1997.

Del Russo, Alessandre, Luini. International Protection of Human Rights. Washington, D.C.: Learner Law Book Co., 1971.

Del Russo, Alessandra Luini. International Protection of Human Rights. Washington, D.C.: Lerner Law Book Co., 1971.

Desai, Meghnad and Paul Redfern, ed. Global Governance: Ethics and Economics of the World Order. London: Pinter, 1995.

Deutsch, Karl W. et al. Political Community and the North Atlantic Area: International Organization in the Light of Historical Experience. New York: Greenwood Press, 1969.

Delmas-Marty, Mireille and Christine, Chodkiewicz, ed. The European Convention for the Protection of Human Rights: International Protection Versus National Restrictions. Dordrecht: Martinus Nijhoff Pub., 1992.

Dijk, P van and G.J.H van Hoof. Theory and Practice of the European Convention on Human Rights. 2nd ed. Deventer: Kluwer Law and Taxation Pub., 1990.

Diamond, Larry and Marc F. Plattner, ed. The Global Resurgence of Democracy. Baltimore, MD: The Johns Hopkins University Press, 1993.

Diemer, Alwin. Philosophical Foundations of Human Rights. Paris: UNESCO, 1986.

Dominguez, Jorge I et al. Enhancing Global Human Rights. New York: McGraw-Hill Book Co., 1979.

Dougherty, James E. and Robert Pfaltzgraff, Jr. Contending Theories of International Relations: A Comprehensive Survey, 2nd ed. Cambridge: Harper & Row, Pub, 1981.

Dominguez, Jorge I et al. Enhancing Global Human Rights. New York: McGraw Hill, 1979.

Donnelly, Jack. Universal Human Rights in Theory and Practice. Ithaca, N.Y.: Cornell University Press, 1989.

Donnelly, Jack and Rhoda E. Howard, ed. International Handbook of Human Rights. New York: Greenwood Press, 1987.

————. International Human Rights, 2nd ed. Boulder, CO: Westview Press, 1998.

Dworkin, Ronald. Take Rights Seriously. Cambridge: Harvard University Press, 1984.

Dwyer, Kevin. Arab Voices: The Human Rights Debate in the Middle East. Berkeley: University of California Press, 1991.

Dyke, Vernon Van. Human Rights, The United States, World Community. New York: Oxford University Press, 1970.

Eastby, John. Functionalism and Interdependence. Lanham, MD: University Press of America, 1985.

Eber, Irene, ed. Confucianism: The Dynamics of Tradition. New York: Macmillan Pub., 1986.

Edwards, R. Randle, Louis Henkin and Andrew J. Nathan. Human Rights in Contemporary China. New York: Columbia University Press, 1986.

Eide, Asbjorn and Jan Helgesen, eds. The Future of Human Rights Protection in a Changing World. Oslo: Norwegian University Press, 1991.

Eide, Asbjorn, et al, ed. The Universal Declaration of Human Rights: A Commentary. London: Scandinavian University Press, 1992.

Ensign, Margee M. Doing Good or Doing Well? New York: Columbia University Press, 1992.

Evans, Tony. US Hegemony and the Project of Universal Human Rights. London: Macmilian Press, 1996.

Eze, Osita C. Human Rights in Africa: Some Selected Problems. Lagos, Nigeria: The Nigerian Institute of International Affairs, 1984.

Edwards, Michael and David Hulme, eds. Beyond the Magic Bullet: NGO Performance and Accountability in the Post-Cold War World. West Hartford, CT: Kumarian Press, 1996.

Edwards, Michael and David Hulme, ed. NGOs, States and Donors: Too Close for Comfort? New York: St. Martin's Press, 1997.

Edwards, Michael and David Hulme, ed. Making a Difference: NGOs and Development in a Changing World. London: Earthscan Pub., 1992.

Eide, Asbjorn and Bernt Hagtvet. Human Rights in Perspective: A Global Assessment. Oxford: Blackwell Pub., 1992.

Emmanuel, Arghiri. Unequal Exchange: A Study of the Imperialism of Trade. New York: Monthly Review Press, 1972.

Etzioni, Amitai. Political Unification. New York: Holt, Rinehart, and Winston, 1965.

Falk, Richard A. Human Rights and State Sovereignty. New York: Holms and Meier, 1981.

Fawcett, J.E.S. The Application of the European Convention on Human Rights. Oxford: Clarendon Press, 1987.

Falk, Richard and Saul H. Mendlovitz. Regional Politics and World Order. San Francisco: W.H. Freeman and Co., 1973.

Falk, Richard. Human Rights and State Sovereignty. New York: Holmes and Meier, 1981.

Farer, Tom, ed. Beyond Sovereignty: Collectively Defending Democracy in the Americas. Baltimore, MD: The Johns Hopkins University Press, 1996.

Fawn, Rick and Jeremy Larkins, ed. International Society after the Cold War: Anarchy and Order Reconsidered. New York: St. Martin's Press, 1996.

Felice, William F. Taking Suffering Seriously: The Importance of Collective Human Rights. New York: State University of New York Press, 1996.

Featherstone, Mike, ed. Global Culture: Nationalism, Globalization and Modernity. London: Sage Pub., 1990.

Feld, Werner J., Robert S. Jordan and Leon Hurwitz. International Organizations: A Comparative Approach, 3rd. ed. London: Praeger, 1994.

Feld, Werner and Roger A. Coate. The Role of International Nongovernmental Organizations in World Politics. New York: Learning Resource in International Studies, 1976.

Fenwick, Charles, G. The Organization of American States: The Inter-American Regional System. Washington: Kaufman Inc., 1963.

Felice, William F. Taking Suffering Seriously: The Importance of Collective Human Rights. New York: State University of New York Press, 1996.

Fine, Robert and Shirin Rai, ed. Civil Society: Democratic Perspectives. London: Frank Cass, 1997.

Fisher, Julie. Non Governments: NGOs and the Political Development of the Third World. West Hartford, CT: Kumarian Press, 1997.

Flood, Patrick James. The Effectiveness of UN Human Rights Institutions. London: Praeger, 1998.

Forsythe, David P. The Internationalization of Human Rights. Lexington, MA: Lexington Books, 1991.

————. Human Rights and World Politics. 2nd ed. Lincoln: University of Nebraska Press, 1988.

————. Human Rights and U.S. Foreign Policy: Congress Reconsidered. Gainesville: University of Florida Press, 1988.

————, ed. Human Rights in the New Europe. Lincoln: University of Nebraska Press, 1994.

Fonseca, G. da. How To File Complaints of Human Rights Violations: A Practical Guide to Inter-Governmental Procedures. Geneva: World Council of Church, 1975.

Frankel, Jeffrey A., ed. The Regionalization of the World Economy. Chicago: The University of Chicago Press, 1998.

Friedman, Edward, ed. The Politics of Democratization: Generalizing East Asian Experiences. Boulder, CO: Westview Press, 1994.

Gamble, Andrew and Anthony Payne, ed. Regionalism and World Order. New York: St. Martin's Press, 1996.

Gellner, Ernest, Legitimacy of Belief. Cambridge: Cambridge University Press, 1974.

————. Conditions of Liberty: Civil Society and Its Rivals. New York: Penguin Books, 1994.

Gelber, Harry G. Sovereignty Through Interdependence. London: Kluwer Law, 1997.

Ghandi, P.R. The Human Rights Committee and the Right of Individual Communication: Law and Practice. Aldershot: Dartmouth, 1998.

Gifford, N.L. When in Rome: An Introduction to Relativism and Knowledge. Albany: State University of New York Press, 1985.

Goodman, Roger and Ian Neary. Case Studies on Human Rights in Japan. Surrey: Japan Library, 1996.

Goldmann, Kjell and Gunnar Sjostedt. Power, Capabilities, Interdependence: Poblems in the Study of International Influence. Beverly Hills, CA: Sage Pub., 1979.

Gormley, W. Paul. Human Rights and Environment: The Need for International Co-operation. Leyden: A.W. Sijthoff, 1976.

Greenstein, Fred I. and Nelson W. Polsy, ed. International Politics. Handbook of Political Science vol. 8. Reading, MA: Addison-Wesley Pub., 1975.

Groom, A J R. and Paul Taylor, ed. Functionalism: Theory and Practice in International Relations. New York: Cran, Russak & Co., 1975.

Haas, Ernst B. Human Rights and International Actions: The Case of Freedom of Association. Stanford, CA: Stanford University Press, 1970.

————. Beyond the Nation-State: Functionalism and International Organization. Stanford: Stanford University Press, 1964.

————. The Obsolescence of Regional Integration Theory. Berkeley, CA: Institute of International Studies, 1975.

————. Tangle of Hopes: American Commitments and World Order. Englewood Cliffs, N.J.: Prentice-Hall, 1969.

————. The Uniting of Europe. Stanford, CA: Stanford University Press, 1957.

Hall, John A, ed. Civil Society: Theory, History and Comparison. Cambridge: Polity Press, 1995.

Hannum, Hurst. Guide to International Human Rights Practice. Philadelphia: University of Pennsylvania Press, 1984.

Harbeson, John W, Donald Rothchild, and Naomi Chazan, ed. Civil Society and the State in Africa. London: Lynne Rienner Pub., 1994.

Hawley, Amos. Human Ecology: A Theory of Community Structure. New York: Ronald Press, 1950.

Hannum, Hurst and Dana D. Fischer, ed. U.S. Ratification of the International Covenants on Human Rights. New York: Transnational Pub., Inc., 1993.

Hannum Hurst. Guide to International Human Rights Practice. 2nd ed. Philadelphia: University of Pennsylvania Press, 1992.

Hannum, Hurst, ed. Guide to International Human Rights Practice. Philadelphia: University of Pennsylvania, 1984.

Harris, David J. and Stephen Livingstone, eds. The Inter-American System of Human Rights. Oxford: Clarendon Press, 1998.

Henkin, Alice. Human Dignity: The Internationalization of Human Rights. New York: Aspen Institute for Humanistic Studies, 1978.

Held, David. Democracy and Global Order: From the Modern State to Cosmopolitan Governance. Stanford, CA: Stanford University Press, 1995.

Henkin, Louis and John Lawrence Hargrove, ed. Human Rights: An Agenda for the Next Century. Washington, D.C.: The American Society of International Law, 1994.

Henkin, Louis. The Age of Rights. New York: Columbia University Press, 1990.

———. The Rights of Man Today. Boulder, CO: Westview Press, 1978.

———. The International Bill of Rights: The Covenant on Civil and Political Rights. New York: Columbia University Press, 1981.

Henkin, Louis and John Lawrence Hargrove, ed. Human Rights: An Agenda for the Next Century. Washington, D.C.: The American Society of International Law, 1994.

Hennelly, Alfred and John Langan, Human Rights in the Americas: The Struggle for Consensus. Washington, D.C.: Georgetown University Press, 1982.

Hevener, N. Kaufman, ed. The Dynamics of Human Rights in U.S. Foreign Policy. New Brunswick, Transaction Books, 1981.

Hill, Dilys M., ed. Human Rights and Foreign Policy: Principles and Practice. New York: St. Martin's Press, 1989.

Hirst, Paul. From Statism to Pluralism: Democracy, Civil Society and Global Politics. London: UCL Press, 1997.

Hirst, Paul and Grahame Thompson. Globalization in Question: The International Economy and the Possibilities of Governance. Oxford: Polity Press, 1996.

Hoffmann, Stanley. Duties Beyond Borders. New York: Syracuse University Press, 1981.

Hook, Steven W. National Interest and Foreign Aid. Boulder, CO: Lynne Rienner Pub., 1995.

———., ed. Foreign Aid Toward the Millennium. Boulder, CO: Lynne Rienner Pub., 1996.

Howard, Rhoda E. Human Rights and the Search for Community. Boulder, CO: Westview Press, 1995.

———. Human Rights in Commonwealth Africa. Totawa, N.J.: Rowman and Littlefield, 1986

Hsing, James C., ed. Human Rights in East Asia: A Cultural Perspective. New York: Paragon House Pub., 1985.

Hunter, Kenneth W. and Timothy C. Mack, ed. International Rights and Responsibilities for the Future. Westport, CT: Praeger, 1996.

Huntington, Samuel P. The Third Wave: Democratization in the Late Twentieth Century. Norman: Oxford University Press, 1991.

———. The Clash of Civilizations and the Remaking of World Order. New York: Simon & Schuster, 1996.

Hoffman, Stanley. Duties Beyond Borders: On the Limits and Possibilities of

Howard, Rhoda E. Human Rights and the Search for Community. Boulder, CO: Westview Press, 1995.

Huntington, Samuel P. The Third Wave: Democratization in the Late Twentieth Century. Norman: University of Oklahoma Press, 1991.

Hunter, Kenneth W. and Timothy C. Mack. International Rights and Responsibilities for the Future. Westport, Conn: Praeger, 1996.

Hunnum, Hurst, ed. Guide to International Human Rights Practice. Philadelphia: University of Pennsylvania, 1984.

International Human Rights Law Group. U.S. Legislation Relating Human Rights to U.S. Foreign Policy. 4th ed. Washington, D.C. 1991.

Jacob, Philip E. and James V. Toscano. The Integration of Political Communities. Philadelphia: J.B. Lippincott Co., 1964.

Jacobson, Harold K. Networks of Interdependence: International Organizations and the Glboal Political System. New York: Alfred A. Knopf, 1979.

Janoski, Thomas. Citizenship and Civil Society: A Framework of Rights & Obligations in Liberal, Traditional, and Social Democratic Regimes. Cambridge: Cambridge University Press, 1998.

Jacobs, Francis G. and Robin C.A. White. The European Convention on Human Rights. 2nd ed. Oxford: Clarendon Press, 1996.

Kaplan, Morton A. System and Process in International Politics. New York: John Wiley & Sons, 1957.

Kaplan, Roger, ed. Freedom in the World: The Annual Survey of Political Rights & Civil Liberties 1997–1998. London: Transaction Pub., 1998.

Kaufman, Natalie Hevener. Human Rights Treaties and the Senate: A History of Opposition. Chapel Hill, N.C.: The University of North Carolina Press, 1990.

Kent, Ann. Between Freedom and Subsistence: China and Human Rights. Oxford: Oxford University Press, 1993.

Kegley, Jr, Charles W. and Eugene R. Wittkoph. The Global Agenda. New York: Random House, 1984.

Keohane, Robert, Joseph Nye. Power and Interdependence: World Politics in Transition. Boston, MA: Little, Brown and Co., 1977.

Kommers, Donald and Gilburt D. Loescher, ed. Human Rights and American Foreign Policy. Notre Dame, IN: University of Notre Dame Press, 1979.

Korea Institute for National Unification. White Paper on Human Rights in North Korea 1997. Seoul: Korea Institute for National Unification, 1997.

Korey, William. NGOs and the Universal Declaration of Human Rights: "A Curious Grapewine." New York: St. Martin's Press, 1998.

Kofman, Elenore and Gillian Youngs, ed. Globalization: Theory and Practice. New York: Pinter, 199

Koizumi, Tetsuo. Intei.   :ndece and Change in the Global System. Lanham, MD: University Press of America, 1993.

Kommers, Donald P. and Gilburt D. Loescher, ed. Human Rights and American Foreign Policy. Notre Dame: University of Notre Dame Press, 1979.

Korhonen, Pekka. Japan and Asia Pacific Integration: Pacific Romances 1968–1996. London: Routledge, 1998.

Korten, David C. Global Civil Society: Reclaiming Our Right to Power. New York: Seven Stories Press, 1998.

————. Getting to the 21st Century: Voluntary Action and the Global Agenda. West Hartford, CT: Kumarian Press, 1990.

————. When Corporations Rule the World. West Hartford, CT: Kumarian Press, 1995.

Korhonen, Pekka. Japan and Asia Pacific Integration: Pacific Romances 1968–1996. London: Routledge, 1998.

Lauterpacht, Hersch. International Law and Human Rights. London: Garland Pub., Inc. 1973.

Lawyers Committee for Human Rights. Human Rights and U.S. Foreign Policy: Report and Recommendations, 1992. New York: Lawyers Committee for Human Rights, 1992.

Ladd, John, ed. Ethical Relativism. Belmont, Calif.: Wadsworth, 1973.

Laqueur, Walter and Barry Rubin., eds. The Human Rights Reader. New York: Penguin USA, 1990.

Lawson, Rick and Matthijs de Blois, ed. The Dynamics of the Protection of Human Rights in Europe. Dordrecht: Martinus Nijhoff Pub., 1994.

LeBranc, Lawrence. The OAS and the Promotion and Protection of Human Rights. The Hague: Martinus Nijhoff, 1977.

Lebra, Takie S. Japanese Women. Honolulu, HI: University of Hawaii Press, 1984.

LeBlanc, Lawrence. The Convention on the Rights of the Child. Lincoln: University of Nebraska Press, 1995.

Lefort, Claude. The Political Form of Modern Society: Bureaucracy, Democracy, Totalitarianism. Cambridge, MA: Massachusetts Institute of Technology, 1986.

Licht, R.A., ed. Old Rights and New. Washington, D.C. American Enterprise Institute, 1993.

Lindberg, Leon and Scheingold, Stuart, ed. Regional Integration: Theory and Research. Cambridge: Harvard University Press, 1971.

Lindberg, Leon. The Political Dynamics of European Economic Integration. Stanford: Stanford University Press, 1963.

Lipschutz, Ronnie D. Global Civil Society and Global Environmental Governance: The Politics of Nature from Place to Planet. New York: State University of New York Press, 1996.

Livezey, Lowell W. Nongovernmental Organizations and the Ideas of Human Rights. Princeton, N.J.: The Center of International Studies, Princeton University, 1988.

Lillich, Richard B and Frank C. Newman. International Human Rights: Problems of Law and Policy. Boston, MA: Little, Brown and Co., 1979.

Locke, John. The Second Treatise on Government. Cambridge: Cambridge University Press, 1993.

Loutfi, Martha F. The Net Cost of Japanese Foreign Aid.New York: Praeger, 1973.

Luard, Evan. Human Rights and Foreign Policy. Oxford: Pergamon Press, 1981.

Lubman, Stanley, ed. China's Legal Reform. Oxford: Oxford University Press, 1996.

Lutz, Ellen, Hurst Hannum and Kathryn J. Burke, ed. New Directions in Human Rights. Philadelphia: University of Pennsylvania Press, 1989.

Luard, Evan, ed. The International Protection of Human Rights. London: Thames and Hudson, 1967.

Matthews, Robert O. and Cranford Pratt, ed. Human Rights in Canadian Foreign Policy. Toronto: McGill-Queens, 1988.

Madison, G.B. The Political Economy of Civil Society and Human Rights. London: Routledge, 1998.

Magdoff, Harry. The Age of Imperialism: Economics of U.S. Foreign Policy. New York: Monthly Review Press, 1969.

Mally, Gerhard. Interdependece. Lexington, MA: D.C. Heath and Co., 1976.

Macdonald, R.St.J., F. Matscher and H. Petzold The European System for the Protection of Human Rights. Dordrecht: Martinus Nijhoff Pub., 1993.

McCarthy-Arnolds, Eileen and David R. Penna and Debra Joy Cruz Sobrepena. Africa, Human Rights, and the Global System: The Political Economy of Human Rights in a Changing World. Westport, CT: Greenwood Press, 1994.

Macfarlane L.T. The Theory and Practice of Human Rights. London: Temple Smith, 1985.

Machlup, Fritz, ed. Economic Integration World Wide, Regional, Sectoral. London: Macmillan Press Ltd., 1976.

Martin, Curtis W. The History and Theory of the Functional Approach to International Organization. Cambridge, MA: Harvard University, unpublished Ph.D dissertation, 1950.

Meron, Theodore, eds. Human Rights in International Law: Legal and Policy Issues. New York: Oxford University Press, 1984.

———. Human Rights and Humanitarian Norms as Customary Law. Oxford: Clarendon Press, 1989.

Meyer, Ann Elizabeth. Islam and Human Rights: Tradition and Politics, 2nd ed. Boulder, CO: Westview Press, 1991.

Mill, John Stuart. On Liberty. London: Fontana Press, 1962.

Ministry of Foreign Affairs of the Kingdom of the Netherlands. Human Rights and Foreign Policy. The Hague: Ministry of Foreign Affairs of the Kingdom of the Netherlands, 1979.

Monshipouri, Mahmood. Islam, Secularism, and Human Rights in the Middle East. London: Lynne Rienner Pub., 1998.

Moskowitz, Moses. The Politics of Dynamics of Human Rights. New York: Oceana Pub., 1968.

Mower, Jr., A Glenn. Human Rights and American Foreign Policy: The Carter and Reagan Experiences. New York: Greenwood Press, 1987.

———. The United States, the United Nations, and Human Rights: The Eleanor Roosevelt and Jimmy Carter Eras. Westport, CT: Greenwood Press, 1979.

Morrison, Jr, Clovis C. The Dynamics of Development in the European Human Rights Convention System. The Hague: Martinus Nijhoff Pub., 1981.

Morrison, Jr, Clovis C. The Developing European Law of Human Rights. Leyden: A.W. Sijthoff., 1967.

Moskowitz, Moses. The Politics of Dynamics of Human Rights. New York: Oceana Pub., 1968.

Mower, Jr. Glenn A. Regional Human Rights: A Comparative Study of the West European and Inter-American Systems. New York: Greenwood Press, 1991.

Mullerson, Rein. Human Rights Diplomacy. London: Routlege, 1997.

Murphy, Sean D. Humanitarian Intervention: The United Nations in an Evolving World Order. Philadelphia: University of Pennsylvania, 1996.

McGrew, Anthony G. and G. Lewis et al. Global Politics: Globalization and the Nation-States. Oxford: Polity Press, 1992.

Melo, Jaime De. and Arvind Panagariya, ed. New dimensions in Regional Integration. Cambridge: Cambridge Unviersity Press, 1993.

Meron, Theodore, ed. Human Rights in International Law: Legal and Policy Issues: Oxford: Clarendon Press, 1984.

Mitrany, David. A Working Peace System. New York: Royal Institute of International Affairs, 1966.

———. The Functional Theory of Politics. London: Martin Robertson, 1975.

Morgenthau, Hans J. Politics among Nations. 5th ed. New York: Knoph 1978.

Muir, Ramsay. The Interdependent World and Its Problems. Port Washington, N.Y.: Kennikat Press, 1971.

Naisbitt, John. Global Paradox. London: Nicholas Brearley Pub., 1994.

Nanda, Ved P., James R. Scarritt, George W. Shepherd, Jr. Global Human Rights: Public Polices, Comparative Measures and NGO Strategies. Boulder, CO: Westview Press, 1981.

Newberg, Paula, ed. The Politics of Human Rights. New York: New York University Press, 1980.

Nelson, Jack L. and Vera M. Green. International Human Rights: Contemporary Issues. New Brunswick, Human Rights Publishing Group, 1980.

Newberg, Paula R. The Politics of Human Rights. New York: New York University Press, 1980.

Newsom, David D, ed. The Diplomacy of Human Rights. Lanham, MD: University Press of America, 1986.

Nickel, James. Making Sense of Human Rights: Philosophical Reflections on the Universal Declaration of Human Rights. Berkeley: University of California Press, 1987.

Newman, Frank and David Weissbrodt. International Human Rights. Cincinnati: Anderson Pub., 1990.

Nedjati, Zim M. Human Rights Under the European Convention. New York: North-Holland Pub., 1978.

Newman, Frank, C. and Lillich Richard B. International Human Rights: Problems of Law and Policy. Boston: Little Brown and Co., 1979.

Nickel, James W., Making Sense of Human Rights: Philosophical Reflections on the Universal Declaration of Human Rights. Berkeley: University of California Press, 1987.

Nye, Joseph S. International Regionalism: Readings. Boston, MA: Little, Brown and Co., 1968.

———. Peace in Parts: Integration and Conflict in Regional Organization. Boston, MA: Little, Brown and Co, 1971.

Ohmae, Kenichi. The Borderless World. London: Collins, 1990.

Ohno, Kenichi and Izumi Ohno, eds. Japanese Views on Economic Development: Diverse paths to the market. London: Routledge, 1998.

Okele, G.N. Controversial Subjects of Contemporary International Law. Rotterdam: University Press, 1974.

Oman, Charles. Globalization and Regionalization: The Challenge for Developing Countries. Paris: OECD Development Center, 1994.

Palmer, Norman D. The New Regionalism in Asia and the Pacific. Lexington, MA: D.C. Heath and Co., 1991.

Pei-heng, Chiang. Non-governmental Organizations at The United Nations: Identity, Role and Function. New York: Praeger, 1981.

Peter, Chris Maina: A Comparative Study of the African Human and Peoples' Rights Charter and the New Tanzanian Bill of Rights. New York: Greenwood Press, 1990.

Porter, Gareth and Janet Welsh Brown. Global Environmental Politics. Boulder, CO: Westview, 1990.

Plannter, Marc, ed. Human Rights in Our Time: Essays in Memory of Victor Baras. Boulder, CO: Westview Press, 1984.

Pollis, Adamantia and Peter Schwab, eds. Human Rights: Cultural and Ideological Perspectives. New York: Praeger, 1979.

Purvis, Hoyt. Interdependence: An Introduction to International Relations. New York: Harcourt Brace Jovanovich College Pub., 1992.

Quiroga, Cecilia Medina. The Battle of Human Rights: Gross, Systematic Violations and the Inter-American System. Dordrecht: Martijus Nijhoff Pub., 1988.

The Report of the Commission on Global Governance. Our Global Neighbourhood. Oxford: Oxford University Press, 1995.

Ramcharan B.G. Implementing the International Covenant on Human Rights Thirty Years After the Universal Declaration. The Hague: Martinus Nijthoff Pub., 1979.

———. International Law and Fact-Finding in the Field of Human Rights. The Hague: Martinus Nijthoff Pub., 1982.

Rawls, John. A Theory of Justice. Cambridge: Harvard University Press, 1971.

———. Political Liberalism. New York: Columbia University Press, 1993.

Reoch, Richard. Human Rights - the New Consensus. London: Regency Press, 1994.

Renteln, Alison Dundes. International Human Rights: Universalism Versus Relativism. London: Sage Pub., 1990.

Riker, William H. Federalism: Origin, Operation, Significance. Boston: Little, Brown and Co., 1964.

Robertson, Roland. Globalization: Social Theory and Global cClture. London: Sage, 1992.

Rosenau, James N. The Study of Global Interdependence: Essays on the Transnationanilzation of World Affairs. London: Frances Pinter, Ltd., 1980.

———. Turbulence in World Politics: A Theory of Change and Continuity. Princeton, N.J.: Princeton University Press, 1990.

Rosenau, James and Hylke Tromp, ed. Interdependence and Conflict in World Politics. Aldershot: Avebury, 1989.

Rehof, Lars Adam & Claus Gulmann, ed. Human Rights in Domestic Law and Development Assistance Policies of the Nordic Countries. Dordrecht: Martinus Nijhoff Pub., 1989.

Reports of the Asia Pacific NGO Conference on Human Rights and NGOs' Statements to the Asia Regional Meeting. Our Voice: Bangkok NGO Declaration on Human Rights. Bangkok: Edison Press, 1993.

Rhoodie, Eschel M. Discrimination Against Women: A Global Survey of the Economic, Educational, Social and Political Status of Women. Jefferson, NC: McFarland & Co., 1989.

Ricoeur, Paul. Philosophical Foundations of Human Rights. Paris: UNESCO, 1986.

Robertson, A.H. Human Rights in the World: An Introduction to the Study of the International Protection of Human Rights. Manchester: Manchester University Press, 1982.

———. The Council of Europe: Its Structures, Functions and Achievements. New York: Frederick A., Praeger, Inc. 1956.

Robertson, A.H. and J.G. Merrills. Human Rights in Europe: A Study of the European Convention on Human Rights. Manchester: Manchester University Press, 1993.

Robertson, A.H. and J.G. Merrills. Human Rights in the World: An Introduction to the Study of the International Protection of Human Rights, 4th ed. Manchester: Manchester University Press, 1996.

Rosenbaum, Alan S., ed. The Philosophy of Human Rights: International Perspectives. London: Aldwhch Press, 1980.

Russell, Ian, Peter Van Ness and Beng-Huat Chua. Australia's Human Rights Diplomacy. Canberra: The Australian National University, 1992.

Russett, Bruce M. International Regions and the International System: A Study in Political Ecology. Chicago: Rand McNally & Co., 1979.

Said, Abdul Aziz. Human Rights and World Order. New York: Praeger Pub., 1978.

Saksena, K.P. ed. Human Rights Perspective & Challenges (In 1990 and Beyond). New Delhi: World Congress on Human Rights, 1994.

Sakamoto, Yoshikazu, ed. Global Transformation: Challenges to the State System. Tokyo: United Nations University Press, 1994.

Saunders, Kate. Eighteen Layers of Hell: Stories From the Chinese Gulag. London: Cassell, 1996.

Saunders, Christopher T., ed. Regional Integration in East and West. New York: St. Martin's Press, 1983.

Schmale, Wolfgang, ed. Human Rights and Cultural Diversity: Europe-Arabic-Islamic World Africa-China. Goldbach, Germany: Keip Publishing, 1993.

Scholte, Jan Aart. International Relations of Social Change. Buckingham, PA: Open Unviersity Press, 1993.

Schemale, Wolfgang. Human Rights and Cultural Diversity: Europe-Arabic-Islamic World Africa-China. Goldbach, Germany: Keip Pub., 1993.

Schwab, Peter and Adamantia Pollis, ed. Toward A Human Rights Framework. New York: Praeger, 1982.

Schwelb, Egon. Human Rights and the International Community. Chicago: Quadrangle Books, 1964.

Schreiber, Anna. Tbe Inter-American Commission on Human Rights. Amsterdam: A.W. Sijthoff/Leiden, 1970.

Seligman, Adam B. The Idea of Civil Society. New York: The Free Press, 1992.

Sewell, James P. Functionalism and World Politics. Princeton: Princeton University Press, 1965.

Shaw, M.N. International Law 3rd ed. Cambridge: Grotius Pub., 1991.

Shaw, William, ed. Human Rights in Korea: Historical and Policy Perspectives. Cambridge: Harvard University Press, 1991.

Shepherd, Jr. George and Ved P. Nanda. Human Rights and Third World Development. Westport, CT: Greenwood Press, 1985.

Shaw, Martin. Civil Society and Media in Global Crises: Representing Distant Violence. London: Pinter, 1996.

Shepherd, Jr., George. and Ved P. Nanda., ed. Human Rights and Third World Development. Westport, CT: Greenwood Press, 1985.

Shute, Stephen and Susan Hurley, ed. Human Rights: the Oxford Amnesty Lectures 1993. New York: Basic Books, 1993.

Shihata, Ibrahim F.I. The World Bank in a Changing World. Dordrecht: Martinus Nijhoff, 1991.

Shue, Henry. Basic Rights: Subsistence, Affluence, and U.S. Foreign Policy. Princeton, N.J.: Princeton University Press, 1980.

Sieghart, Paul. The International Law of Human Rights. Oxford: Clarendon Press, 1983.

Soderberg, Marie, ed. The Business of Japanese Foreign Aid: Five case studies from Asia. London: Routledge, 1996.

Steiner, Henry and Philip Alston. International Human Rights in Context: Law, Politics, Morals. Oxford: Clarendon Press, 1996.

Steiner, Henry J. Diverse Partners: Non-Governmental Organizations in the Human Rights Movement. Cambridge, MA: the Harvard Law School Human Rights Program and Human Rights Internet, 1991.

Svensson, Marina. The Chinese Conception of Human Rights: the Debate on Human Rights in China, 1898–1949. Lund, Sweden: Studentlitteratur's Printing Office, 1996.

Spirer, Herbert and Louise Spirer. Data Analysis for Monitoring Human Rights. Washington, D.C.: American Association for Advancement of Science. 1994.

Spybey, Tony. Globalization and World Society. Cambridge, MA: Polity Press, 1996.

Steenbergen, Bart van, ed. The Condition of Citizenship. London: Sage Pub., 1994.

Stormorken, Bjorn. HURIDOCS Standard Formats for the Recording and Exchange of Information on Human Rights. Dordrecht: Martinus Nijhoff Pub., 1985.

Sweeney, Joseph Modeste, Covey Oliver T. and Noyes Leech E. The International Legal System. New York: The Foundation Press, Inc. 1988.

Shaw, William, ed. Human Rights in Korea: Historical and Policy Perspectives. Cambridge, MA: Harvard University Press, 1991.

Smith, Jacqeline, ed., Human Rights: Chinese and Dutch Perspectives. The Hague: Martinus Nijhoff Pub., 1996.

Sohn, Louis and Thomas Buergenthal. International Protection of Human Rights. New York: The Bobbs-Merrill Co., 1973.

Steiner, Henry and Philip Alston. International Human Rights in Context: Law, Politics, Morals. Oxford: Clarendon Press, 1996.

Tan, Joseph L, ed. Regional Economic Integration in the Asia-Pacific. Singapore: Institute of Southeast Asian Studies, 1993.

Taylor, Paul. and A.J.R. Groom, ed. Internaitonal Organization: A Conceptual Approach. London: Frances Pinter Ltd., 1978.

Teubner, Gunther, ed. Global Law Without a State. Aldershot: Dartmouth, 1997.

Thakur, Ramesh and Carlyle A. Thayer, ed. Reshaping Regional Relations: Asia-Pacific and the Former Soviet Union. Boulder, CO: Westview Press, 1993.

Tang, James T. H., ed. Human Rights and International Relations in the Asia-Pacific Region. London: Pinter, 1995.

Teson, Fernando R. Humanitarian Intervention: An Inquiry into Law and Morality. New York: Transnational Pub., 1997.

Thompson, Kenneth W., ed. The Moral Imperatives of Human Rights: a World Survey. Washington, D.C.: University Press of America for the Council on Religion and International Affairs, 1980.

Tardu, M.E. The International Petition System. Dobbs Ferry, 1985.

Tomasevski, Katarina. Development Aid and Human Rights: A Study for the Danish Center of Human Rights. New York: St. Martin's Press, 1989.

———. Development Aid and Human Rights Revisited. New York: Pinter Pub., 1993.

Thoolen, Hans and Berth Verstappen. Human Rights Missions: A Study of the Fact-Finding Practice of Non-governmental Organizations. Dordrecht: Martinus Nijhoff Pub., 1986.

Tolley, Jr. Howard B. The International Commission of Jurists. Philadelphia: University of Pennsylvania, 1994.

Umozurike, U. Oji. The African Charter on Human and Peoples' Rights. The Hague: Martinus Nijhoff Pub., 1997.

United Nations. Manual on Human Rights Reporting. Geneva: United Nations Human Rights Center, 1991.

United Nations. United Nations Actions in the Field of Human Rights. 1994.

United States House Committee on Foreign Affairs, Human Rights in the World Community: A Call for U.S. Leadership. Washington, D.C.: March 27, 1974.

Vernon, Raymond. Sovereignty at Bay. New York: Basic Books, 1971.

Van Dyke, V. Human Rights, the United States, and the World Community. New York: Oxford University Press, 1970.

Van Ness, Peter, ed. Debating Human Rights: Critical Essays from the United States and Asia. London: Routledge, 1999.

Vasak, Karel, ed. The International Dimensions of Human Rights. Westport, CT: Greenwood Press, 1982.

Vincent, R.J. Human Rights and International Relations. New York: Cambridge University Press, 1991.

————. ed. Foreign Policy and Human Rights: Issues and Responses. Cambridge: Cambridge University Press, 1986.

Vogelgesang, Sandy. American Dream Global Nightmare: The Dilemma of U.S. Human Rights Policy. New York: W.W. Norton & Co., 1980.

Vincent, R.J., ed. Foreign Policy and Human Rights. Cambridge: Cambridge University Press, 1986.

Vasak, Karel, ed. The International Dimensions of Human Rights. Westport, CT: Greenwood Press, 1982.

Wallerstein, Immanuel. The Capitalist World-Economy. Cambridge: Cambridge University Press, 1979.

Walker, R.B.J. One World, Many Worlds: Struggle for a Just World Peace. Boulder, CO: Lynne Rienner, 1988.

Walzer, Michael, ed. Toward A Glboal Civil Society. Providence, RI: Berghahn Books, 1995.

Ward, Barbara. Spaceship Earth. New York: Columbia University Press, 1966.

Waters, Malcolm. Globalization. London: Clays Ltd., 1995.

Wacks, Raymond, ed. Human Rights in Hong Kong. Oxford: Oxford University Press, 1992.

————. Hong Kong, China and 1997: Essays in Legal Theory. Hong Kong: Hong Kong University Press, 1993.

Waldron, Jeremy, ed. Theories of Rights. Oxford: Oxford University Press, 1984.

Warner, Daniel, ed. Human Rights and Humanitarian Law: The Quest for Universality. The Hague: Martinus Nijhoff Pub., 1997.

Weiss, Thomas George. International Burequcracy: An Analysis of the Operation of Functional and Global International Secretariats. Lexington, MA: D.C. Heath and Co, 1975.

Weiss, Thomas G. and Leon Gordenker, ed. NGOs, the UN, and Global Governance. Boulder, CO: Lynne Rienner Pub., 1996.

Welch Jr. Claude E. and Virginia A. Leary. Asian Perspectives on Human Rights. Boulder, CO: Westview Press, 1990.

Welch Jr. Claude E., and Ronald I. Meltzer, ed. Human Rights and Development in Africa. Albany, NY: State University of New York, 1984.

Weil, G.L. The European Convention on Human Rights. Leyden: A.W. Sijthoff, 1963.

Welch, Claude E. and Virginia A. Leary. Asian Perspectives on Human Rights. Boulder, CO: Westview Press, 1990.

Welch, Claude E. Protecting Human Rights in Africa: Roles and Strategies of Non-Governmental Organizations. Philadelphia: University of Pennsylvania Press, 1995.

White, L. International Non-Governmental Organizations: Their Purpose, Methods and Accomplishments. New Brunswick: Rutgers University Press, 1951.

Whitman, Marina N. Reflections of Interdependence: Issues for Economic Theory and U.S. Policy. Pittsburgh, PA: University of Pittsburgh Press, 1979.

Wiarda Gerard J. Protecting Human Rights: The European Dimension Berlin: CarlHeymanns Verlag KG, 1988.

Wu, Hongda Harry. Laogai - The Chinese Gulag. Boulder, CO: westview Press, 1992.

Wu, Yuan-li, et al. Human Rights in the People's Republic of China. Boulder, CO: Westview Press, 1988.

Wilson, Richard, ed. Human Rights, Culture & Context: Anthropological Perspectives. London: Pluto Press, 1997.

Winston, Morton E. The Philosophy of Human Rights. Belmont, CA: Wadsworth Pub., 1989.

World Assembly, ed. Citizens: Strengthening Global Civil Society Washington, D.C.: World Alliance for Citizen Participation, 1994.

Yalem, Ronald. Regionalism and World Order. Washington, D.C.: Public Affairs Press, 1979.

Yamamoto, Tadashi, ed. Emerging Civil Society in the Asia Pacific Community: Nongovernmental Underpinnings of the Emerging Asia Pacific Regional Community. Singapore and Tokyo: Institute of Southeast Asian Studies and Japan Center for International Exchange, 1995.

Yasutomo, Dennis T. The New Multilateralism in Japan's Foreign Policy. New York: St. Martin's Press, 1995.

Young, Oran R, ed. Global Governance: Drawing Insights from the Envirnmental Experience. Cambridge, MA: The MIT Press, 1997.

Zolo, Danilo. Cosmopolis: Prospects for World Government. Cambridge: Polity Press, 1997.

Zuijdwijk, T.J.M. Petitioning the United Nations: A Study in Human Rights. New York: St. Martin's Press, 1982.
Zwart, Tom. The Admissibility of Human Rights Petitions: The Case Law of the European Commission of Human Rights and the Human Rights Committee. Dordrecht: Martinus Nijhoff Pub., 1994.

ARTICLES

Alston, Philip. "UNESCO's Procedure for Dealing With Human Rights Violations" *Santa Clara Law Review* 20 (1980): 665–696.
———. "U.S. Ratification of the Covenant on Economic, Social and Cultural Rights: The Need for an Entirely New Strategy" *American Journal of International Law* (1990): 365–393.
Alston, Philip. "Conjuring Up New Human Rights: A Proposal for Quality Control" *American Journal of International Law* (July 1984): 607–621.
Asante, S.K.B. "Nation Building and Human Rights in Emergent Africa" *Cornell International Law Journal* 2 (1969): 72–107.
Ahn, Chung-Si. "Economic Development and Democratization in South Korea" *Korea and World Affairs* 15 (1991): 740–754.
Ahn, Choong Yong. "Economic Cooperation in Northeast Asia: Feasibility or Illusion?" *Jounrnal of Economic Development* 18 (June 1993): 81–100.
Alker, Hayward R. "A methodology for design research on interdependence alternatives" *International Organization* (1977): 29–63.
Askin, Kelly Down. "Issues Surrounding the Creation of a Regional Human Rights System for the Asia-Pacific" *ILSA Journal of International & Comparative Law* (Spring 1998): 599–601.

Baehr, Peter. "Human Rights: A Common Standard of Achievement?" *Netherlands Quarterly of Human Rights.* 9 (1991): 5–18.
Baldwin, David A. "Interdependence and Power: A Conceptual Analysis" *International Organization* (1980): 471–506.
Barsh, Russel Lawrence. "The Right to Development as a Human Right: Results of the Global Consultation" *Human Rights Quarterly* 13 (1991): 322–338.
Badawi El-Shikh, Ibrahim "The African Commission on Human and Peoples' Rights: Prospects and Problems" *Netherlands Quarterly of Human Rights* 7 (1989): 272–283.
Ball, M. "The Organization of American States and the Council of Europe," *British Yearbook of International Law* 26 (1949):150–176.
Barkin, J. Samuel and Bruce Cronin. "The state and the nation: changing norms and the rules of sovereignty in international relations" *International Organization* 43 (Winter 1994): 107–130.
Baehr, P.R. "Concern for Development Aid and Fundamental Human Rights: The Dilemma as Faced by the Netherlands" *Human Rights Quarterly* (1982): 39–52.
Beg, Mirza Hameedullah. "Human Rights and Asia" *Santa Clara Law Review* 20 (Spring 1980): 319–350

Bell, Daniel. "The East Asian Challenge to Human Rights: Reflection on an East West Dialogue" *Human Rights Quarterly* 18 (1996): 641–667.

Beer, Lawrence W. "Group Rights and Individual Rights in Japan" *Asian Survey* 21 (April 1981): 437–453.

Beer, Lawrence W. and C.G. Weeramantry. "Human Rights in Japan: Some Protections and Problems" *Universal Human Rights* (1979): 1– 33.

Benedek, Wolfgang. "The African Charter and Commission on Human and Peoples' Rights: How to make it more effective." *Netherlands Quarterly of Human Rights* 11 (1993): 25–40.

Bell, Daniel. "American exceptionalism" revisited: the role of civil society. *The Public Interest* (Fall 1975): 38–56.

Berger, Peter L "Are Human Rights Universal?" *Commentary* 64 (September 1977): 60–63.

Bielefeldt, Heiner. "Muslim Voices in the Human Rights Debate." *Human Rights Quarterly* 17 (1995): 587–617.

Bilder, R.B. "Human Rights and U.S. Foreign Policy: Short-Term Prospects" 14 *Virginia Journal of International Law* (1974): 597–609.

Bilder, Richard B "Rethinking International Human Rights: Some Basic Questions" *Human Rights Journal* 2 (December 1969): 557–608.

Blaser, Arthur W. "How to Advance Human Rights Without Really Trying: An Analysis of Nongovernmental Tribunals" *Human Rights Quarterly* (1992): 339–370.

Boerefijn, Ineke and Koen Davidse "Every Cloud..? The World Conference on Human Rights and Supervision of Implementation of Human Rights" *Netherlands Quarterly of Human Rights* (1993): 457–468.

Boven, Theo van. "The United Nations Sub-Commission on Prevention of Discrimination and Protection of Minorities" *Netherlands Quarterly of Human Rights* (1989): 464–471

Bradlow, Daniel D. and Claudio Grossman. "Limited Mandates and Intertwined Problems: A New Challenge for the World Bank and the IMF" *Human Rights Quarterly* 17 (1995): 411–442.

Bouvier-Azam, Solange. "The Thirteenth Conference of the United Nations Nongovernmental Organizations" *Review of Contemporary Law* No.2 (1976): 182.

Boyan, Callestio and Harold Burnham. "Eurocontrol: A Reapraisal of Functional Integration" *Journal of Common Market Studies* 13 (January 1975): 345–367.

Boven, Theo van. "Combating Racial Discrimination in the World and in Europe" *Netherlands Quarterly of Human Rights* 11 (1993): 163–172.

Brar, P. "The Practice and Procedures of the Human Rights Committee under the Optional Protocol of the International Covenant on Civil and Political Rights" 25 *Indian Journal of International Law* (1985):

Buergenthal, Thomas. "Human Rights in the Americas: View from the Inter-American Court." *Connecticut Journal of International Law* 2 (1987): 387–389.

———. "The Inter-American Court of Human Rights" *American Journal of International Law* 76 (April 1982): 231–245.

———. "International and Regional Human Rights Law and Institutions: Some Examples of Their Interaction" *Texas International Law Journal* 12 (Spring/Summer 1977): 321–330.

———. "The Revised OAS Charter and the Protection of Human Rights" *American Journal of International Law* 69 (October 1975): 828–836.

———. "The American Convention on Human Rights: Illusions and Hopes" *Buffalo Law Review* 21 (1971–1972): 121–136.

———. "The American and European Convention on Human Rights: Similarities and Differences" *American University of Law Review* 30 (Fall 1980): 155–166.

———. "The Evolution of the European Convention on Human Rights" *American Journal of International Law* 57 (October 1963): 804–827.

Brownlie, Ian. "The Place of the Individual in International Law" *Virginia Law Review* 50 (March 1964): 435–462.

Brett, Rachel. "The Role and Limits of Human Rights NGOs at the United Nations." *Political Studies* 43 (1995): 96–110.

Brems, Eva. "Enemies or Allies? Feminism and Cultural Relativism as Dissident Voices in Human Rights Discourse" *Human Rights Quarterly* 19 (1997): 136–164.

Cabra, Monroy and Gerardo, Marco. "Rights and Duties Established by the American Convention on Human Rights" *The American University Law Review* 30 (Fall 1980): 21–64.

Cabranes, Jose. "Human Rights and Non-Intervention in the Inter-American System" *Michigan Law Review* 65 (Fall 1967): 1147–1182.

———. "The Protection of Human Rights by the OAS" *American Journal of International Law* 62 (October 1968):889–908.

Camargo, P.P. "The American Convention on Human Rights" *Human Rights Journal* III-2 (1970): 333–356.

Carey, John. "The United Nations' Double Standard on Human Rights Complaints" *American Journal of International Law* 60 (October 1966): 792–803.

———. "Procedures for International Protection of Human Rights" *Iowa Law Review* 53 (October 1967): 291–324.

Carlos, Abranches and Dunshee, de Alberto. "The Inter-American Court of Human Rights" *The American University Law Review* 30 (Fall 1980): 79–125.

Carleton, D. and M. Stohl. "The role of human rights in U.S. foreign assistance policy: A critique and reappraisal" *American Journal of Political Science* (1987): 1002–1018.

Cassese, Antonio. "A New Approach to Human Rights: The European Convention for the Prevention of Torture" *American Journal of International Law* 83 (1989): 128–153.

Caporaso, James A. "Dependence, Dependency, and Power in the Global System: A Sturctural and Behavioral Analysis" *International Organization* (Winter 1978): 13–43.

————. "Regional Intergration Theory: Understanding of Our Past and Anticipating Our Future" *Journal of European Public Policy* (March 1998): 1–16.

Cerna, Christina M. "Universality of Human Rights and Cultural Diversity: Implementation of Human Rights in Different Socio-Cultural Contexts" *Human Rights Quarterly* 16 (1994): 740–752.

————."The Inter-American Commission on Human Rights" *Connecticut Journal of International Law* 2 (1987): 311–318.

Charnovitz, Steve. "Two Centuries of Participation: NGOs and International Governance" *Michigan Journal of International Law* 18 (Winter 1997): 183–286.

Christenson, Gordon A. "World Civil Society and the International Rule of Law" *Human Rights Quarterly* 19 (1997): 724–737.

Claude, Richard Pierre. "Human Rights Education: The Case of the Philippines" *Human Rights Quarterly* 13 (1991): 453–524.

Chew, Melanie. "Human Rights in Singapore" *Asian Survey* 34 (November 1994): 933–948.

Cingranelli, D and T. Pasquarello. "Human Rights Practices and the Distribution of U.S. Foreign Aid to Latin American Countries" *American Journal of Political Science* (1986): 539–563.

Claude, Jr, Inis L. "The Nature and Status of the Sub-Commission on Prevention of Discrimination and Protection of Minorities" *International Organization* (May 1951): 300–312.

Cobbah, Josiah A.M. "African Values and the Human Rights Debate: An African Perspective." *Human Rights Quarterly* 9 (1987): 309–331.

Coblentz, W. and Warshaw R. "The European Convention for the Protection of Human Rights and Fundamental Freedoms" *California Law Review* 44 (March 1956): 94–104.

Cohen, Cynthia Price, Stuart N. Hart, and Susan M. Kosloske. "The UN Convention on the Rights of the Child: Developing an Information Model to Computerize the Monitoring Treaty Compliance" *Human Rights Quarterly* 14 (19920: 216–231.

Cook, Helena M. "International Human Rights Mechanism: The Role of the Special Procedures in the Protection of Human Rights The Way Forward After Vienna" *The Review* (June 1993): 31–55.

D'Costa, Bina. "Challenge for An Independent Asian Human Rights Commission" *ISLA Journal of International & Comparative Law* (Spring 1998): 615–621.

D'Amato, Anthony. "The Concept of Human Rights in International Law" *Columbia Law Review* 82 (1982): 1110–1159.

Dae Jung, Kim. "Is Culture Destiny? The Myth of Asia's Anti-Democratic Values" *Foreign Affairs* 73 (Nov/Dec. 1994): 189–194.

Davidse, Koen."Many Happy Returns? The 50th Session of the UN Commission on Human Rights" *Netherlands Quarterly of Human Rights* 12 (1994): 165–175.

Davis, Michael C. "The Price of Rights: Constitutionalism and East Asian Economic Development" *Human Rights Quarterly* 20 (1998): 303–337.

Danelius, Hans. "The United Nations Fund for Torture Victims: The First Years of Activity" *Human Rights Quarterly* (May 1986): 294–305.

de Oliveira, Miguel Darcy. "Civilization - Sociological Aspects" *National Civic Review* 84 (Spring 1995):

Donnelly, Jack. "Human Rights in the New World Order" *World Policy Journal* (Spring 1992): 251–277.

———. "The United Nations and Human Rights: More Than A Whimper Less Than A Roar" *Human Rights Quarterly* 9 (1987): 550–586.

Duvall, Raymond D. "Dependence and Dependencia Theory: Notes Toward Precision of Concept and Argument" *International Organization* (Winter 1978): 51–78.

Denys, Myres P. "Human Rights in Europe" *American Journal of International Law* 48 (April 1954): 299–301.

de Zayas, Alfred M. et al. "Application of the International Covenant on Civil and Political Rights under the Optional Protocol by the Human Rights Committee" 28 *German Yearbook of International Law* 9 (1985): 9–64.

Devine, D.J. "The Protection of Human Rights in the Case of Supranational Economic Integration" *South African Journal on Human Rights* 6 (1990): 48–59.

Diokno, Jose W. "Asian Lawyers, People's Rights and Human Rights" *New Zealand Law Journal* (February 1980): 43–47.

Dreier, J.C. "New Wine and Old Bottles: The Changing Inter-American System" *International Organization* 22 (Spring 1968): 477–493.

de Neufville, Judith Innes "Human Rights Reporting as a Policy Tool: An Examination of the State Department Country Reports" *Human Rights Quarterly* (Nov. 1986): 681–699.

Dijk, P. Van and A. Bloed. "The Conference on Security and Cooperation in Europe, Human Rights and Non-Intervention" *The Liverpool Law Review* (Spring 1983): 117–142.

Ding, Yi. "Opposing Interference in Other Countries' Internal Affairs Through Human Rights" *Beijing Review* 32 (1989): 10–12.

Donoho, Douglas Lee. "Relativism Versus Universalism in Human Rights: The Search for Meaningful Standards." *Stanford Journal of International Law* (Spring 1991): 345–391.

Donnelly, Jack. "Cultural Relativism and Universal Human Rights" *Human Rights Quarterly* 6 (1984): 400–419.

———. "Human Rights and Human Dignity: An Analytic Critique of Non-Western Conceptions of Human Rights" *American Political Science Review* 76 (June 1982): 303–316.

———. "How are Rights and Duties Correlative?" *Journal of Value Inquiry* 16 (1982): 287–297.

Emerson, Ruper. "The Fate of Human Rights in the Third World" *World Politics* (January 1975): 201–226.

Eissen, Marc-Andre "The European Convention on Human Rights and the United Nations Covenant on Civil and Political Rights: Problems of Co-Existence" *Buffalo Law Review* 22 (Spring 1973):187–216.

Evans, Malcolm and Rod Morgan. "The European Convention for the Prevention of Torture: Operational Practice" *International and Comparative Law Quarterly* 4 (July 1992): 590–614.

Farer, Tom J. "Intervention and Human Rights: The Latin American Context" *California Western International Law Journal* 12 (19870: 503–507.

Farer, Tom. "The Rise of the Inter-American Human Rights Regime: No Longer a Unicorn, Not Yet an Ox" *Human Rights Quarterly* 19 (1977): 510–546.

Falk, Richard. "Global Civil Society: Perspectives, Initiatives, Movements" *Oxford Development Studies* 26 (Feb 1998): 99–110.

Fawsett J.E.S. "The European Commission of Human Rights at Work" *The World Today* 5 (May 1972): 209–215.

Farer, Tom. "New Players in the Old Game: The De Facto Expansion of Standing to Participate in Global Security Negotiations" *American Behavioral Scientist* 38 (May 1995): 842–866.

Feld, Werner. "Nongovernmental Entities and the International System: A Preliminary Quantitative Overview" *Orbis* (Fall 1971): 879–922.

Fisher, Danda D. "Reporting under the Covenant on Civil and Political Rights: The First Five Years of the Human Rights Committee" *American Journal of International Law* (January 1982): 142–153.

Fournier, Fernando. "The Inter-American Human Rights System" *De Paul Law Review* 21 (Winter 1971): 376–396.

Franck, Thomas. "The Emerging Right to Democratic Governance" *American Journal of International Law* 86 (1992): 46–91.

Frost, Lynda E. "The Evolution of the Inter-American Court of Human Rights: Reflections of Present and Former Judges" *Human Rights Quarterly* 14 (1992): 171–205.

Frowein, Jochen. "The European and the American Conventions on Human Rights - A Comparison." *Human Rights Law Journal* 1 (1980): 44–65.

Forsythe, David P. "The United Nations and Human Rights, 1945–1985" *Political Science Quarterly* 100 (Summer 1985): 249–269.

Fukuyama, Francis. "Capitalism & Democracy: The Missing Link" *Journal of Democracy* 3 (July 1992): 100–110.

Ghai, Yash. "Human Rights and Governance: The Asia Debate" The *Australian Yearbook of International Law* 15 (1994): 1–34.

Galtung, Johan. "A Structural Theory of Integration" *Journal of Peace Research* 5 (1968): 375–394.

Gladwyn, Lord. "World Order and the Nation-State - A Regional Approach" *Daedalus* 95 (Spring 1966): 694–703.

Gaer, Felice D. "First Fruits: Reporting by States Under the African Charter on Human Peoples' Rights" *Netherlands Quarterly of Human Rights* 10 (1992): 29–42.

Garcia, Bauer, Carlos. "The Observance of Human Rights and the Structure of the System for their Protection in the Western Hemisphere" *The American University Law Review* 30 (Fall 1980): 5–20

Ghandhi, P.R. "The Human Rights Committee and the Right of Individual Communication" *British Yearbook of International Law* 57 (1986): 201–251.

Gold, Thomas. "The Resurgence of Civil Society in China" *Journal of Democracy* (Winter 1990): 18–31.

Good, Martha H. "Freedom of Expression in Comparative Perspective: Japan's Quiet Revolution" *Human Rights Quarterly* 7 (August 1985): 429–445.

Greenberg, Jack and Shalit Anthony R. "New Horizons for Human Rights: The European Convention Court and Commission on Human Rights" *Columbia Law Review* 63 (January 1963): 1384–1412.

Gormley, Paul W. "An Analysis of the Future Procedural Status of the Individual Before International Tribunals." *University of Detroit Law Journal* 39 (1961): 38–88.

Gross, Bertram. "Towards a Human Rights Century" *Human Rights Quarterly* 13 (1991): 387–395.

Gillies, David. "Human Rights, Democracy, and "Good Governance" Stretching the World Bank's Policy Frontiers," a paper presented at the International Conference on Human Rights in a New World Order, Prague, Czech Republic, June 9–12, 1992.

———. "Cultural Absolutism and the Nostalgia for Community" *Human Rights Quarterly* 15 (1993): 315–338.

Haver, Peter. "The United Nations Sub-Commission on the Prevention of Discrimination and the Protection of Minorities" *Columbia Journal of Transnational Law* 21 (1982): 103–134;

Hollenbach, David. "Human Rights and Religious Faith in the Middle East: Reflections of a Christian Theologian" *Human Rights Quarterly* 4 (1982): 94–109.

Haas, Ernst B. and Philippe C. Schmitter. "Economics and Differential Patterns of Poltical Integration: Projections About Unity in Latin America" *International Organization* 18 (Autumn 1964): 705–737.

Haas, Ernst B. "Regionalism, Functionalism and International Organization" *World Politics* (1956): 238–263.

———and Mario Barrera."The Operationalization of Some Variables Related to Regional Integration: A Research Note. *International Organization* 23 (Winter 1969): 150–160.

———. "The Challenge of Regionalism" *International Organization* 12 (Autumn 1958): 440–458.

Hansen, Roger D. "Regional Integration: Reflection on a Decade of Theoretical Efforts" *World Politics* 21 (1969): 242–271.

Halderman, John W. "Advancing Human Rights Through the United Nations" *Law and Contemporary Problems* 43 (Spring 1979): 275–287

Haver, Peter. "The United Nations Sub-Commission on the Prevention of Discrimination and the Protection of Minorities" *Columbia Journal of Transnational Law* (1982): 103–134.

Hobe, Stephan. "Global Challenge to Statehood: The Increasingly Important Role of Nongovernmental Organizations" *Global Legal Studies Journal* (Fall 1997): 191–209.

Holsti, Kal J. "A New International Politics? Diplomacy in Complex Interdependence" *International Organization* (Spring 1978): 513–530

Howard, Rhoda. "Evaluating Human Rights in Africa: Some Problems of Implicit Comparison" *Human Rights Quarterly* 6 (May 1984): 160–179.

Huntington, Samuel P. "The Clash of Civilization?" *Foreign Affairs* 72 (1993): 22–49.

———. "Human Rights and American Power" *Commentary* (September 1981):

Hassan P. "The International Covenant on Human Rights: An Approaches to Interpretation" *Buffalo Law Review* 19 (1968–1969): 35–50.

Henkin, Louis. "The United Nations and Human Rights" *International Organization* 19 (1965): 504–517.

Heyns, Christof. "African Human Rights Law and the European Convention" *South African Journal on Human Rights* 11 (1995): 252–263

Higgins, Rosalyn. "Derogations under Human Rights Treaties" *British Yearbook of International Law* 47 (1975–1976): 645–657.

Hsiao, Hsin-Huang Michael. "Emerging Social Movement and the Rise of a Demanding Society in Taiwan" *The Australian Journal of Chinese Affairs* (July 1990): 163–179.

Howard, Rhoda. "Evaluating Human Rights in Africa: Some Problems of Implicit Comparisons" *Human Rights Quarterly* 6 (May 1984): 160–179.

Ignatieff, Michael."On Civil Society: Why Eastern Europe's Revolutions Could Succeed" *Foreign Affairs* (March/April 1995): 128–136.

Iwasawa, Yuji. "The Impact of International Human Rights Law on Japanese Law - The Third Reformation for Japanese Women" *The Japanese Annual of International Law* 34 (1991): 21–68.

———. "Legal Treatment of Koreans in Japan: The Impact of International Human Rights Law On Japanese Law" *Human Rights Quarterly* 8 (May 1986): 131–179.

Ishaque, Khalid M. "Human Rights in Islamic law" *Review of the International Commission of Jurists* 12 (1974): 30–39.

Jung, Kim Dae. "Is Culture Destiny? The Myth of Asia's Anti-Democratic Values" *Foreign Affairs* (Nov./Dec. 1994): 189–194.

Jones, Sidney. "Regional Institutions for Protecting Human Rights in Asia" *Australian Journal of International Affairs* 50 (1996): 269–277.

Johnston, Douglas M. "Functionalism in the Theory of International Law" *The Canadian Yearbook of International Law* (1988): 3–59.

Kamminga, M.T. "The Thematic Procedures of the UN Commission on Human Rights" *Netherlands International Law Review* (1987): 299–323.

Kathree, Fayeeza. "Convention on the Elimination of All Forms of Discrimination Against Women" *South African Journal of Human Rights* 11(1995): 421–437.

Kaufman, N. Hevener and David Whitman. "Opposition to Human Rights Treaties in the United States Senate: The Legacy of the Bricker Amendment" *Human Rights Quarterly* (August 1988): 309–338.

Kausikan, Bilahari. "Asia's Different Standard" 92 *Foreign Policy* (1993): 24–41.

Kawashima, Yoshio. "The International Covenants on Human Rights and the Japanese Legal System" *The Japanese Annual of International Law* 22 (1978): 54–74.

Kim, Sunhyuk. "Civil Society in South Korea: From Grand Democracy Movements to Petty Interest Groups?" *Journal of Northeast Asian Studies* (Summer 1996): 81–97.

———. "State and Civil Society in South Korea's Democratic Consolidation: Is the Battle Really Over?" *Asian Survey* 37 (Dec. 1997): 1135–1144.

Khadduri, Majid. "Human Rights in Islam" *The Annals* 243 (1946): 77–81.

Kaiser, Ronn. "Toward the Copernican Phase of Regional Integration Theory" *Journal of Common Market Studies* (March 1972): 207–232.

Katzenstein, Peter. "International Interdependence: Some long-Term Trends and Recent Changes" *International Organization* (Autumn 1975): 1021–1034.

Kaufman, Edy. "Prisoner of Conscience: the Shaping of A New Human Rights Concept." *Human Rights Quarterly* 13 (August 1991): 339–367.

Keohane Robert O. and Joseph S. Nye Jr. "Power and Interdependence in the Information Age" *Foreign Affairs* (September/October 1998): 81–94.

Kim, Sunhyuk. "State and Civil Society in South Korea's Democratic Consolidation" *Asian Survey* 37 (Dec. 1997): 1135–1144.

Kowack, Glenn. "Internet Governance and the Emergence of Global Civil Society" *IEEE Communications Magazine* (May 1997): 52–57.

Khushalani, Yougindra. "Human Rights in Asia and Africa" 4 *Human Rights Law Journal* 406 (1983): 403–442.

Kirkpatrick, Jeane. "Human Rights and American Foreign Policy" *Commentary* (November 1981): 42–46.

———. "Dictatorship and Double Standard" *Commentary* 68 (November 1979): 34–45.

Lipschutz, Ronnie D. "Emerging World Politics: The Emergence of Global Civil Society" *Millenium* (Winter 1992): 389–420.

Livezey, Lowell W. "Human Rights and the NGOs." *The Center Magazine* (May/June 1984): 30–37.

Lansing, Paul and Tamra Domeyer. "Japan's Attempt at Internationalization and Its lack of Sensitivity to Minority Issues" *California Western International Law Journal* 22 (1991): 135–157.

Lawrence J LeBlanc "The Inter-American Commission on Human Rights" *Human Rights Journal* 4 (July/December 1976): 645–657

Landy, Ernest A. "The Implementation Procedures of the International Labor Organization" *Santa Clara Law Review* (Summer 1980): 633–663.

Lee, Seung-Hwan. "Was there a concept of rights in Confucian virtue-based morality? *Journal of Chinese Philosophy* 19 (1992): 241–261.

Li, Xiaorong. "Asian Values and the Universality of Human Rights" *Philosophy & Public Policy*. 16 (Spring 1996): 18–23.

Manglapus, Raul. "Human Rights Are Not A Western Discovery" *Worldview* 4 (1978): 4–6.

Marfording, Annette. "Cultural Relativism and the Construction of Culture: An Examination of Japan." *Human Rights Quarterly* 19 (1997): 431–448.

Mahmud, Sakah S. "The State and Human Rights in Africa in the 1990s: Perspectives and Prospects" *Human Rights Quarterly* 15 (1993): 485–498.

Meyer, Ann Elizabeth "Universal Versus Islamic Human Rights: A Clash of Cultures or a Clash with Construct?" *Michigan Journal of International Law* 15 (1994): 317–392.

Mills, Kurt. "Reconstructing Sovereignty: A Human Rights Perspective" *Netherlands Quarterly of Human Rights* (September 1997): 267–290.

Moller, Nicholas H. "The World Bank: Human Rights, Democracy and Governance" *Netherlands Quarterly of Human Rights* (March 1997): 21–45.

Moynihan, Daniel P. "The Politics of Human Rights" *Commentary* (Aug. 1977): 19–26.

Mathews, Jessica T. "Power Shift" *Foregin Affairs* 76 (January/February 1997): 50–66.

Mitrany, David. "The Functional Approach to World Organization" *International Affairs* (July 1948): 350–363.

Montias, J.M. "Problems of Integration" *World Politics* 18 (July 1966): 718–726.

Marfording, Annette. "Cultural Relativism and the Construction of the Culture: An Examination of Japan" *Human Rights Quarterly* 19 (1997): 431–448.

MacDonald R St. J. "The OAS in Action" *University of Toronto Law Journal* 15 (1963–1964): 358–429.

Marfording, Annette. "Cultural Relativism and the Construction of Culture: An Examination of Japan" *Human Rights Quarterly* 19 (1997): 431–448.

Medina, Cecilia. "The Inter-American Commission on Human Rights and the Inter-American Court of Human Rights: Reflections on a Joint Venture." *Human Rights Quarterly* 12 (November 1990): 439–464

———. "The Role of Country Report in the Inter-American System of Human Rights" *Netherlands Quaterly of Human Rights* 15 (Dec. 1997): 457–473.

Morrison, Clovis C. "The European Human Rights Convention System as a Functional Enterprise" *Universal Human Rights* (Oct.-Dec. 1979): 81–92.

Mower, Jr. A. Glenn. "The American Convention on Human Rights: Will it Be Effective?" *Orbis* 15 (1972): 1147–1172.

———. "The Implementation of the United Nations Covenant on Civil and Political Rights" Human Rights Journal 10 (1977): 271–295.

Mutua, Makau. "The African Human Rights System in a Comparative Perspective: The Need for Urgent Reformation" *The Nairobi Law Monthly* 44 (July 1993): 27–30.

———. "The African Human Rights Court: A Two-Legged Stool?" *Human Rights Quarterly* 21 (1999): 342–363.

Murphy, Jr. Cornelius F. "Objections to Western Conceptions of Human Rights" *Hofstra Law Review* 9 (Winter 1981): 433–447.

Nawaz, M.K. "The Concept of Human Rights in Islamic Law" *Howard Law Journal* (1965): 325–332.

Neier, Aryeh. "Asia's Unacceptable Standard" *Human Rights Law Journal* 406 (1983): 42–51.

Murphy, Jr Cornelius F. "Objections to Western Conceptions of Human Rights" 9 *Hofstra Law Review* (1981): 433–447.

Nawaz, M.K. "The Concept of Human Rights in Islamic Law" *Howard Law Journal* 2 (Spring 1965): 325–332.

Nielsen, Kai. "Skepticism and Human Rights" *Monist* 52 (1968): 573–594.

Nathanson, Nathaniel L. "Human Rights in Japan Through the Looking-Glass of Supreme Court Opinions" *Howard Law Journal* 11 (1965): 316–324.

Nishimura, Kunio. "The New Volunteerism: Japanese NGOs - Helping Hands" *Transnational Association* (1993): 13–16.

Norris, Robert E. "Bringing Human Rights Petitions before the Inter-American Commission" *Santa Clara Law Review* 20 (Summer 1980): 733–772.

———. "Observation in Loco: Practice and Procedure of the Inter-American Commission" *Texas International Law Journal* 15 (Winter 1980): 46–95.

Nolan, Cathal J. "The Influence of Parliament on Human Rights in Canadian Foreign Policy" *Human Rights Quarterly*

Nowicki, Marek Antoni. "NGOs before the European Commission and the Court of Human Rights." *Netherlands Quarterly of Human Rights.* 14 (September 1996): 289–302.

Nye, Joseph S. "Comparative Regional Integration: Concept and Measurement" *International Organization* 22 (Autumn 1968): 855–880.

———. "Patterns and Catalysts in Regional Integration" *International Organization* 19 (Autumn 1965): 870–884.

Nowak, Manfred. "Proposals for Improving the UN Human Rights Programme" *Netherlands Quarterly of Human Rights* (1993): 153–162.

Obilade, A.O. "The Individual as A Subject of International Law" *The Indian Journal of International Law* 14 (Jan-Mar. 1974): 90–99.

Ojo, Olusola and Amadu Sesay. "The O.A.U. and Human Rights: Prospects for the 1980s and Beyond" *Human Rights Quarterly* 89–103.

Obilade, A.O. "The Individual as a Subject of International Law" *The Indian Journal of International Law* 14 (Jan- Mar. 1974): 90–99.

Ohmae, Kenichi. "Putting Global Logic First" *Harvard Business Review* (January-February 1995): 119–125.

Odinkalu, Anselm Chidi. "Proposals for Review of the Rules of Procedure of the African Commission of Human and Peoples' Rights" *Human Rights Quarterly* 15 (1993): 533–548.

Okere, Obinna. "The Protection of Human Rights in Africa and the African Charter on Human and Peoples' Rights: A Comparative Analysis with the European and American Systems." *Human Rights Quarterly* 6 (1984): 141–59.

Omozurike, U.O. "The Protection of Human Rights under the Banjul Charter on Human and Peoples' Rights" *African Journal of International Law* 1 (1988): 82–83.

Onuma, Yasuaki. "Interplay Between Human Rights Activities and Legal Standards of Human Rights: A Case Study on the Korean Minority in Japan" *Cornell International Law Journal* 25 (1992): 515–540.

Otto, Dianne. "Nongovernmetal Organizations in the United Nations System: The Emerging Role of International Civil Society" *Human Rights Quarterly* 18 (1996): 107–141.

Panikkar, R. "Is the Notion of Human Rights A Western Concept?" *Digenes* (Winter 1982): 75–102.

Pease, Kelly Kate and David P. Forsythe. "Human Rights, Humanitarian Intervention, and World Politics" *Human Rights Quarterly* 15 (1993): 290–314.

Peek, John M. "Buddhism, Human Rights and the Japanese State" 17 *Human Rights Quarterly* (1995): 527–540.

Perry, Michael. "Are Human Rights Universal? The Relativist Challenge and Related Matters" *Human Rights Quarterly* 19 (1997): 461–509.

Panikkar, Raimundo. "Is the Notion of Human Rights a Western Concept?" *Diogenes* (Winter 1982): 75–102.

Peace, Kelly Kate and David P. Forsythe "Human Rights, Humanitarian Intervention, and World Politics" *Human Rights Quarterly* 15 (1993): 290–314.

Pollis, Adamantia. "Cultural Relativism Revisited: Through a State Prism" *Human Rights Quarterly* 18 (1996): 316–344.

Posner, Michael H. and Candy Whittome. "The Status of Human Rights NGOs" *Columbia Human Rights Law Review* 25 (1994): 269–290.

Potter, Pitman. "Universalism Versus Regionalism in International Organization" *American Political Science Review* (1943): 850–862

Puchara, Donald J. "Reviews and Other Discussion: The Pattern of Contemporary Regional Integration" *International Studies Quarterly* 12 (March 1968): 38–64.

———."The Pattern of Contemporary Regional Integration" 12 *International Studies Quarterly* (March 1968): 38–64.

Peek, John M. "Japan, the United Nations, and Human Rights" *Asian Survey* (March 1992): 217–229.

Peerenboom, R.P. "What's Wrong with Chinese Rights?: Toward a Theory of Rights with Chinese Characteristics" *Harvard Human Rights Law Journal* 6 (1993): 29–57.

Pena, Benito. "Note: Human Rights The Statute of the Inter-American Court of Human Rights" *Harvard International Law Journal* 21 (Fall 1980): 735–742.

Port, Kenneth L. "The Japanese International Law "Revolution": International Human Rights Law and Its Impact in Japan" *Stanford Journal of International Law* 28 (Fall 1991): 139–172.

Powell, G.L. "The Council of Europe" *International Law Quarterly* 3 (1950): 164–196.

Prasad, Maya. "The Role of Non-Governmental Organizations in the New United Nations Procedures for Human Rights complaints" *Denver Journal of International Law and Policy* 5 (1975): 441–462.

Poe, Steven C. "Human Rights and US Foreign Aid: A Review of Quantitative Studies and Suggestions for Future Research" *Human Rights Quarterly* 12 (November 1992): 499–512.

Pollis, Adamantia. "Cultural Relativism Revisited: Through a State Prism." *Human Rights Quarterly* 18 (1996): 316–344

Qazilbash, Ali Mohsin."NGOs Efforts towards the Creation of a Regional Human Rights Arrangement in the Asia-Pacific Region" *ILSA Journal of International & Comparative Law* (Spring 1998): 603–614.

Renteln, Alison Dundes. "The Unanswered Challenge of Relativism and the Consequences for Human Rights" *Human Rights Quarterly* 7 (November 1985): 514–540.

Ramcharan, B.G. "Strategies for the International Protection of Human Rights in the 1990s" *Human Rights Quarterly* 13 (1991): 155–169.

Ray, Jr. Philip L and J Sherrod Taylor. "The Role of Nongovernmental Organizations in Implementing Human Rights in Latin America." *Georgia Journal of International and Comparative Law* 7 (1977): 477–506.

Robertson, Roland. "Globlization and Social Modernization: A Note on Japan and Japanese Religion" *Sociological Analysis* (1987): 35–43.

———. "Globalization Theory and Civilization Analysis" *Comparative Civilizations Review* (1987): 20–30.

Robinson, Mary. "Human Rights at the Dawn of the 21st Century" *Human Rights Quarterly* 15(1993): 629–639.

Robertson, A.H. "European Court of Human Rights" *American Journal of Comparative Law* 3 (1960): 1–28.

———. "Revision of the Charter of the OAS" *International and Comparative Quarterly* 17 (April 1968): 345–362.

———. "The United Nations Covenant on Civil and Political Rights and the European Convention on Human Rights" *British Yearbook of International Law* 43 (1968–1969): 36–48

Rolin, Henri. "Has the European Court of Human Rights a Future?" *Howard Law Journal* (Spring 1965): 508–526

Rosecrance R , et al "Whither Interdependence?" *International Organization* 31 (Summer 1977): 425–445.

Rosecrance, Richard and Arthur Stein "Interdependence: Myth or Rality" *World Politics* (Oct. 1973): 1–27.

Said, Abdul Aziz. "Precept and Practice of Human Rights in Islam" *Universal Human Rights*. I (April 1979): 63–80.

Sanders, Douglas. "Collective Rights" *Human Rights Quarterly* 13 (1991): 368–386.

Skogly, Sigrun I. "Human Rights Reporting: The Nordic Experience" *Human Rights Quarterly* (Nov. 1990): 513–528.

Sikkink, Kathryn "Human Rights, Principled Issue-Networks, and Sovereignty in Latin America" 47 *International Organization* (Summer 1993): 411–441.

Schmitter, Philippe. "Three Neo-Functional Hypotheses About International Organization" *Internaitonal Organization* 23 (Winter 1969): 161–166.

Sandifer, V.D. "Human Rights in the Inter-American Commission System" *Howard Law Journal* (Spring 1965): 508–526.

Scheman, L.Ronald. "The Inter-American Commission on Human Rights" *American Journal of International Law* 59 (April 1965): 335–344

Shelton, Dinah. "Improving Human Rights Protection: Recommendations for Enhancing the Effectiveness of the Inter-American Commission and the Inter-American Court of Human Rights" 3 *American University Journal of International Law and Policy* (1988):

Schwelb, Egon. "Entry Into Force of the International Covenant on Civil and Political Rights" *American Journal of International Law* 70 (July 1976): 511–518.

———. "The International Measures of Implementation in the United Nations Covenant on Human Rights and of the Optional Protocol" *Texas International Law Journal* 12 (Spring/Summer 1977): 141–186.

———. "Civil and Political Rights: The International Measures of Implementation" *American Journal of International Law* 62 (October 1968): 827–860

———. "The Abuse of the Right of Petition" *Human Rights Journal* III-2 (1970): 313–332.

———. "Some Aspects of the Measures of Implementation of the Covenant on Economic, Social and Cultural Rights" *Human Rights Journal* 3 (1968): 363–377.

———. "On the Operation of the European Convention on Human Rights" *International Organization* 18 (1964): 558–585.

Sepulveda, Cesar. "The Inter-American Commission on Human Rights of the Organization of American States" *German Yearbook of International Law* 28 (1985); 65–87.

Sohn, Louis B. "United Nations Machinery for Implementing Human Rights" *American Journal of International Law* 62 (October 1968): 267–272

Spjur R.L. "Torture Under the European Convention Systems" *American Journal of International Law* 75 (April 1979): 267–272.

Starr, Robert. "Procedures for International Protection of Human Rights" *Iowa Law Review* 53 (1967): 291–324.

———. "International Protection of Human Rights and the United Nations Covenants" *Wisconsin Law Review* 1 (Winter 1967): 863–890.

Schmidt, Markus G. "Achieving Much With Little: The Work of the United Nations Center for Human Rights." *Netherlands Quarterly of Human Rights* 8(1990): 371–380.

Schreuer, Christoph. "The Waining of the Sovereing State: Towards a New Paradigm for International Law?" *European Journal of International Law* (1993): 447–471.

Schoener, Wendy."Non-Governmental Organizations and Global Activism: Legal and Informal Approaches" *Indiana Journal of Global Legal Studies* 4 (1997): 537–569.

Shelton, Dinah. "The Participation of Nongovernmental Organizations in International Judicial Proceedings" *American Journal of International Law* 88 (Oct. 1994): 611–642.

Shestack, Jerome J. "Sisyphus Endures: The International Human Rights NGO" *New York Law School Law Review* 24 (1978): 89–123.

Smith, Jackie, Ron Pagnucco, and George A. Lopez. "Globalizing Human Rights: The Work of Transnational Human Rights NGOs in the 1990s" *Human Rights Quarterly* 20 (1998): 379–412.

Spiro, Peter J. "New Global Communities: Nongovernmental Oragnizations in International Decision-Making Institutions" The *Washington Quarterly* (Winter 1995): 45–56.

Stikker, D.U. "The Functional Approach to European Integration" *Foreign Affairs* (April 1951): 436–444.

Tardu, M.E. "United Nations Response to Gross Violations of Human Rights: The 1503 Procedure" *Santa Clara Law Review* 20 (Summer 1980): 559–601.

Teson, Fernando " International Human Rights and Cultural Relativism" *Virginia Journal of International Law* 25 (1985): 869–898.

Tibi, Bassam. "Islamic/Shari'a, Human Rights, Universal Morality and International Relations." *Human Rights Quarterly* 16 (1994): 277–299.

Tardu, M.E. "The Protocol to the United Nations Covenant on Civil and Political Rights and the Inter-American System: A Study of Co-Existing Petition Procedures" *American Journal of International Law* 70 (October 1976): 778–801.

Thomas, Ann Van Wynen and Thomas Jr. A.J. "Human Rights and the OAS" *Santa Clara Lawyer* 12 (1972): 319–376.

Thomas, A.Wynen. "The Inter-American Commission on Human Rights" 20 *South Western Law Journal* (June 1966): 282–309.

Tucker, Carol M. "Regional Human Rights Models in Europe and Africa: A Comparison" *Syracuse Journal of International Law and Commerce* 10 (1983): 135–168.

Tollison, Robert D. and Thomas D. Willett. "International Integration and the Interdependence of Economic Variables" *International Organization* (Spring 1973): 255 271.

Tetreault, Mary Ann. "Measuring interdependence" *International Organization* (Summer 1980): 429–443.

Turner, Scott. "Global Civil Society, Anarchy and Governance: Assessing An Emerging Paradigm" *Journal of Peace Research* 35 (January 1998): 25–42.

Tremewan, Christopher. "Human Rights in Asia" *The Pacific Review* 6 (1993): 17–30.

Ullman, R.H. "Both National Security and Human Rights Can Be Served Simultaneously" *The Center Magazine* (March/April 1984):

Umozurike, U.O. "The African Charter on Human and Peoples' Rights" *American Journal of International Law* 77 (October 1983):

Upham, Frank K. "The Years of Affairmative Action for Japanese Burakumin: A Preliminary Report on the Law on Special Measures for Dowa Projects" 13 *Law in Japan: Annual* (1980): 39–73.

Van Ness, Peter. "Human Rights and International Relations in East Asia" *Ethics and International Relations* 16 (July 1992): 43–52.

Vesak, Karel. "The European Convention on Human Rights beyond the Frontiers of Europe" *International and Comparative Law Quarterly* 12 (October 1963): 1206–1231.

Volio, Fernand. "The Inter-American Commission on Human Rights" *The American University Law Review* 30 (Fall 1980): 65–78.

van Dijk, Peter. "A Common Standard of Achievement. About Universal Validity and Uniform Interpretation of International Human Rights Norms" *Netherlands Quarterly of Human Rights* 13 (1995): 105–121.

Veverka, Vladimir "The Question of Universality in the Theory of Human Rights" *Bulletin of Czechoslovakia Law*, Prague 25 (1967): 9–28.

Vernon, Raymond. "Economic Sovereignty at Bay" *Foreign Affairs* (October 1968): 110–122.

Washburn, W.E. "Cultural Relativism, Human Rights, and the AAAS," *American Anthropologist* 3 (1987): 30–37.

Weissbrodt, D. "Human Rights Legislation and U.S. Foreign Policy" 7 *Georgia Journal of International and Comparative Law* (1977): 231– 287.

Walter, Michael. "The Idea of Civil Society" *Dissent* (Spring 1991): 293–304.

Wapner, Paul. "Environmental Activism and Global Civil Society" *Dissent* (Summer 1994): 389–393.

Weigle, Marcia A. and Jim Butterfield. "Civil Society in Reforming Communist Regimes: The Logic of Emergence" *Comparative Politics* (October 1992): 1–23.

Weissbrodt, David and James McCarthy "Fact-Finding by International Nongovernmental Human Rights Organizations" *Virginia Journal of International Law* 22 (1981): 1–89.

Weissbrodt, David. "The Role of International Nongovernmental Organizations in the Implementation of Human Rights." *Texas International Law Journal* 12 (1977): 293–323.

White, Gordon. "Civil Society, Democratization and Development (I): Clearing the Analytical Ground" *Democratization* 1 (Autumn 1994): 375–390.

Wiseberg, Laurie S. "Protecting Human Rights Activists and NGOs: What More Can Be Done?" *Human Rights Quarterly* 13 (1991): 525–544.

Wiseberg, Laurie S. and Harry M. Scoble. "The International League for Human Rights: The Strategy of a Human Rights NGO" *Georgia Journal of International and Comparative Law* 7 (1977): 289–313.

Weissbrodt, D and Rose Farley. "The UNESCO Human Rights Procedure: An Evaluation" *Human Rights Quarterly* (1994): 391–414.

Wiseberg, Laurie. "Access to United Nations Human Rights Documentation" *Human Rights Quarterly* (1997): 350–364.

Waldock, Humphrey. "The Effectiveness of the System set up by the European Convention on Human Rights." *Human Rights Law Journal*1 (1980): 1–12.

———. "The European Convention for the Protection of Human Rights and Fundamental Freedoms" *British Yearbook of International Law* 34 (1958): 356–363.

Walsh, Brian. "The European Court of Human Rights" *Connecticut Journal of International Law* 2 (1987): 271–281.

Weil, Gordon L. "Decisions on Inadmissible Application by the European Convention on Human Rights" *American Journal of International Law* 54 (October 1960): 874–881.

———. The European Convention on Human Rights" *American Journal of International Law* 57 (October 1963): 804–827.

Welch, Jr, Claude E. "The African Commission on Human Rights: A Five-Year Report and Assessment" *Human Rights Quarterly* 14 (1992): 43–61.

Weston, Burns, Robin Ann Lukes, and Kelly M. Hnatt. "Regional Human Rights Regimes: A Comparison and Appraisal." *Vanderbilt Journal of Transnational Law* 20 (October 1987): 585–637.

Wilde, Ralph. "NGOs Proposals for an Asia-Pacific Human Rights System" *The Yale Human Rights Development Law Journal* (1998): 1–8.

Yokota, Yozo. "How Japan Can Contribute to Human Rights" *Japan Review of International Affairs* (Spring 1995): 137–146.

Young, Nick. "Are there any real NGOs in China?" *Alliance* 4 (March 1999): 16–19.

Zakaria, Fareed. "Culture is Destiny: A Conversation with Lee Kuan Yew" *Foreign Affairs* 73 (March/April 1994): 109–125.

Index

Admissibility, 93
African Charter on Human and
    Peoples' Rights, 1, 49, 64, 97,
    123
African Commission on Human and
    Peoples' Rights, 98
African Court on Human and Peoples'
    Rights, 98
African Development Fund, 79
African Development Fund, 79
Ainu, 108
All China Women's Federation, 111
All Japan Federation of Buraku
    Liberation Movement, 124
Alston, Philip, 65
American Convention on Human
    Rights, 4, 90, 95
Americanization, 30
Amnesty International, 34, 37, 140
Amnesty International/USA, 124
American Declaration of Independence,
    48, 60
American Declaration of the Rights
    and Duties of Man, 64, 95
Anman Workshop, 115
Annan, Kofi, 57, 59, 65
Arab Charter on Human Rights, 64
Arab Commission on Human Rights, 5
Asia Pacific Resource Center for

Human Rights Education, 43
Asia-Pacific Network for International
    Education and Value Education,
    43
Asia-Pacific Human Rights
    Information Center, 124
Asian Human Rights Charter, 43–44,
    45, 103, 135, 136, 140, 141,
    144
Asian Human Rights Commission, 43,
    124
Asian Development Bank (ADB),
    86–87, 146
Asian Coalition of Human Rights
    Organization, 119
Association of Southeast Asian Nations
    (ASEAN), 9, 119
Asian Center for the Progress of
    Peoples, 124
Asia Monitor Resource Center, 124
Asian Values, 50, 51
Association for Solidarity with Foreign
    Migrant Workers, 124

Banjur Charter on Human and
    Peoples' Rights, 4
Bangkok NGO Declaration, 57, 117
Bielefeldt, Heiner, 57
Bricker Amendment, 77

243

Bureau of Human Rights and Humanitarian Affairs, 79
Burakumin, 108

Canadian International Development Agency (CIDA), 82
Carter, Jimmy, 79
Center for Justice and International Law, 96, 97
Cerna, Christina, 125
Chi Young Pak, 125
Charter of the International Military Tribunals at Nuremberg and Tokyo, 66
Chinese Declaration of Human Rights, 111
Chinese Human Rights Alliances, 111
Chinese Association for Human Rights, 108
China Federation of Disabled Persons, 111
Christian Conference of Asia, 124
Chiu, Hungda, 125
Civil Society, 30–32, 109, in China, 111
Clash of Civilizations, 47
Comfort Women, 108
Council of Europe, 1, 36, 64
Council of the League of Arab States, 64
Commission on Human Rights, 67
Commission on the Status of Women, 69, 70
Commission on Crime Prevention and Criminal Justice, 70
Committee on the Elimination of Racial Discrimination, 70
Committee Against Torture, 70
Committee on the Elimination of All Forms of Discrimination Against Women, 71
Committee on Economic, Social and Cultural Rights, 72
Committee on the Rights of the Child, 72
Convention on the Elimination of All

Forms of Discrimination Against Women, 61
Convention against Torture and Other Cruel, Inhuman or Degrading Treatment, 62
Code of Conduct for Law Enforcement Officers, 62
Convention on the Rights of the Child, 62
Cross-fertilization, 23
Complex interdependence, 23, 24
Cultural relativism, 52, 54
Cultural Relativism, 52
Cultural Imperialism, 55
Conditionality of aid, 85

Datsua Nyuo, 143
Deutsch, Karl, 19
Dependency, 27–28
Declaration of the Rights to Development, 62
Dias, Clarence, 125, 130
Donnely, Jack, 53

Economic and Social Council Resolution 1296, 36
English Bill of Rights, 48
European Convention on Human Rights and Fundamental freedoms, 2, 64, 91
European Court of Human Rights, 33, 53, 92
European Convention for the Protection of Human Rights and Fundamental Freedoms, 4, 64, 91
European Social Charter, 64, 92
European Convention for the Prevention of Torture, and Inhuman or Degrading Treatment or Punishment, 64

Farer, Tom, 97
Ferguson, Adam, 32
Final Act of the Conference on Security and Cooperation in Europe, 64, 78

Food Agricultural Organization, 14
Foreign Assistance Act, 38, 77, 80
Forsythe, David, 59
Four Freedoms, 77
Fraser, Donald, 78
Framework for Regional Technical
      Cooperation in the Asia-Pacific,
      146
Functionalism, 2, 11–15;
   functional integration, 42
Freedom House, 34
French Declaration of the Rights of
      Man and the Citizen, 48, 60

Genocide Convention, 61
Geneva Conventions, 88
Ghai, Yash, 58
Globalization, 6, 29
Global civil society, 6, 32–34
Global governance, 6
Greenpeace, 34

Haas, Ernst, 15
Habeas Corpus Act, 48
Harkin Amendment, 79
High politics, 14
Human rights education, 38
HURIGHTS Osaka, 43, 108, 118, 134
Human Rights Committee, 70
Humanitarian Intervention, 87–88
Human Rights Committee of the Korea
      Youth Progress Party, 124
Human Rights in China, 124
Human Rights Watch/Asia, 124
Hume, David, 32

Information Center for Human Rights
      and Democratic Movement, 124
Inter-American Commission on Human
      Rights, 1
Interdependence, 5, 22–28,
   economic interdependence, 26–27
   moral interdependence, 44
International Association for the
      Protection of Child Welfare, 14
International Telecommunications, 14

International Labor Organization
      (ILO),14, 34, 36, 72
Inter-American Commission on Human
      Rights, 33, 95
Inter-American Court of Human
      Rights, 33, 96
Inter-American Convention on the
      Forced Disappearance of
      Persons, 64
International Bill of Rights, 60
International Red Cross, 34
International Commission of Jurists, 36
International Covenant on Civil and
      Political Rights, 60, 61
International Covenant on Economic,
      Social and Cultural Rights, 60,
      61
International Convention on the
      Elimination of All Forms of
      Racial Discrimination, 61
International Court of Justice (ICJ), 61
International Year for Human Rights,
      74
International Development and Food
      Assistance Act, 78
International Security Assistance and
      Arms Export Control Act, 78
Inter-American Development Bank, 79
International Human Rights of Korea,
      124
International Association for the
      Protection of Child Welfare, 14
International Bank for Reconstruction
      and Development (IBRD), 85
International Development Association
      (IDA), 85
International Finance Corporation
      (IFC), 85
Investigation Team on the Truth About
      Forced Korean Labors in Japan,
      124

Japanese NGO Center for International
      Cooperation (JANIC), 108
Japan Federation of Bar Association,
      124

Japanese Committee of World
     Conference on Religion and
     Peace, 124
Jakarta Workshop, 113
Jesuit Social Center, 124
Jendrzejczyk, Mike, 125, 130, 131,
     135

Kathmandu Workshop, 114, 115
Kim Dae Jung, 17, 30, 42
Kim, Jong Il
Kissinger, Henry, 79
Kjaerum, Morten, 39,
Korean War, 143
Kodena, Sayoko, 125
Koran, 50, 51
Kutner, Luis, 30

LAWASIA Human Rights Committee,
     119, 122
Lawyers for a Democratic Society, 124
Lawyers Committee for Human Rights,
     80
Lee Kuan Yew, 50, 125
Lindberg, Leon, 15
Li, Xiaorong, 55–56, 125
Low politics, 14,

Manila Workshop, 112
Mandate of Heaven, 50
Marfording, Annette, 58
Mitrany, David, 2, 3
Mill, John Stuart, 49
Mongolian Human Rights Committee,
     124
Mohamad, Mahathir, 125
Multilateral Investment Guarantee
     Agency (MIGA), 85

Nana N. Soeyonon Ma, 125
Nanking Massacre, 129
Neo-functionalism, 15 -16
Nongovernmental organization , 13,
     28, 34–35; 94, 98, 99,
     human rights NGOs, 34–42;
     strengths and weaknesses of, 39

problems of , 39
involvements in the European sys-
     tem, 94
involvements in the Inter-
     Americansystem, 96, 97
involvements in African system, 98,
     99
New Delhi Workshop, 116
Nye, Joseph, 15

Official Development Aid (ODA), 8 -9,
     84
Office of the High Commissioner for
     Human Rights, 70
Onuma, Yasuaki, 59
Organization of African Unity (OAU),
     1, 36, 64, 97
Organization of American States
     (OAS), 1, 34, 36, 64, 95; Charter
     95

Pacific Charter of Human Rights, 122
Pae Keun Park, 125
People's Solidarity for Participatory
     Democracy, 124
Planetary citizenship, 34
Principles of Medical Ethics, 62

Quiet diplomacy, 79

Rawls, John, 57
Realpolitik, 79
Regional inter-governmental organiza-
     tion, 1
Regional integration, 4, 17–22,
     economic integration, 20
     social integration, 21
     political integration, 21–22
Regional Council on Human Rights in
     Asia, 119
Resolution 1235, 67
Resolution 1503, 67

Seoul Workshop, 113, 114
Sen, Amartya, 125
Sharia, 51, 51n

Shock therapy, 31
Shin Hae Bong, 125
Shue, Henry, 55
Sierra Club, 34
Smith, Adam, 32
South Asian Association for Regional
    Cooperation (SAARC), 9, 121
Spill-over, 3, 14, 15, 17
Special Rapporteur, 69
Standard Minimum Rules for the
    Treatment of Prisoners, 62
Sub-Commission on the Promotion and
    Protection of Human Rights, 69
Sunna, 51

Taiwan Association for Human Rights,
    124
Teheran Workshop, 115, 116
Tobin, John J., 125
Transnational Corporation (TNC), 28,
    34

United Nations High Commissioner for
    Human Rights, 70
United Nations Commission on
    Human Rights, 67, 136
United Nations Educational, Scientific
    and Cultural Organization
    (UNESCO), 36, 73, 74
Universal Telegraphic Union, 14

Universal Postal Union, 14
Universal Declaration of Human
    Rights, 49, 56, 65, 106
Universality of Human Rights, 55, 60
US Constitution, 48

Vance, Cyrus, 79
Vasak, Karel, 60
Vienna Declaration and Programme of
    Action, 57, 75, 120
Voluntary Fund for Victims of Torture,
    62

Women's Democratic Club, 124
Working peace system, 11
World Trade Organization ,14, 34
World Meteorological Organization ,
    14
World Health Organization (WHO),
    14
Working Group, 69
Working Group for an ASEAN Human
    Rights Mechanism, 120, 124
World Conference on Human Rights,
    74
World Bank, 85